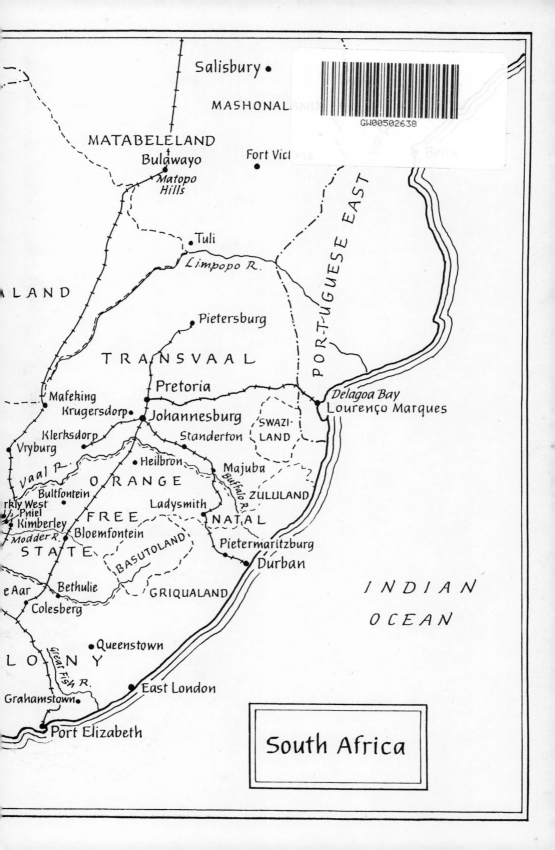

Salisbury

MASHONALAND

MATABELELAND

Bulawayo

Matopo Hills

Fort Victoria

Beira

PORTUGUESE EAST

Tuli

Limpopo R.

Pietersburg

T R A N S V A A L

Pretoria

Delagoa Bay
Lourenço Marques

Mafeking

Krugersdorp

Johannesburg

SWAZI-LAND

Klerksdorp

Standerton

Vryburg

Heilbron

Majuba

Buffalo R.

ZULULAND

Vaal R.

O R A N G E

Bultfontein

Ladysmith

rkly West

F R E E

NATAL

Pniel

Kimberley

Bloemfontein

Pietermaritzburg

Modder R.

S T A T E

BASUTOLAND

Durban

e Aar

Bethulie

GRIQUALAND

I N D I A N

Colesberg

O C E A N

Queenstown

L O N Y

Great Fish R.

East London

Grahamstown

Port Elizabeth

South Africa

Rhodes & Barnato

RHODES & BARNATO

The Premier and the Prancer

by
James Leasor

LEO COOPER

LONDON

First published in Great Britain in 1997 by
LEO COOPER
an imprint of
Pen & Sword Books Ltd
47 Church Street
Barnsley
South Yorkshire
S70 2AS

ISBN 0 85052 545 4

A catalogue record for this book is
available from the British Library

Typeset by Phoenix Typesetting, Ilkley, West Yorkshire

Printed in England by Redwood Books, Trowbridge, Wiltshire

CONTENTS

ACKNOWLEDGEMENTS

I am indebted to many people in South Africa, Zimbabwe and England for their generous help, and would like to express my warm thanks and gratitude to the following:

Dr Jeremy Catto, Rhodes Fellow and Tutor in Modern History, Oriel College, Oxford; Elizabeth Boardman, Archivist, Oriel College; Margaret Kirwin, Librarian, Oriel College; Lieut-Col F K Horne (Retd), Harare, Zimbabwe; Diana Barnato Walker MBE; Theo Aronson; Stella Coles; Elizabeth Cartmale Freedman; Jane Harriss; Sandra Kibble-White, Rhodes Trust, Oxford; my wife, Joan Leasor; Jenny McNally; Brian Roberts; Juliet Waters; the Librarians and staff of the British Newspaper Library at Colindale; the Librarians and staff of the London Library; Salisbury Library, Wiltshire, and the National Archives of Zimbabwe, Harare.

I am also greatly in debt to members of the staff of De Beers and associated companies, especially to Andrew Lamont, Manager, Group Corporate Communications, CSO Valuations AG; Helen Chesterfield, Lesley Coldham, and Helen Hackett, also of CSO Valuations AG; John Imrie, P. Bunkell, John Lang and Rosemary Burke of the Chamber of Mines of South Africa, in Johannesburg; Dennis Knox of De Beers Consolidated Mines Limited in Kimberley; Estrilita Forbes and Ivan Morrow of CDM (Proprietary) Limited in Oranjemund, and Gino Noli in Lüderitz and Kolmanskop.

Any errors are my own.

J. L.

CHAPTER 1

TWO FUNERALS, FIVE YEARS AND SEVEN THOUSAND MILES APART

All through that June Sunday morning the West End of London had become steadily more crowded. Everyone seemed cheerful, in carnival mood, and every few minutes special trains from suburbs and provinces poured out hundreds more to throng the streets.

Horse buses packed with sightseers and day-trippers moved slowly along Piccadilly and Oxford Street, around the Marble Arch and up and down the Edgware Road. They were following the route that Queen Victoria would take on the following Tuesday for her ceremonial progress through London to mark her Diamond Jubilee. Sunday was the one free day most people had from work. They were determined to make the most of this particular Sunday which marked the start of an historic week in the capital of the world's greatest empire.

Windows and balconies overlooking the streets were framed with flags and patriotic swathes of red, white and blue bunting. The rooms on to which these windows opened had all been booked months in advance. Here spectators could watch the procession from the comfort of cushioned seats. At the same time they could enjoy, at a cost of two guineas each, (twice as much as most people earned in a week and in present-day values more than £500) collations of lobster mayonnaise, cold roast beef, lamb, pressed tongue, smoked ham and chicken, with vanilla and strawberry ice creams, aerated water, claret cup and tea.

Huge triumphal arches of real and artificial flowers spanned doorways and side streets, spelling out simple messages of loyalty such as 'God bless our Queen'. The crowds had come to admire these decorations and to walk through the parks, now dotted with the white tents of army and navy contingents from New Zealand, Malaya, India, Ceylon, South Africa, Australia, Hong Kong and Canada. Everyone was infused by the feeling of goodwill and national pride. Poor most of these people might be, but these vast and visible preparations for the Queen's Jubilee made them all feel important

1

members of the family of nations from which these troops in strange uniforms had come to 'the old country' to pledge loyalty to their Sovereign.

Against a background of hoarse cries of hawkers touting miniature flags and specially printed booklets listing the many achievements of Queen Victoria's reign, the constant beat of martial music from a dozen different bands rehearsing for the parade added to an intoxicating sense of great occasion and involvement.

Then, into the queues of buses and private carriages and costers' carts bringing people from London's less fashionable suburbs a number of magnificent black carriages, with windows closed and blinds drawn, began to appear. They stopped in line outside one of London's most fashionable addresses, No 6, Hyde Park Mansions, Marble Arch. Passers-by counted more than a hundred of them, waiting patiently one behind the other, their polished lacquer glittering like glass in the sunshine, coachmen sitting motionless on their boxes, reins in hand. In front of this long assembly of carriages of the very rich waited a magnificent hearse. Its black horses stood with plumed heads bowed gravely in deference to the dead.

Two police inspectors and a dozen uniformed policemen now arrived and did their best to hold back hundreds of inquisitive people, who soon blocked the pavement around the entrance to No 6. Whose funeral was this? they were asked. Time and again the policemen patiently explained that this was the funeral of Barney Barnato; he was to be buried in the Jewish cemetery in Willesden, four miles north up the Edgware Road. The great house outside which they waited belonged to his widowed sister, Mrs Kate Joel, known to some in the crowd as the former landlady of The King of Prussia public house, near Petticoat Lane in the East End.

The two words 'Barney Barnato' were repeated with awe, even reverence. Obviously most of those on the pavement had never met him, but in some strange way they all felt a strong kinship with him. Of course they had seen his photograph often enough in the illustrated newspapers: a small, perky character, with fair hair and very blue eyes, wearing a stiff white butterfly collar and a polka dot tie, invariably smoking a cigarette, pince-nez perched on his nose, one thumb cheekily in his waistcoat pocket.

To Londoners of all ages and classes, Barney Barnato had been more than a man, more than a name, much more than a card. He was an icon, positive proof that someone born in the humblest of backgrounds, with little education and no influence whatever, could, simply by his own natural abilities, and perhaps a little bit of luck, win international fame and fortune.

They approved his simple, pugnacious philosophy expressed in such maxims as: 'Never let a man put his hand on you without giving him what for – and always 'it 'im first,' and: 'Always wind up with a good curtain, and bring it down before the public gets tired – or has had time to find you out!'

Now the curtain had come down on him for the last time, and his life had been more dramatic than many of the plays he had so greatly admired.

Born in a two-room shack above a shop where his father sold cast-off clothes, Barney had left school at 14, worked in his sister's public house as part-time barman and chucker-out, and as an occasional juggler and comic in the poorest East End music halls. Somehow he had scratched together enough money to buy a single ticket, steerage class, to South Africa.

Then, in that faraway, almost mythical land of sunshine and opportunity, he had been transformed – miraculously, it seemed to some – like the frog in the fairy story, who became a prince. In a few years Barney had achieved enormous wealth, power and influence – all qualities the crowd admired and for which they secretly yearned. He had done it. So, in theory, could they.

On the day Barney Barnato died his private fortune was estimated at £20,000,000 – billions in present-day values. He made five pounds for every minute of his working day, at a time when a skilled craftsman felt fortunate to earn that amount in a month and a country labourer in two.

Barney had become a life governor of De Beers, the company that controlled virtually the world's entire diamond output, and a member of Cape Town's parliament. His London house in Park Lane, built on land bought from the Duke of Westminster, was on a palatial scale in keeping with his achievements. It contained two billiard rooms, a ballroom with 2,000 square feet of parquet flooring and a central marble staircase which soared up for four floors, lit by a vast glass dome in the roof.

When the Duke learned that a former East Ender wished to buy the site for £70,000 cash, he quickly had a clause put into the contract stipulating that any house Barney was to build on it must not cost less than £20,000. Barney was incensed at what he felt was condescension.

'Tell the Duke I'm going to spend that on the stables alone,' he retorted angrily.

But despite Barney Barnato's prodigious wealth, he had never forgotten his original poverty, or friends he had known when he was poor who had been kind to him. Every morning, when in London, he would dispatch a servant to the East End carrying a portmanteau stuffed with envelopes containing pound notes to hand out to anyone with a hard luck story.

Then, returning from South Africa shortly before his forty-fifth birthday, Barney had died tragically. He fell from the liner's top deck. A ship's officer immediately dived into the sea to try and rescue him, but too late. Barney was already dead.

Now the crowd stood in silence as the plain oak coffin, without any name plate, was loaded into the hearse – a strange contrast to the gilded carriage and four which, with liveried outriders, he used in Johannesburg, a city he had helped to found and much of which he had owned.

There was subdued clapping as William Tarrant Clifford, the merchant navy officer who had so gallantly attempted to save him, came out of the house with other mourners.

Newspaper reports of Barney's strange death at sea, and the coroner's verdict that he had committed suicide 'while temporarily insane', were fresh in everyone's mind. Solly Joel, Barney's nephew, had been on the deck of the Union Royal Mail steamer *Scot* with him. Suddenly Barney had rushed to the deck rail, seemingly determined to throw himself overboard. Solly managed to catch hold of his uncle's coat, but could not prevent him from falling. Inexplicably the cry of 'Murder!' was heard as Barney Barnato fell to his death.

Now, Barney's widow stayed inside the house with her three young children, watching from an upper window as the cortege left for the cemetery. As the reporter from *The Daily News* tactfully explained her absence from the mourners in the carriages, 'in harmony with the merciful custom of the community', she and other women in the family were not required to take part in the proceedings.

The chief mourners were Barney's elder brother, Harry, and his three nephews, Woolf, Solly and Jack Joel, all of course, millionaires. Others present included Sir Joseph Renals, recently created a baronet, and Lieutenant for the City of London. As Lord Mayor, he had given a banquet in the Mansion House, at the end of his year in office, in honour of Barney and his achievements.

In another carriage rode Lord Marcus Beresford, an extra equerry to the Queen and manager of Her Majesty's thoroughbreds and the Sandringham Stud. He had also managed Barney's racehorses. Further carriages contained representatives of the Rothschild family, Members of Parliament, doctors, clergymen, business leaders from South Africa and diamond merchants from Antwerp. That so many important people should have come to Barney Barnato's funeral was eloquent testimony to the very high regard in which he had been held, socially, professionally and personally.

Slowly the hearse set off, and, side by side, the carriages followed. Travelling two abreast, they occupied virtually the whole width of the Edgware Road, so that traffic coming south to London had to pull into the side and stop. Men passengers got out of carriages to stand, hats off, heads bowed in respect, as the hearse slowly went by. Crowds on the pavement also stood silently, the men baring their heads, until the last carriage had passed.

Every cab driver along the Edgware Road had wrapped black ribbon around his whip. As Barney's hearse approached, they each lowered their whips in silent tribute, as cavalry officers lower their swords in ceremonial salute to a departed colleague.

This was not simply the funeral of a very rich man, but of someone they all felt had been a friend, one of the family. They could identify with him, and what he had done, and approve the prodigal ease with which he had apparently made – and certainly spent – his millions. Now, poor though many of them might still be, they had one enormous advantage over him. They were alive on that sunny afternoon, and, despite his millions, Barney Barnato was not.

In the mortuary chapel at the cemetery, the Rev J. Singer, the Rabbi from the West End synagogue in St Petersburgh Place, read the brief burial service in Hebrew. The mourners wore their hats 'as a mark of reverence among their people'. Then the casket was slowly lowered into the grave, next to the grave of his father, who had died three years previously, and handfuls of earth thrown on top of it. At the express wish of the family, there were no flowers.

The funeral party united in prayer in English and then the Rabbi gave a brief and poignant address on the frailties and shortness of human life.

Slowly and in silence, heads bowed, the mourners left. Their carriages turned in the cemetery gateway, past the huge and respectful crowd that had by now gathered outside it, and came down the Edgware Road, towards Marble Arch, at a brisker pace than they had kept on the outward journey.

Such was Barney Barnato's international importance that reporters wired descriptions of the funeral to newspapers around the world. In South Africa Cecil Rhodes, whose life had for years crossed and uncrossed with Barney's, and who, like him, was a life governor of De Beers, was travelling by train from Cape Town north to Bulawayo. At about eleven o'clock that night a telegram describing Barney's funeral was received at Vryburg station, where the train stopped briefly, and handed to Rhodes' male secretary, Gordon Le Sueur.

He was unwilling to wake up his master at that hour with such sad news, so waited until the following morning before he gave Rhodes this telegram. Rhodes was extremely angry that he had not been given it the moment it arrived.

'I suppose you thought this would affect me, and I shouldn't sleep?' Rhodes asked him testily. 'Why? Do you imagine I should be the *least* affected if *you* were to fall under the wheels of this train now?'

This outburst did not surprise Le Sueur.

'He tried to give the impression of being without feeling, but nothing is more absurd,' he wrote later.[1] 'He was crammed with sentiment to his fingertips, but adopted a brutal manner and rough exterior to cover up the

[1] *Cecil Rhodes, the Man and his Work*, Gordon Le Sueur, FRGS, John Murray, London, 1913.

weakness of sentiment, and thus many a broken-hearted man and woman left him with the impression – entirely erroneous – that he was a callous brute lacking in human sympathy.'

A few days after Barney's death the dividend due to him as a De Beers life governor was announced, a matter of £30,000. Rhodes proposed that this should be paid to Barney's widow and was not best pleased when Barney's company, Barnato Brothers, claimed it for themselves.

*   *   *

Five years later, in 1902, at three minutes to six on the evening of 26 March, Rhodes died. He was 48, three years older than Barney.

Rhodes died as he had lived for much of his adult life, in deliberately simple and spartan surroundings. Not for him the butlers and footmen who looked after Barney in his huge houses in London, the English countryside and the Cape, or hangers-on like the ex-pugilist Barney had employed just in case he felt like a few rounds to keep himself fit. For years Rhodes did not even have a pillow on his bed, but used a Gladstone bag. Once, travelling to England, the trousers of his only suit were so threadbare that he had to ask a ship's steward to patch them for him.

Rhodes died in a small cottage he owned near Muizenberg on the edge of the sea outside Cape Town. The cottage had three rooms, a kitchen and a bathroom, and was infernally hot under an iron roof. To help his breathing, because of the heart condition from which he suffered, holes had been knocked in the ceiling above his bed and blocks of ice placed in tins to cool in breezes from the Atlantic.

In one corner of the room a washbasin stood on a metal stand. On a wall hung a print of Oriel College, Oxford, where, after nine years in which, as he said, he had 'oscillated between Oxford and Kimberley', he had finally graduated with a pass degree.

From boyhood Rhodes had been haunted by the feeling and the opinions of various doctors that he would die young. He had a constant preoccupation with the shortness of human life. In his last entry for *Who's Who* he wrote that he was 'fond of nearly all old fashions, fond of old things, particularly of old oak chests'.

'Everything in the world is too short,' he said once. 'Life, and fame and achievement, everything is too short. . . . From the cradle to the grave, what is it? Three days at the seaside.'

Now he had died at the seaside, his face bloated and purple, as he sweated and gasped for breath. His last words, according to his friend and physician, Dr Leander Starr Jameson, who was with him, were, 'So little done, so much to do'. Someone else recalled that Rhodes' final request was an appeal to a male secretary, as he struggled for breath, 'Turn me over, Jack'.

Next day newspapers in Cape Town and elsewhere appeared with black borders. *The New York Tribune* declared, 'Not for half a century has Great Britain, or any nation, produced a more powerful or more successful empire builder. He was not the aggressor against the Boer states; his marching empire strode past their petty borders.'

An anonymous friend, writing in the London *Daily Telegraph*, described Rhodes as 'the greatest Englishman who has ever been associated with the fortunes of Great Britain in her south African possessions.'

The New York Sun noted that 'South Africa has been a grave of many reputations, and some of them great ones. There is no one who will occupy a more prominent place in its history than Rhodes – not so much because he was great in what he accomplished, but because of the greatness of his ambitions and calibre, and the methods he relied upon for their realisation.'

The Giornale d'Italia obituarist wrote more cautiously that 'The Napoleon of the Cape dies without the secret of his life being revealed. On him, as on the real Napoleon, the verdict can only be passed by future generations.'

The New York Times summed up his character as 'a typical captain of industry – a man of great energy, large conceptions – and little scruple'.

In the Kimberley Club, of which he had been a founder, members walked over the metal arrow pointing north, which Rhodes had embedded in the tiles of the hall, as a continual reminder of his endeavours to link the Cape by rail with Cairo and help to bring all Africa within the British Empire. In silence they draped the club balconies and stoep – the verandah – with black cloth.

Work stopped in every diamond mine throughout South Africa. Shops ceased trading and shuttered their windows. A writer in *The Diamond Fields Advertiser* in Kimberley noted: 'The noisy iron-tongued clatter of the machinery ceased, as it never ceases save on Christmas Day, and the sun rose on many workmen, serious-faced, hastening sombrely homeward. A great silence had fallen on the busy mining city.'

In Cape Town the body of Cecil Rhodes lay in state at his main house, Groote Schuur – literally The Great Barn in Dutch – while arrangements were being made for his state funeral. More than 20,000 filed past his open coffin every day.

In London a public service in St Paul's Cathedral to honour his memory was announced. The King, then cruising in the Royal yacht around the Scilly Isles, would be represented, along with foreign ambassadors and representatives from Empire countries.

Such tributes marked the passing of a remarkably successful man. The stark consequences of failure in that year were sharply illustrated by the case of an 80 year-old man, Edward Jeffrey, seven thousand miles away, at West Malling, in Kent. Jeffrey had never left his village, and, being unable to read, had probably never heard of Rhodes. Now he stood to face the serious charge of attempted suicide.

The magistrates were told that he had worked conscientiously as a labourer in the parish for 60 years. More recently the parish guardians had allowed him three shillings a week relief, but at his age he could not find work and, in his wife's absence from their cottage one morning, he had tried unsuccessfully to end his miserable life by cutting his throat with a table knife.

The Chairman: 'Why did you want to end your life in this way?'

The accused: 'There was nothing but poverty and starvation before me, and I didn't want to enter the workhouse if I could avoid it. I tried hard to get work, but couldn't. I was very thankful for what the guardians allowed me, but it wasn't enough to keep us.'

A doctor gave evidence that the accused was an excellent character and had diligently tried to get work. At this Jeffrey broke down.

'I'm very willing to work and earn my own living although I am more than four score years old,' he insisted tearfully. But no one had any work to offer him and, since there was also no charitable agency available, the court discharged him on condition he entered the workhouse he had tried to kill himself to avoid.

After a funeral service in the Anglican cathedral in Cape Town Rhodes' coffin was borne under a Union flag on the carriage of the gun nicknamed Long Cecil, built in the mine foundry in Kimberley, and which had been used to help to raise the siege by the Boers on that town.

The route was lined by soldiers who stood, rifles reversed, heads bowed. Cape Town station was draped in black crepe; the train which waited, steam up, to carry the coffin north, was swathed in purple and black. Six years earlier Rhodes had travelled to the Matopo Hills, 45 miles out of Bulawayo, when he had settled a revolt by the Matabeles. Here the solitary and uncompromising grandeur of a huge rock formation that soared up in the middle of a vast green space had touched his heart. Here, too, the old African king, Mzilikazi, the father of Lobengula, the Matabele ruler with whom Rhodes had dealt, had been buried, sitting up so that even in death he could face a view he had loved so much in life. Rhodes called this magnificent panorama 'one of the world's views' and he decided that he would also be buried here in the country named Rhodesia after him.

On the way north, whenever the funeral train stopped at small stations, all draped in black cloth, crowds of English and Boer settlers stood in silence on the platform until it left. Local bands played the Dead March from *Saul* or buglers sounded the Last Post.

At four o'clock in the morning the train reached Kimberley, where Rhodes and Barnato had made their prodigious wealth from diamonds. Thousands of people were already at the station waiting for it. A guard of honour of the Kimberley Regiment filled the platform with a band ready to strike up the Dead March as soon as the train stopped. Before the train left six hours later, more than 15,000 people passed along the platform in single file, looking through the open window of the carriage which contained Rhodes' coffin.

Finally, five days after leaving Cape Town, the train came slowly into Bulawayo station. The whole town turned out to meet it. All work had stopped; every shop was shut; every office closed. The station roof was covered with black crepe and flags flew at half mast.

Next morning the mourners, including Rhodes' three brothers, all Army officers, and Dr Jameson, left Fuller's Hotel, where they had stayed overnight, and led a procession for five miles across hills and through gorges. Some mourners walked, others rode cycles or horses, or travelled in Cape carts. All wore black.

A mile from the grave everyone who had been riding dismounted and covered the rest of the distance on foot. Even with all vehicles and horses excluded, the line of mourners extended for more than a mile. The military march with arms reversed, while their band played and replayed the Dead March.

The place of burial was a stone kopje or small hill, so steep and rugged that it was almost inaccessible. Twelve oxen were required to draw the coffin on its gun-carriage up to the heights, watched by more than 2,000 natives, many of them murmuring, 'My father is dead'.

The procession finally reached its destination and at noon the Bishop of Mashonaland began the funeral service. Many wept openly as the Bishop said, 'I consecrate this place for ever as his grave. Here he fought, here he lived and died for the Empire, fully alive to the great mystery of death.'

The grave had been cut deeply into the rock and was encircled by six boulders. The Union flag still lay on the coffin with Rhodes' masonic regalia. On the flag was a wreath from Queen Alexandra, and others from Rhodes' brothers and Dr Jameson. As the coffin was lowered by chains into the grave one of the African chiefs spoke:

'I am an old man on the brink of the grave,' he said, his voice hoarse with emotion. 'I was content to die knowing that my children and my people would be safe in the hands of Mr Rhodes, who was at once my father and mother. That hope has been taken from me, and I feel that the sun indeed has set for me.'

The 'Old Hundredth' was sung and then the hymn, 'Now the labourer's task is o'er', and mourners passed round the grave in turn, throwing flowers on to the coffin. Soon the whole area around the grave was covered with flowers and wreaths.

That night local natives slew fifteen oxen as a sacrifice; so far as they were concerned, Cecil Rhodes, who they mourned genuinely as their chief, was buried with the same honours as their king who had first chosen this place for his grave. A brass plate was fitted on the rock with the words: Here lie the remains of Cecil John Rhodes.

Two funerals, five years and seven thousand miles apart, for two men who, despite differences in background and outlook, were both creatures of their time. Had they arrived in South Africa even a few years – maybe even months – earlier or later, their lives might have been as unspectacularly unsuccessful as those of most other new emigrants.

But they had landed in Africa at a time of momentous changes. First, there was the discovery of diamonds, initially on a small scale, and then in quantities that rivalled the legendary mines of India and Brazil. Gold had already been found on the west coast – hence the name the Gold Coast – and much more was soon to be found elsewhere in the country.

Second, France and Germany were showing increasing interest in acquiring colonies in Africa, which made the British government realize the importance of a country which hitherto had been of little more value to them than a useful staging post for ships on the Eastern run.

Europeans who visited Africa for the first time were invariably astonished – and not infrequently dismayed – by the country's sheer size. This had the opposite effect on Rhodes and Barnato; statistics were always only a challenge to them: the harder the task, the greater the prize.

Africa had a coastline of 19,000 miles and was more than three times as large as Europe. Its smallest rivers dwarfed the Thames; the Congo river was larger than the Mississippi. The country's two extreme points, Cape Blanc in the north west and Cape Agulhas in the south, were nearly 5,000 miles apart; and from east to west, Cape Verde to Ras Hafun, only a few hundred miles less.

To many new arrivals the heart of South Africa, near the vast Orange and Vaal Rivers, seemed to epitomize much of this huge and largely unknown continent. Plains stretched to infinity, shimmering in heat, so that it was often difficult to determine where land ended and sky began. Thorn trees sprouted among acres of silvery grass that moved in the wind like waves on an immense land-locked sea. The earth, often grey as ash raked from a furnace, felt hot and abrasive, and under the sun's ferocious heat dry ground would split with wide fissures. Winds blew clouds of dust so thick that they could choke men and beasts. When the rains came the cracked parched earth at first absorbed the water gratefully, but such became the strength of the deluge that soon foaming torrents spread out and rivers became impassable.

In the south-west seas were so rough that ships could only land on a few days every year. Here winds blew so strongly and unpredictably that entire villages could disappear overnight under miles of shifting sands. By next morning the winds might change and the villages reappear.

Fevers were endemic. For most, there was no known cure. Natives were often strange in appearance, with even stranger customs, and therefore to be feared and distrusted; they represented the unknown. Several tribes lived in the south between the Atlantic and Indian oceans: the Bushmen, the Hottentots, the Bantus, sometimes known as Kaffirs. The Bushmen, who occupied the Kalahari Desert, were small in stature, usually between four and five feet tall. Their life-style had not changed much since the Stone Age. They did not cultivate the ground, nor did they own any domestic animals, not even dogs. They lived in caves and holes, and by hunting. When this failed they ate insects, worms, roots, snakes. Their language was a series of clicking sounds, in the opinion of one South African, 'the language of the higher apes'.[2] They had no apparent religion, marriage rites or family ties.

Yet these primitive people, or their forebears, had been responsible for some remarkable rock paintings. They were so fit physically that they could lope alongside a wild animal for perhaps 20 miles until the beast began to tire. Then they would bring it down with a poisoned arrow.

The Hottentots were nomads of medium height, with light brown complexions, and possessing considerable skills in wood carving and metal-work. The Bantus, who comprised Bechuanas, Zulus and Basutos, were collectively described as Kaffirs, from the Arab word meaning unbelievers, first given to them by Mohammedans on the coast. They lived in large groups under their own chiefs.

The first European to sail round the Cape was the Portuguese navigator, Bartolomew Diaz, in 1487. Because of the ferocious seas and winds he encountered, he called it the Cape of Storms. King John II of Portugal preferred a more optimistic name: the Cape of Good Hope.

Vasco da Gama followed 10 years later, and during the next hundred years English and Dutch vessels sailed round the Cape regularly in some numbers, on their way to India and the Spice Islands. At that time Europe did not possess any satisfactory way of keeping large quantities of cattle alive during winter months. Each autumn most animals had to be killed and the beef salted. When spices were discovered in the East they were instantly in great demand (and at very high prices) to add flavour to preserved meat.

The return trip from Europe to the Spice Islands could take at least six months, sometimes a year. Seas were rough, distances great and the ships very small. On their homeward voyage pirates would often ambush them, seize their immensely valuable cargoes and slaughter the crews.

To shorten the distance between ports, and so reduce this ever-increasing

[2] *Ex Africa*, Dr Hans Sauer, Geoffrey Bles, 1937

risk, the English established bases on the Indian coast. Here their ships could pause long enough to carry out any repairs and take on fresh vegetables and water before continuing their journey. A similar facility in South Africa was required, but initial efforts here were unsuccessful. For the time being English ships used the small island of St Helena, about 1,000 miles off South-West Africa. St Helena was originally discovered by the Portuguese in 1501 and taken over by the British East India Company 150 years later.

Meanwhile, the Dutch East India Company had heard from Dutch seamen shipwrecked on the South African coast that, surprisingly, the natives had not harmed them. Also, fruit and vegetables grew there in abundance, helped by the warm climate. In 1652 a Dutch surgeon, Jan Van Riebeck, led three small ships to the Cape, where they anchored and the crews went ashore to explore the possibilities of settling in the area.

They built a small fortress and reached an accommodation with local Hottentots who sold them cattle, (and then stole them back to resell a second or third time). These early Dutch settlers were frequently threatened by sailors from English and French ships, but they stayed, and slowly their settlement grew and prospered.

Then Louis XIII of France revoked the Edict of Nantes, which a previous monarch, Henry IV, had issued to give French Protestants legally defined rights of worship and allow them to hold political and judicial office. By abrogating this law, Louis XIII drove thousands of Protestant French Huguenots into exile. Most came to England or Germany, but about 500 sailed south to the Cape to join the Dutch settlers, known as Boers, from the Dutch word for peasant or husbandman.

Their life was frugal and austere, virtually their only reading the Bible and books of psalms. Many large Boer families had a living-in teacher, Scots, English or Irish, who taught the young children reading, writing and arithmetic. Some of these teachers married Boer girls.

If a young Boer wished to court a girl, the custom was for him to buy a highly coloured saddle cloth and set out on a specially trained horse to the home of the girl to whom he wished to propose. This horse had been schooled as a *Kopspieler*, which meant that as the animal cantered it moved its head up and down smartly. This would allow the girl's family to realize that the rider was not simply a casual caller but on a highly important mission.

He would also take a bowl of crystallized plums and a thick candle to the girl's house, which, because of the sparseness of the population and the distance between each house, could be many miles away.

If her parents approved of him as a potential son-in-law, he would give the plums to the girl's mother as an introductory present and evidence of his serious intentions. The mother would then stick a pin into the candle an inch or two from the top, light the wick and leave the young people on their own – possibly the first time they had been alone together – for as long as it took for the flame to reach this pin.

Their rigid and austere way of life, based on the most literal interpretation of the Bible, might have continued indefinitely had not war broken out thousands of miles away between England and France. The French had earlier threatened British supremacy in India, and Britain was determined that neither France nor any other European country would do so a second time. Britain therefore felt she needed complete dominance of the sea route to India. Possession of a strong naval base at the Cape was of vital importance because all European ships had to pass the Cape on their way to or from the East. The British Government decided to acquire the Cape and so preempt the possibility of the French seizing it first. Accordingly, Britain paid £6,000,000 to Holland for the legal title.

The Dutch East India Company had no intention of founding an empire in South Africa. Like the old British East India Company, their concern was with trade. The Cape was a convenient and valuable base on the way to or from the East and the Boers grew vegetables and reared cattle to revictual the ships that called in regularly.

Behind their original coastal settlement lay an enormous amount of land, which they found useful for growing more vegetables or rearing more cattle. Accordingly, with the Huguenots, they moved north, away from their original base – and new English arrivals.

The Boers were fundamentalists. They felt superior, intellectually and racially, to the Hottentots they used as labourers on their farms. With the move inland, their farms grew larger and increasingly prosperous, helped by the very low wages paid to the native labourers. Success encouraged and increased a natural spirit of robust individuality among the Boers and reinforced their reluctance to accept the authority of any outside government or governor.

The British, who were now settling in the Cape in some numbers, had also initially no intention of founding a new empire. They were concerned with safeguarding the route to India which had come to be regarded as the most important country in the British Empire.

With the new British settlers in the Cape came missionaries, largely Scottish. The Boers were unsympathetic to their stated intentions; first, to evangelize the natives and then to emancipate them. In 1833 the British Parliament passed the Abolition of Slavery Act, which became law in South Africa and meant that the Boers could no longer rely on very cheap African labour and, indeed, set free 39,000 virtual slaves.

English also became the official language instead of Dutch and, after a native police force was formed, about 10,000 Boers decided to leave and form their own state where they believed they would be free from such foreign intervention. Their exodus north became known as The Great Trek, from the verb *trekken*, meaning to move on to new and better pastures.

They travelled in huge wagons painted red, green and yellow, each drawn by up to eighteen oxen. Throughout their journey they had to live off the land. Each night they formed the wagons up in a circle and camped within this ring, like the pioneers in North America.

An apparent infinity of pasture land for cattle and to grow crops stretched in every direction, so there was no need for them all to remain in a single group. Some established camps on the banks of the Orange and Vaal Rivers (from which came the name Transvaal, across the Vaal). Others settled in fertile plains between the mountains and the Indian Ocean. This was called Natal (*terra Natalis*) because Vasco da Gama had landed there for the first time on Christmas Day, 1497.

Natal contained a number of Zulus under their own chief, and English settlers with a local governor at Port Natal. Neither the Zulus nor the English welcomed the arrival of the Boers and attempted to repulse them. They were unsuccessful and the Boers set up their first independent republic with Pietermaritzburg its capital.

All this was happening a long way from London and, since the speediest communications could take months, the British government could conveniently ignore this situation for some time. Eventually hostility between Dutch and English in Port Natal grew so strong that Sir George Napier, the Governor of the Cape, declared Natal a British colony. This had the added benefit of removing all foreigners from the coast, where conceivably they could pose a threat to shipping going to or from India.

The Boers remained determined to live their lives as they wished, not subject to the decrees of another country, so back they trekked and joined their compatriots north of the Orange and Vaal Rivers.

Here they founded two small autonomous republics, the Orange Free State and Transvaal, and here they stayed until once more the British, anxious now to secure the land frontiers of Cape Colony against any possible predators, annexed the Orange Free State.

A Liberal Government in power in England did not relish either the expense or the responsibility of a colonial war, so, in 1852, Britain recognized the independence of Transvaal, and two years later gave similar recognition to the Orange Free State.

These republics conducted their own government under their own parliaments, elected by the Dutch farmers and traders, who were known as Burghers. The British in Cape Colony were also given a constitution and an elected assembly, with powers to vote a budget, operating under the Governor and a Council.

Thus, by the third quarter of the 19th century, when Rhodes and Barnato arrived, Southern Africa contained two Boer republics and two British crown colonies. Throughout the country, indigenous natives far outnumbered whites: 3,000,000 to less than 400,000, most involved with agriculture or breeding cattle. From time to time, however, attempts were made in the Cape to produce cotton and silk on a large scale.

To the south stretched the Great Karoo, a huge and unfriendly landscape, home to several native tribes, including the Bastards. These were in fact originally bastards, born from unions between Dutch traders and Hottentot women. When Scottish missionaries arrived, they attempted to persuade the Bastards to live in settlements. As an initial base, they selected a site near a freshwater spring, named Klaarwater, around which it was hoped they would build permanent dwellings and abandon their rootless, nomadic way of life. The Rev John Campbell, of the London Missionary Society, decided that in this new life they needed a new name. So the Bastards henceforth became known as the Griquas, Klaarwater became Griquatown, and eventually the area where they lived became Griqualand West. One Sunday the Griqua chief Adam Kok saw a Boer farmer leaving the Dutch church at Bethulie wearing a magnificent hat made of beaver skin. Kok wanted this so badly that he offered the farmer a huge farm in exchange for it. The offer was accepted.

From Griquatown the nearest town with white settlers was Colesberg, 200 miles south-east, and originally a London Missionary Society mission station. White farmers, living on isolated farms between Colesberg and Griquatown, decided to found a town of their own with a church and a store. For this purpose they bought land from a Boer farmer, Siewert Christiaan Wiid, for £1,125, and diplomatically named their new settlement Hopetown, after Major William Hope, then Acting Secretary of the Cape Colonial government.

Hopetown was roughly 500 miles north-east of Cape Town, and for the next five years the authorities there took little notice of it. Then they sent a surveyor, W.F.J. Von Ludvig, to survey crown lands in the area. This routine assignment was to have momentous consequences for the future of South Africa, as was the decision of Siewert Christiaan Wiid to buy another farm, named De Kalk, with his stepson, Schalk Jacobus Van Niekerk.

Ludvig's survey took several months to carry out and, in between his journeys on horseback, he used De Kalk as his base. Ludvig's life was solitary, and whenever he returned to the farm he was glad to have Niekerk as a companion with whom he could discuss his hobby, collecting unusual stones. He had with him several books on this subject and, on his travels as a surveyor, would try to identify any new stone he found against pictures in these books.

When Ludvig's survey was complete and he was due to return to Cape Town he gave one of his books to Niekerk as a parting present and told him that, if he found any unusual stone, the pictures and explanations would help him to identify it. His last words to the farmer were, 'Keep your eyes open'.

This Niekerk did. He was pleased to have a new diversion, apart from Bible readings, to help pass spare time in his isolated farmhouse, and began enthusiastically to collect any unusual stones he could find, usually from the beds of dried-up rivers. Gradually, the profitability of De Kalk farm dwindled and Niekerk decided to sell his share and try his luck elsewhere.

A Boer family, the Jacobs, who lived in a thatched two-room cottage on the farm's boundary, expressed interest in the property. They had five children and, by living extremely quietly and cutting out unnecessary expenditure, Daniel Jacobs had saved enough money to buy Niekerk's share of the farm for £1,125 – exactly the same amount that Niekerk's stepfather had received for the whole site of Hopetown.

One day towards the end of 1866 Niekerk called on the Jacobs family, apparently to discuss some aspects of the sale. In the cottage porch he saw the Jacobs children playing with a handful of shiny pebbles. Niekerk picked up one to examine it more closely. The stone had a rough texture, was semi-transparent and appeared to be quite different from the others.

He remarked on this to Mrs Jacobs and offered to buy it for his collection. She would not hear of this, explaining that it was only an odd stone one of the children had picked up somewhere out in the veld. If Niekerk wanted it, he was welcome to have it as a gift. So Niekerk took back this stone to add to his collection.

Three months later a travelling trader, John O'Reilly, called on him. O'Reilly was one of many itinerants who made a living by buying and selling elephant tusks, ostrich feathers, the skins of wild animals and anything else on which they believed they could make a profit.

There were no inns or hotels where travellers could stay and it was the custom for Boers to offer hospitality to them, knowing that, should they also ever be on the road, others would extend the same kindness to them. In the evenings on such occasions, after a meal, guest and host would sit by candle-light, grateful for the opportunity to discuss with a stranger whatever news they had to give to each other.

Niekerk showed O'Reilly his collection of stones and then brought out the pebble Mrs Jacobs had given to him.

'Is it of any value?' he asked. 'Could it be a diamond?'

He asked this because there had been stories of people who had picked up diamonds in the area in the past, but no one ever seemed to have actually met anyone who had done so. Rumours also persisted that old maps used by the early missionaries were marked with such legends as 'Here be diamonds'. In addition, there was the experience of a German missionary, Hermann Heinrich Cleft, who, years before Hopetown existed, was said to have found a cluster of diamonds. Holding a fortune in his hand, he deliberately threw away all the stones, saying that in his opinion they would only bring tragedy to the country and its people.

O'Reilly examined Niekerk's stone thoroughly and agreed that it might indeed be a rough diamond, but he could not say for sure because he had never seen one. However, he was on his way to Hopetown and then to Colesberg, so Niekerk asked if he would take the stone with him and see whether any expert in either town could identify it, and O'Reilly agreed.

In Hopetown O'Reilly showed the stone to various traders in bars and asked their opinion. They all laughed at him. One offered him a bet – a dozen bottles of beer – that the stone was valueless. In a billiard hall that night O'Reilly asked other players for their opinion. *Could* it be a diamond? They ridiculed this idea so vehemently that he was on the point of throwing away the stone. On second thoughts, however, he decided to keep it, reasoning that if he threw it away, he could never make a profit, while if he kept it, he just might, somewhere, somehow, from someone.

He carried the stone on to Colesberg, where his reception was exactly the same. He was an idiot, a madman; anyone could see that the stone was just a piece of glass, probably made opaque by rubbing against stones at the bottom of a river. Some men to whom he showed it took such exception to his claim that it could be valuable that they seized the stone and threw it out of the window. O'Reilly had to search for several hours before he found it.

For a final opinion O'Reilly showed the stone to the Acting Civil Commissioner, Lorenzo Boyes, and asked him for his opinion. Boyes was initially as sceptical as everyone else, but there was no denying that the stone seemed totally unlike any other he had seen. It might just have *some* value, if only as a curiosity.

He took it to a local chemist who was said to know something about precious stones. The chemist declared that it was a topaz. Lorenzo Boyes was not entirely convinced, so the chemist promised that he would buy Boyes a new hat if the stone was valuable. Boyes thanked him and, with O'Reilly's consent, sent the stone on to the nearest genuine geologist he knew, Dr William Atherstone, in Grahamstown, the nearest town of any size.

Atherstone was an unlikely physician and surgeon to be practising in such a remote part of South Africa at that time. He was a true medical pioneer. Twenty years earlier he had performed the first operation in South Africa in which ether was used as an anaesthetic when he amputated a man's leg. Atherstone had also surveyed for copper in Namaqualand and was highly regarded as a reliable geologist and naturalist.

He was sitting in the garden of his house when the postman delivered the letter from Lorenzo Boyes. Although Boyes had felt that the stone might have some value, he had not bothered to register the letter or even seal the envelope. As Dr Atherstone opened it, the stone fell out on the lawn. When he read Boyes' letter, he called his daughter from the house and together they searched the grass on their hands and knees until they found it.

Although Dr Atherstone also thought at first that this was probably only a stone from the bottom of a river, washed by years of rushing water, like O'Reilly he had never seen a rough diamond, so he took it to a local jeweller for his opinion. The jeweller attempted to file it, but the stone was so hard that it blunted his files. Atherstone then carried out two tests of his own, examining the stone by polarized light and taking its specific gravity. Finally, he sought the opinion of a friend, the local Catholic priest. The priest picked up the stone and scratched his initials and the date on the window of his study. Both men agreed that no ordinary stone could do that. This must be a diamond.

Dr Atherstone wrote back to Lorenzo Boyes that he considered that it was indeed a valuable stone and added, as his opinion, 'Where that came from there are lots more'. Boyes gave Dr Atherstone permission to send the stone to the Colonial Secretary in Cape Town. In the covering letter he said that it weighed 20 carats, and so could be worth about £800.

Diamonds were so valuable because they were so rare, and also the hardest of all known substances. The word diamond comes from the Greek adamus, meaning the unconquerable; their Latin name was *diamas*. They are formed from crystallized carbon forced up from the centre of the earth by the enormous heat and pressure of volcanic eruptions. When they had first been discovered in India, near Hyderabad, the Mogul emperors believed that by possessing diamonds they could personally absorb their qualities. Diamonds represented wealth, and wealth was equated with power.

Originally, diamonds, like pearls, were weighed against dried carob seeds, which curiously, but conveniently, all weighed virtually the same. Gradually, the name carob changed to carat, possibly from the Greek word for the carob tree, *keration*.

Experts in Cape Town pronounced this stone to be a genuine diamond. One offered to buy it for £400, but the Colonial Secretary was not prepared to sell and sent it on to London. Here Garrards, the Crown jewellers, also agreed that it was a diamond, which they valued at £500.

Niekerk's discovery was now given a name, the Hope diamond. This was later changed to Eureka, after the cry of Archimedes, the Greek mathematician, when he discovered the scientific principle that still carries his name: 'Eureka, I have found it!' But no one seemed particularly interested in the fact that a diamond had been found in South Africa. Disbelief and disagreement surrounded the discovery.

The Colonial Secretary wanted the diamond sent to the *Exposition Universelle* in Paris where Cape Colony had a stand displaying their products, but the man in charge of the stand could not arouse much enthusiasm in the diamond. He attempted to persuade the *Illustrated London News* to publish a photograph of it, but they refused.

Then Garrards announced that they were not interested in the discovery of a single diamond and would delay final opinions until diamonds had been discovered in quantities that might affect the diamond market as a whole. Sir Roderick Murchison, of the Museum of Practical Geology, declared publicly that he would stake his entire professional reputation on the fact that there were no diamonds to be found in South Africa.

The Governor of the Cape, Sir Philip Wodehouse, while interested in personally buying for himself any diamonds found in South Africa, was more concerned in his official capacity with the possibility of silver being discovered in South-West Africa. He believed that the territory adjoining Cape Colony could be rich in such deposits and suggested to the Government in Whitehall that it might profitably annexe it. The Secretary of State was not interested, so this subject was dropped, like any official interest in the Hope diamond.

Some of a more acutely commercial character were, however, already pondering what might happen if more diamonds were found in South Africa. When another diamond of 15½ carats was discovered nearby, a diamond polisher, Louis Hond, moved to Hopetown in the expectation of more business, and a London merchant, Harry Emanuel of Bond Street, was particularly interested in the possibility of diamonds being found in large numbers. He feared that this could conceivably devalue diamonds found in the traditional mines in India and Brazil.

Shortly before 'Eureka' was discovered, he had published a book, *Diamonds and Precious Stones*, in which he explained how 'European traders, who had never seen or dreamt of any other but the Indian diamond, and who feared that if an indefinite number were thrown on the market by this discovery of new mines (in Brazil) their stocks would thus be depreciated, and perhaps become valueless, endeavoured by every means to discourage their sale and spread a report that the so-called Brazilian diamonds were only the refuse of the Indian mines exported from Goa to Brazil, and thence to Europe; and at first succeeded in preventing their sale.

'The Portuguese merchants, however, turned the tables on them by exporting diamonds from Brazil to Goa and then offering them for sale as Indian diamonds.'

Mr Emanuel decided that the matter was too important to rely on hearsay and second-hand opinions, and engaged Mr James R. Gregory, who, according to him was 'a gentleman well known in geological and mineralogical circles', to travel to South Africa and report back to him personally. On Gregory's return, Mr Emanuel published a letter in *The Geological Magazine* in which he ridiculed the idea of any diamonds being found in South Africa:

'Some months ago my attention was called to the report of diamonds having been discovered in or near to the Orange River and I was shown a diamond of fair quality (resembling Indian Rough material) said to have been found thereabouts,' he wrote.

'Being naturally desirous of discovering or developing a new source of supply . . . I commissioned Mr J.R. Gregory . . . thoroughly to explore the districts where diamonds were said to have been found.

'Mr Gregory has just returned and reports having carefully visited the Orange, Vaal, Buffalo and Fish rivers, as well as the adjacent country as far as 120 miles in Griqualand, and has failed to find anywhere these geological and mineralogical signs which have hitherto been invariably seen whenever diamonds have been found, and nowhere does the formation of the country warrant the inference that diamonds could exist there.'

He claimed that Mr Gregory, whom he described as 'a perfectly competent authority' had covered over 2,000 miles of Cape Colony in his researches and was 'of opinion that no diamonds have or ever will be found in the Cape Colony – saving such as are deposited there for a purpose.'

In South Africa this comment was greeted with anger and disbelief. Some said that Gregory had never visited the sites, but had only spent a fortnight beyond the Orange River. When someone showed Gregory a diamond, he claimed that it must have been dropped there by an ostrich, and that any others must also have been dropped by ostriches.

O'Reilly wrote to the local newspaper, *The Colesberg Advertiser*, claiming that Gregory had told several people he hoped to return to the Cape shortly. Mr O'Reilly left the public 'to draw their own conclusions and judge for themselves which is most likely to be the true way of accounting for the nature and style of his report.'

The general feeling was that Mr Emanuel was anxious to ridicule any possibility of more discoveries in case they reduced the value of his own stock.

Gregory suggested that some citizens of Hopetown could have found diamonds elsewhere and deliberately deposited them around their village in the hope that this might increase the value of their land. He published a report of his findings in *The Geological Magazine* in which he claimed that he 'saw no indication that would suggest the finding of diamonds or diamond-bearing deposits in any of these localities. The geological character of that part of the country renders it impossible, with the knowledge in our present possession of diamond-bearing rocks, that any could have been discovered there.'

Dr Atherstone and John O'Reilly vigorously defended their belief that diamonds *were* there and probably in large quantities. The controversy burned on inconclusively until a Griqua shepherd boy named Swartboy found another unusual stone and took this to Van Niekerk for his opinion. Van Niekerk instantly recognized this stone as a diamond and bought it from the boy for 500 sheep, ten oxen and a horse. Swartboy was delighted; so was Van Niekerk. The diamond weighted 83.5 carats and he quickly sold it on for £11,200.

This diamond became known as 'The Star of Africa'. Cut and polished, it was eventually sold for £30,000 to the Earl of Dudley. He gave it to his second wife to wear in her hair.

Gregory's name came to have a certain significance in South Africa for years thereafter. Any claim or statement involving diamonds which was manifestly untrue or exaggerated was called a 'Gregory'.

Few now doubted that other diamonds of great value remained in the Cape, waiting to be found. A large number of people immediately decided to find them. South Africa would never be the same again.

CHAPTER 2

A VICAR'S SON SETS OUT
TO GROW COTTON

When Cecil Rhodes was a small boy he was taken to visit a retired Admiral, then in his eighties. He found the old man in his garden, planting acorns.

With all the directness of the very young, Rhodes asked him a question. 'Why are you planting acorns, sir, when you cannot expect to see them growing into oaks?'

'My boy,' the Admiral replied gravely, 'I have the imagination, and I already see them as trees, with people walking in their shade. I have the pleasure of the conception of their glory.'

All through his life Cecil Rhodes would remember the Admiral's reply. Whatever he did, he would strive to build for a future that others could enjoy, but which he doubted he would ever live to see himself. As a child of relatively elderly parents – his father was 46 and his mother 36 when Cecil was born on July 5, 1853, and his mother died when he was 20 – he was unusually conscious of the shortness of human life. Years later, when Rhodes laid out a road in South Africa, he turned to a friend, Sir Thomas Fuller, a member of the Legislative Assembly, and later Agent General for the Cape, and, echoing the Admiral's words, remarked, 'I love to think that human beings will walk that road long after I am gone.'

Originally the Rhodes family came from Cheshire. In 1720 an ancestor, William Rhodes, moved to a farm east of what is now Gray's Inn Road in London, where Mecklenburgh and Brunswick Squares now stand. His ambition was to own 1000 head of breeding stock. When Cecil Rhodes was asked about this forebear, he would only reply enigmatically, 'I believe that my ancestor was a keeper of cows.'

Later the family bought two and a half acres north-east of London in Dalston, which they still owned when Cecil Rhodes was born. Rhodes' father, Francis William Rhodes, was educated at Harrow and Trinity College, Cambridge, and became curate of Brentwood in Essex. Here, because of his charitable nature, he was known as 'the good Mr Rhodes'. He built, at his own expense, a church to serve the needs of a hamlet in the nearby parish of South Weald. The vicar of this parish was also Precentor of St Paul's Cathedral and the alternate patron of the living of Bishop's Stortford in Hertfordshire, to which he appointed Francis Rhodes as vicar. Here he stayed until his retirement.

Cecil Rhodes' grandfather had speculated successfully in land and owned a factory making tiles and bricks for which there was great demand as the fields around London were steadily covered by streets of houses. Then he became involved in an unfortunate court case that dragged on for eleven years and which eventually he lost. Legal costs diminished his wealth and the blow to his family was possibly one reason why his son decided to eschew a career in business and become a cleric. However, despite this financial setback, the Vicar of Bishop's Stortford had the considerable private income of £2666 a year from his father's investments.

He married when he was 27; his wife died two years later, having given birth to a daughter. Eleven years later he married again. Cecil Rhodes made a number of wills throughout his life; in each, he pointedly excluded his half-sister.

His father married for the second time the 28-year-old daughter of a wealthy Lincolnshire banker. She bore him eleven children, two of whom died in infancy. She was a plump, cheerful woman, a very early riser every morning, and always regarded as the mainstay of their home.

'My mother got through an amazing amount of work,' Cecil Rhodes said once. 'She must have had the gift of organization, for she was never flustered and seemed always to have ample time to listen to all our many and, to us, vastly important affairs.'

Cecil was the vicar's fourth son. The fifth, Frederick, lived for only five weeks and the sixth, Elmhirst, was not born until 1858, so for four years Cecil was the youngest and, according to the family's manservant, 'his mother's boy, her favourite'.

She called him 'my darling', an endearment she did not use with her other sons. This closeness lasted unbroken until her death. She was the only person in his family who wrote to him when he went to South Africa, and to his mother alone he described in detail his early life there and his hopes and ambitions.

Rhodes' father hoped that his seven sons would become clergymen. He described them, in the description of Revelations, as 'the seven angels of the seven churches'. In fact, none followed their father's career. Three emigrated to South Africa; the others made the Army their career. In later life Rhodes could either appear almost excessively loyal to his brothers or else waspishly dismissive.

'I have four brothers,' he said once, 'each in a different branch of the British Army, and not one of them could take a company through Hyde Park Gate.'

Of another brother, Bernard, he remarked caustically, 'Bernard is a charming fellow. He rides, shoots and fishes; in fact, he is a loafer.'

Rhodes' sharpness of tongue was noted by a friend who at his death wrote an appreciation of his character.

'If there is anything in the theory of heredity,' he declared, 'it is quite certain that he was not a southerner. The shrewdness, tenacity and, I may add, the tendency to vindictiveness of Cecil John Rhodes bears every stamp of a northern origin.'

The vicar sent one of his sons, Herbert, to Bishop's Stortford grammar school, then to Winchester; his brother, Frank, went on to Eton. Cecil did not progress beyond the grammar school. Why is not clear. Certainly, shortage of money was unlikely to be the reason. The vicarage had a large staff: a manservant, a nurse and an under-nurse, a cook, a parlour maid, plus housemaids and boys to clean shoes and run errands, and two gardeners.

Contemporaries remembered Cecil Rhodes at school as 'a grubby little boy with ruffled hair'. He always had an unusually serious outlook and was nicknamed 'Long-headed Cecil' because he invariably took his time before reaching any decision, and considered all possible consequences before making up his mind. He appears to have inherited this prudence from his father who 'soon taught me to consider a question from every possible point of view'.

The Rev Francis Rhodes prided himself on giving a sermon every Sunday that lasted for exactly 10 minutes. Despite his tall, austere and rather aloof appearance he was a kindly man. When he heard that a poor parishioner was ill, he would take a bottle of wine to the house and, if money was needed, he would help. When he learned that someone else was suffering from what locals called 'a bad chest' in the cold weather, he would visit the patient wearing a poultice of camphor and lard on his own chest. He would then remove this and give it to the sick man.

When Cecil Rhodes was 13 and was asked the question, 'What is your motto?' for his answer to be included in a family album of autographs and sayings, he simply replied, 'To do or to die'. Answering another question about marriage, he replied that in his view to remain single was preferable. This outlook he maintained all his life, not only for himself, but for his male friends and associates. Of the vicar's seven sons, only one married, an unusually low proportion in an age when most men of their class did marry.

His nurse recalled that as a boy Cecil was always shy of women. He was, in her view, 'never like an ordinary child'. He was very quiet and withdrawn, and if irritated or upset would hide under a table or beneath the staircase. He was also a voracious reader and would often retreat to the summerhouse in the garden with a book.

Cecil Rhodes thought of becoming a lawyer instead of a clergyman, although, after the family's experience of the law, his father was unenthusiastic.

His mother's unmarried sister, Sophia Peacock – Aunt Sophy – lived in a large house in Sleaford in Lincolnshire. Cecil would spend school holidays with her; she taught him to ride and was always a ready listener when he wanted to discuss possible careers. He knew that to become a barrister or a clergyman he had to go to university, but to enter Oxford or Cambridge a certain proficiency in Greek and Latin was essential, not feasible to achieve at the local grammar school.

Perhaps because it seemed that to go to Oxford (rather than to his father's university) was apparently impossible, his determination to do so became an obsession. 'No' was never an easy answer for Cecil Rhodes to accept. He came to regard Oxford as the gateway to a totally new and infinitely more rewarding future. He believed that to have been a member of this university was the most important event in any man's life.

Years later, at De Beers, a visitor expressed surprise when he saw the total proceeds of a day's mining being taken away by one man, unguarded and on his own, to be weighed and registered.

'Oh, that's all right,' Rhodes explained casually. 'Mr So-and-so takes charge of the diamonds and he is an Oxford man and an English gentleman. Perhaps if there were two, they might conspire.'

At school he won a medal for elocution, although he was never a gifted public speaker, but would carry a meeting by his total belief in whatever cause he might be promoting. He was also a member of the school's cricket team, but otherwise seemed quite unexceptional at work or at games. Then, when he was 16, he began to suffer from shortness of breath.

The local doctor decided that Rhodes could be consumptive, although he showed none of the other usual symptoms of that condition. It was thought that possibly his heart was weak and the doctor suggested that a long sea voyage – a useful curative panacea proposed to those who could afford it – would restore his health.

His brother Herbert, then 25, had already emigrated to Natal in South Africa, so it seemed an ideal solution for Cecil to join him there. Not only would he have the benefit of weeks of fresh sea air on the voyage, but South Africa's warm climate would surely be beneficial to him.

Whereas Cecil often seemed to have been born middle-aged, Herbert was a cheerful, casual fellow, a show-off, unable or unwilling to settle down to any project for very long.

One of Herbert's schoolmasters, Mr Henry Wilson, described him as 'a born actor, with a face like india rubber and extraordinary command of expression', which showed when a master gave him a beating.

'Herbert was sobbing bitterly, and big tears were dropping on the floor. On the master's turning for a moment the other way, all signs of grief disappeared like magic, and a hideous grimace took their place. The master, aware from a titter that something was going on, turned sharply back to see an agonized countenance and tears again rolling down. . . .

'He might have excelled in another calling, that of Blondin. . . . Out for a walk . . . we passed an unfinished house. He ran up the ladder and out on a horizontal pole, where, without apparent effort, he would stand unsupported, haranguing his schoolfellows.'[1]

Once he dived into a local river from a revolving mill-wheel while others looked on in horrified amazement. Herbert resented his father's authority, and on one occasion lined up his brothers, gave a stick to each one – and then led them in a pointlessly destructive charge through rows of peas in the vicarage kitchen garden. In his mother's opinion, Herbert had 'every sort of sense' except one, common sense.

Herbert had gone – or been sent – abroad in response to an offer from the Land and Colonisation Company in Natal, a colony seeking new settlers. The company promised to provide each successful applicant with fifty acres of land and the option to buy 100 acres more by paying £120 over a period of twelve years. The qualifications required were not onerous. Candidates had to be of good character and familiar with country life, neither very difficult accomplishments for the son of a country clergyman.

Herbert Rhodes received his land in the Umkomaas Valley, near Pietermaritzberg. Here he cleared forty acres of euphorbia bush and planted cotton. Older settlers told him that this venture would never succeed. They were right regarding his first crop, but Herbert was confident he would eventually succeed, no matter what anyone else thought. Although he knew nothing about cotton or how to grow it successfully, he planted his land a second time.

Years later, when Cecil Rhodes was asked why he had gone to Africa in the first place, he would reply with rather heavy wit: 'They will tell you that I came on account of my health or from a love of adventure. And to some extent that may be true. But the real fact is that I could no longer stand cold mutton.'

[1] *Cecil John Rhodes*, Sir Lewis Michell, Edward Arnold, quoting a letter from Mr Wilson to *The Times*, April, 1902.

When he told Aunt Sophy he was leaving, she generously gave him £2,000 as a nest-egg. As a further insurance against any future problems, Rhodes prudently found someone in England who knew the manager of the Land and Colonisation Company in Durban and took a letter of introduction, to use in an emergency.

None of Cecil Rhodes' family came to wish him well when, just 17, he went aboard *Eudora*, a wooden sailing ship.

'I did not see my father to say goodbye to and shake hands with, but I daresay we shall some day meet again,' he wrote to his mother sadly.

Passengers on the South Africa run were mostly migrants, going out for the first time, or returning to South Africa from a furlough in England. After dark, cabins and companion-ways were lit by swinging oil lamps, weighted to keep stable as the ship rolled. At ten o'clock every night these lights were put out. After that hour it was forbidden to light candles or strike matches in cabins because of the risk of fire at sea.

On the voyage, scheduled to take seventy days, Rhodes spent a great deal of his time studying maps of South Africa, trying to familiarize himself with a country about which little was known, and also reading Plutarch's *Lives of the Greeks and Romans* and the *Meditations* of Marcus Aurelius, which became his favourite book. He would frequently quote from it: 'Put an end once for all to this discussion of what a good man should be, and be one.' 'Adapt thyself to the estate which is thy portion.' 'Bethink thee how much more grievous are the consequences of our anger than the acts which arouse it.' 'Execute every act of thy life as though it were thy last.'

There was, in fact, little to do for someone of his temperament; conditions were crude and there was, of course, no means of communication between ship and shore. From the moment they set sail until they reached their destination, everyone in the ship was cut off from all outside news. Thus none of those aboard *Eudora* heard of the outbreak of war between France and Germany, or could guess how this might affect the future of South Africa and their own.

Cecil Rhodes left no record of his voyage, but shortly after he made it, another 17-year-old, Sam Kemp, who later joined him in South Africa, wrote his account.

'The 6,000 mile voyage to Durban, Natal, began my education. My teachers were the gamblers, adventurers and loosely principled women who largely made up the passenger list. . . . I suppose I felt my boyhood slipping behind me and regretted it, for to this day I remember the fifth night out, after days of severe seasickness.

'I stood at the stern and strove to visualize my English home, far across the black waters. In the cabin behind me were hilarious women, noisy gambling, the rough and tumble of drunkenness. If I wept a little because of the ache in my heart, it was the last time I ever privileged myself. My skin was beginning to thicken.'[2]

As the ship drew alongside the quay in Durban, Rhodes scanned the small welcoming crowd on shore, hoping to see Herbert, but he was not there. Then he heard that a Dr Sutherland was asking if a Mr Cecil Rhodes was aboard and introduced himself.

Peter Cormack Sutherland explained that he was the Surveyor General of Natal and a neighbour of Herbert Rhodes, who had unexpectedly gone north, prospecting for diamonds. Before Herbert left he had asked Sutherland to look after his younger brother.

Sutherland had the job of welcoming new arrivals and explained how, after the first isolated finds of diamonds, an organized party of prospectors had set out under an experienced explorer, Captain Loftus Rolleston, to try their luck. Herbert went with them, but then returned to the farm and now had gone north for a second visit. The doctor and his wife invited Cecil to stay with them until Herbert returned. In the meantime Herbert had sent £20 to help his young brother.

The Sutherlands lived outside Pietermaritzberg. Rhodes had his first experience of the sheer size of Africa when it took nine hours and five changes of horses for the coach to reach their house. Mrs Sutherland felt that, in the saying of the time, Rhodes had outgrown his strength. He seemed very reserved and she thought him a quiet lad who was never happier than when he was reading.

Dr Sutherland showed him something of the countryside and took him for a trek through African villages. He felt that, despite Rhodes' evident interest in everything he saw, he would still go back to England and, like his father, become a country vicar. Rhodes wrote long descriptions of Natal to his mother.

'The Kaffirs rather shock your modesty,' he declared. 'Many of them have nothing on, excepting a band round the middle. They are fine-looking men, and carry themselves very erect. They all take snuff, and carry their snuff-boxes in a hole, bored through their ears. They also pay great attention to their hair and carry porcupine quills in it, with which they dress it. You often see them sitting down in groups, dressing each other's hairs, and picking the fleas out. The most disagreeable thing about them is their smell. I don't think anything equals the smell of a party of Kaffir women on a hot day if you pass on the lee side of them.'

When Herbert returned from prospecting for diamonds he took Cecil to

---

[2] *Black Frontiers, Pioneer Adventures with Cecil Rhodes' Mounted Police in Africa*, Sam Kemp, Harrap.

his farm in the Valley 110 miles away, where, within a few months, they planted a further fifty acres of cotton. Herbert had discovered some small diamonds in the north, but not enough to make him give up farming. However, the possibility that prodigious wealth could apparently be discovered so easily had unsettled him; growing cotton now seemed distinctly less attractive.

Cecil Rhodes, however, thoroughly enjoyed his new life. He was working out of doors and rapidly came to believe that everyone should have a job involving physical labour, which he personally found fulfilling. Those who didn't were, in his view, loafers.

'Every man should have active work in life,' he would say. Once, when someone said he would like to become a writer, Rhodes strongly advised against it. 'Shouldn't do that. It's not a man's work – mere loafing.'

The farm had two small huts. The brothers slept in one and used the other as a sitting room, with a table for their meals and space for stores. Life was simple and pastoral, and Rhodes' health soon improved. The sun always seemed to be shining. Around them lay green valleys, thick with flowers; above them cloudless blue skies. They employed an African servant to cook. Sometimes they would go out to share a meal with a neighbour. Every Sunday they went to church in Pietermaritzburg. From time to time Herbert would take a day off from farming to play cricket in the village of Richmond a few miles away.

Cecil wrote regularly to his mother to tell her how much he was enjoying his work. In an early letter, he explained: 'I have lent a good deal of money to the Kaffirs as it is the hut-tax time,[3] and they want money, and if you lend it them, they will come and work it out whenever you want them, besides it's getting a very good name among them and Kaffirs are really safer than the Bank of England.'

Despite Rhodes' satisfaction with his new life, he had no intention of growing cotton as a career. He simply wanted to grow enough to produce sufficient money for him to pay his fees at Oxford. This intention he explained to another young man of his own age, Henry Caesar Hawkins, the son of the Resident Magistrate. Hawkins shared Rhodes' liking for the classics and quite understood his determination to go to Oxford. He had been an undergraduate at Oriel College, where his uncle was Provost.

In another letter to his mother Rhodes asked her: 'Have you ever thought how it is that Oxford men figure so largely in all departments of public life? The Oxford system in its most finished form looks very unpractical, yet, wherever you turn your eye – except in Science – an Oxford man is at the top of the tree.'

[3] Kaffirs paid an annual tax on their living quarters of 10 shillings (50p) or £1.

As a means of making money to add to whatever profits the cotton project might bring, Rhodes asked Dr Sutherland to invest some of Aunt Sophy's money in shares in the first railway in Natal: two miles had already been built from the harbour. At that time South Africa possessed minimal manufacturing possibilities and so most goods had to be imported. Rhodes calculated that, looking ahead, this railway would become extremely profitable.

He also considered certain basic problems on their farm. Whereas Herbert had plunged into the business of growing cotton without much thought, with the result that caterpillars had eaten most of the first crop and monkeys devoured what they left, 'long-headed' Cecil viewed their project in a more scientific way.

He planted the cotton shoots farther apart, with a patch of maize every few feet to attract insects, reasoning that they would then spare the cotton. As a result the crop that the brothers grew together was much more successful than the first, which Herbert had grown on his own. They exhibited it at the Pietermaritzburg Agricultural show and were second in line for a £5 prize.

This achievement might be modest, but it gave Cecil considerable self-confidence. He had proved that his plan had worked; he could do what he had intended, despite the doubts of others. Years afterwards, when people would try to dissuade him from embarking on a plan, because they claimed it was impossible to achieve, he would reply, 'Ah, they told me I couldn't grow cotton.'

He could, but the profit was very small for all the effort involved. He could never hope to pay his Oxford fees from a few acres in this remote colony which seemed about to become even more neglected in future than it had been in the past.

Originally, Holland and Britain had found the Cape important because it was a major point halfway between Europe and the East, where both had increasingly important interests. It stood at the meeting of the Atlantic and Indian Oceans, where the waters were in such constant turmoil that generations of sea captains called Cape Town 'The Tavern of the Seas', where they could rest and revictual.

But in November, 1869, the year before Rhodes landed, the Cape's importance dwindled rapidly because the Suez Canal opened for shipping. Now vessels going to the East, or returning from it, had no need to sail round the Cape of Good Hope. As a result Cape Town and Durban lost much of their usefulness as ports.

There was now little need for suppliers of food or engineers with workshops who could carry out repairs on ships, for now there were far fewer ships. Indeed, South Africa seemed in danger of becoming another written-off tract of land where settlers bred cattle and sheep, and exported ostrich feathers, wool and wine. It did not possess more than sixty miles of railway. The main towns were little better than English villages; only twenty had populations in excess of 1000 people.

Then, shortly before Rhodes' arrival, diamonds were discovered. Newspapers reported how some people had become rich almost overnight, apparently just by scratching the earth to reveal these precious stones. The fever for diamonds spread as swiftly as it had done for gold in California twenty years earlier. Two American writers, Charles and Mary Beard, described what had happened then, when 'Artisans dropped their tools, farmers left their cattle to die and their crops to rot, lawyers fled from clients, teachers threw aside their books, preachers cast off their cloth, sailors deserted their ships in the harbours, and women left their kitchens – all in one overwhelming rush for the gold-bearing districts. Business ceased in the towns; real estate slumped; deserted houses and shops sank into decay. From every direction, fortune hunters swept down like locusts.'[4]

This rush for instant wealth now spread to South Africa and inspired Herbert Rhodes, despite his previous lack of success by the Vaal River, to go north once more, at what were called 'the dry diggings' at Dutoitspan. Henry Caesar Hawkins followed him and Cecil Rhodes wrote to his mother: 'People out here do nothing but talk diamonds. Everyone is diamond mad.'

Some people found that diamonds brought quick profits. Captain Rollestone was one. Rhodes wrote home: 'To hear Rollestone talk and see his diamonds makes one's mouth water. Three whoppers, one worth £8,000, another £10,000 and another £9,000. The man who found the £10,000 diamond had offered his claim the evening before for fifteen shillings, but nobody would buy it.'

Against such prodigious returns, potential profits from growing cotton seemed pathetic. Even so, Rhodes' natural caution made him hold back before joining his brother. He now had thirty Africans working for him and was considering buying another farm. He even sent home a sample of the cotton grown to show his parents how good his last crop had been.

Then Herbert Rhodes found several more diamonds, including stones of 14, 16 and 28 carats, and it was said that every week diamonds worth at least £40,000 were being discovered in the area. Cecil realized he would never make such money from growing cotton on a farm of their size and he decided to go digging for diamonds. He calculated that he had a far greater chance of making sufficient money quickly to pay his university fees by discovering even a few diamonds than by growing cotton. Despite reaching this

---

[4] *The Rise of American Civilisation*, Charles A. Beard & Mary R. Beard, Vol I, The Macmillan Company, New York.

conclusion, he characteristically waited until the cotton harvest was over before he set out for the north, 400 miles away.

He had several means of reaching the dry diggings. There were no roads, of course, and the route lay through desert areas, inhabited by wild animals. The journey could be made by post-cart, the quickest and most expensive way, in a huge coach capable of carrying fifteen passengers and pulled by mules, or by the slower but less crowded ox-cart, pulled by teams of oxen. Some carts used as many as eighteen.

Rhodes decided on a compromise; he would load his baggage on an ox cart and ride a pony himself alongside it. He packed his cabin trunk with all his belongings, including volumes of Homer, Plutarch, Marcus Aurelius and a Greek lexicon, and set off.

The cart was hung with spades and metal sieves with a fine mesh, in which, so Herbert had told him, the earth they dug could be shaken, hopefully leaving any diamonds on the wire screen. The cart itself was enormous. It weighed four tons and had low wooden sides with a canvas roof like a tent top supported on four poles, one at each corner.

On both sides and at the back canvas curtains were rolled up and held in place by leather straps. These curtains could be lowered to shelter the occupants from sun or rain. The vehicle was hung about with canvas pouches holding tins of meat and sardines, bottles of water, cured hams, loaves of bread and flasks of whisky and brandy. Canvas buckets to collect water from any rivers they passed were hooked to the cart sides.

The driver sat up front and behind him were three hard benches, each wide enough to sit three people. Under the driver's feet were rolled coils of rope and several wooden pegs, straps and wedges to jam under the wooden wheels to prevent the cart from rolling backwards if they had to stop on a hill. The driver held a whip like a fishing rod, about fifteen feet in length, with a long lash of narrow plaited strips of bullock hide. At the tip was a small hairy tuft of antelope skin, with which he could flick the backs of the oxen to increase their pace. Sometimes a wheel would strike a hidden boulder or a tree stump with a force that could snap the spokes. When the route was through such very rough country, the driver would walk alongside, shouting encouragement by name to any of the oxen he thought were not accepting their fair share of the work. The Boers called the laziest ox in the team 'Rooinek' or 'Englishman'.

When the wagon approached a steep downward slope the driver would run to the rear of the wagon to screw on the brakes that bore on the edges of the back wheels. This was essential to prevent the wagon from gathering speed and plunging into the oxen, possibly killing them.

There was little hope of buying more than the bare essentials of life in New Rush (see p. 37) and even these were hugely expensive because they had to be transported for hundreds of miles, so visitors carried with them every-thing they might need.

The journey would take more than a month and the aim was to stop each night near a Boer farmhouse. The Boer farmers were generally poor, strug-gling to survive in a harsh environment, but their strict religious beliefs made them regard helping wayfarers as a duty – even the disliked foreigners, the *uitlanders*, who were now coming in such unwelcome numbers to search for diamonds.

If travellers could not reach a farmhouse by nightfall then they could outspan – unhitch – the oxen and sleep in the cart. If several carts were trav-elling in convoy, they could arrange them in a circle and sleep in the centre. There was a real danger from wild animals, and some travellers who had unwisely slept beneath their carts had been dragged off by lions.

The increasing number of ox carts, horsemen and even marchers who now were on the road north astonished the Boers. These travellers wanted to buy far more food than the farmers were accustomed to produce, which led to a strange reaction from some of the farmers they approached. For years they had eked out a bare existence, and yet now some could not comprehend this totally unexpected opportunity to make more money in a month than previ-ously they might have earned in a year.

Thomas Fuller, a traveller visiting the diamond fields, had first-hand experience of this attitude. He was travelling in what he called an American coach, drawn by six horses, with relays of other horses following in loose formation, taking their turn as required, and so reached their destination in twelve days.

For the first night of the journey the coach stopped at a Boer farmhouse, where the owner complained to Fuller that strangers were calling on him by day and night, all eager to buy forage for horses and mules, and food for themselves. Sometimes they would even try to buy a sheep from him to kill for meat. The farmer told Fuller that he could no longer tolerate all this commotion. He was about to abandon the farm and move elsewhere for a quieter life.

Fuller looked around the sparsely furnished little room where they were standing; the man's children were wearing rags and his wife was heavily pregnant.

'I think you ought to be ashamed of yourself,' he told the farmer bluntly. 'By a little industry and attention to your farm you have now a golden chance of earning a good income and putting your children to school instead of letting them pig about the sand half-clad. And now, you want to run away from the opportunity of a lifetime. How a fine, healthy man at your age should surrender such a chance is past understanding. My advice to you is, sow more oats, grow more vegetables, and reap the harvest while you can.'

The farmer was astonished at Fuller's advice, but he accepted it and soon he became one of the most prosperous farmers for miles around.

Despite the riding lessons Rhodes' Aunt Sophy had arranged, Rhodes was never a very good rider. He sat with his body slightly hunched, head forward, his thoughts apparently miles away. Heat beat down on him and on the travellers in the cart like the blast from a suddenly opened furnace door. When the driver lowered the side curtains, the passengers sat sweating, bracing their bodies against the jerk and lumbering movement of the unsprung vehicle, swatting swarms of greedy flies that followed them. Sometimes, when they stopped briefly, groups of men heading for the diamond fields on foot would pass them shouting cheerfully, 'On your way! You're blocking up the road!'

Each man carried a small pack and blankets on his back, military fashion, with an axe and a large knife stuck into his belt. They walked with long easy strides, heads down against the sun until, trailing a cloud of dust, they would disappear into the shimmering distance on their way, they felt certain, to fortune.

From time to time the passengers would climb down from their hard seats in the cart to walk for a few miles and relieve cramp that gripped leg and back muscles as a result of sitting for hours on a wooden bench. Those who did not do so began to complain of pains in their legs and feet. When they removed their shoes, ankles and feet swelled so much they could not put them on again. At night, when the wagon stopped, they would lie down on a blanket on the dry ground, with their feet propped up on a log or flat stone, above the level of their heads, until the swelling subsided.

This was the first time Rhodes had travelled with an ox-cart; he could not have imagined what a large part of his life he would now spend in one on his travels across Southern Africa. An ox-cart then was much more than a home on wheels. It could also become a mobile fortress, capable of being roped down precipices, hoisted up over mountains and driven through steep and stony drifts, over rocks and ant heaps.

The huge distances these wagons had to cover and the total lack of roads meant that they had needed a primitive form of independent suspension. The front and back parts of the undercarriage were linked by a long wooden beam which would yield to every inadequacy of the track. The front axle pivoted loosely on a bolt and so could draw out a little to relieve the tilting of the wagon when one of the wheels went up on a rock or across an ant-hill.

In England a network of lanes and roads linked villages and towns, which were only a few miles apart. Between them, hedges or fences divided fields into neat squares so that in spring the countryside resembled a patchwork quilt of different crops. Here emptiness often stretched on every side.

Sometimes the earth was grey, sometimes brown and hot, like fire-bricks. They passed eucalyptus trees with long thin trunks and branches twenty-odd feet above the ground. Then they would come to a patch of greenish grass or weed or an area of chalky sand. The Boer homesteads they passed were often no more than square shacks, with thatched roofs, surrounded by fields of corn to feed their animals and themselves, and others bright yellow with sunflowers. The farmers would squeeze the seeds to make cooking oil.

Sometimes, in the distance, the sky of cerulean blue was reflected in the hot sand, so that it seemed that not a desert but the sea lay ahead, blue and cool and peaceful. And then the mirage would vanish and the desert return, all a trick of light on dazzled, aching eyes. Often they would see the detritus of other less fortunate travellers: a broken wheel with wooden spokes twisted out of its hub, the bleached bones of skeletons, picked white by vultures.

They came across unexpected pools of water, known locally as pans. In some the water was fresh, in others bright green with algae or glowing with phosphorescent decay, poisoned by the body of a dead animal. One day they might be trundling through valleys with ferns and yellow broom on either side. The next they would be negotiating a pass that led to a plateau floored with round pebbles, each burning hot to the touch, or stretches of dried grass scattered with dead shrubs or burned-out bushes. The whole landscape could be so flat that no plant stood more than six inches out of the ground; the only shadows were those thrown by the ox-cart and Rhodes' pony.

His pony did not survive the journey. Poor food and a punishing pace over rough ground in constant, burning heat proved too much, and the animal died before they reached the outskirts of their destination. The desert was by then falling behind them. Clumps of long grass like pampas rattled in the wind. They came upon trees, and pools of water coloured green, orange or purple from mineral deposits in the ground. Then they were on an unmade track, thick with dust, but at least better than anything they had previously encountered on their journey.

In the distance they could see a mass of tin huts reflecting the sun like heliographs, with covered carts and wagons and rows of dusty tents. This was their destination, which had grown with great speed – like 'the river diggings' – through a series of seemingly unconnected incidents, simple in themselves, but complicated by lawsuits and the threat of violence.

After Swartboy, the Griqua shepherd, had found 'The Star of Africa' diamond, controversy arose as to exactly where he had found it. Some claimed he had discovered it north of the Orange River and at once carried it across the river in case the Griqua chief, Nicolaas Waterboer, claimed it as being found on his territory. The only person known to be interested in unusual stones was Schalk Van Niekerk, to whom he sold it. Lorenzo Boyes, who had passed the Eureka diamond to Dr Atherstone, now joined with some others in Colesberg to form a prospecting company, the Diamond Metal & Mineral Association.

This association came to an arrangement with Nicolaas Waterboer, promising to pay him one-fifteenth of whatever they made prospecting in his territory.

They now challenged the buyers of this diamond, Lilienfeld Brothers, who had paid Niekerk £11,200 for it, on the grounds that it had been found in an area over which they had an exclusive agreement. They lost their case in the court, but the resulting publicity aroused great interest, and further controversy as to the extent of Griqua territory.

The early river diggings had been in a politically sensitive area, with the Boer republics – Orange Free State and the Transvaal – to the east and north-east, Cape Colony to the south-west, and the Griquas also making their claims to much of the land. The Boer president of the Transvaal, Marthinus Pretorius, declared a diamond monopoly to three diggers working along the north bank of the Vaal River, which he claimed as Boer territory. This would last for twenty-one years from June, 1870.

British diggers refused to accept this ruling. A former Royal Navy seaman, Stafford Parker, was voted president of what they called The Diggers' Mutual Protection Union, locally known as 'The Diggers' Republic'.

This uneasy state of affairs lasted for several months until the British authorities in Cape Colony dispatched a magistrate with orders to protect the interests of British subjects. The 'Diggers' Republic' collapsed and the area came under British suzerainty.

Then more diamonds were discovered on two farms, Dorstfontein and Bultfontein, 25 miles south of Pniel, a German mission station on the Vaal River. Dorstfontein later changed its name to Dutoitspan, after a previous owner, Abraham Paulus du Toit. Thousands of fortune hunters now swarmed over these farms and also over another farm nearby, Vooruitzicht, which was owned by two Boer brothers named De Beer. Then a group of diggers from Colesberg found more diamonds about a mile away, on a small hill called Colesberg kopje, which prompted a 'New Rush' from which the area then took its name.

A young digger, Richard Jackson, had been searching for diamonds on the Vaal River without much success. One day an African labourer mentioned that he had seen, or heard about, a white man farther south who was apparently digging up diamonds from dry ground every day. Jackson was sceptical. Such stories were not uncommon, but few people ever seemed to have met these solitary and successful diggers. Stories about them had the attraction of legend rather than truth.

Then Jackson's brother-in-law told him that he had overheard two labourers also discussing this man and they decided to discover whether his existence and activities were true or simply imagined.

They took two friends with them in two Scotch carts and set off towards Vooruitzicht, a three-day journey over the dry veld. As they approached the farm they saw that a tent had been pitched and a wooden table set up outside it. A middle-aged man was sitting at this table, sorting through gravel in a casual, unhurried way. Jackson believed that people only sorted gravel for one reason – to search for diamonds. He and his colleagues therefore decided to approach this man with the utmost caution. They did not want him to suspect that they could also be interested in finding diamonds.

The man was friendly and admitted, without any subterfuge, that he was not only looking for diamonds, he was finding them. He explained that the owner of the farm, Johannes Nicolaas De Beer, had given him permission to do this on the understanding he paid De Beer a quarter of anything he found. To show he was not boasting, he produced a matchbox half-full of small diamonds. Jackson and his friends had never seen such a collection, worth what to them was a fortune.

Jackson realized that the moment for truth had arrived. He explained that he and his companions would also like to search for diamonds. The man advised them to wait until De Beer's son-in-law, who valued his finds every week, was due to arrive. They could then ask him for permission to search for diamonds on their own account.

This young man was not particularly forthcoming. In fact Jackson later called him 'a most offensive and objectionable fellow'. But they were not there to become friends; they were there to do a deal. After some discussion, they did so. The son-in-law agreed that they could each have a claim, thirty feet by thirty feet, on the same basis: that De Beer took a quarter of the proceeds. In addition, they could, if they wished, reserve a few more claims for other friends.

Back on the river diggings, they told several others that they had pegged out claims for them in advance; it was clearly in all their interests to return to Vooruitzicht as quickly and quietly as possible.

This proved easier to say than to do. They required eight wagons to carry all their belongings and it was impossible for eight loaded wagons suddenly to leave at once with a number of diggers and not arouse suspicions that they must have found diamonds elsewhere. No one wished to be left behind. Before the wagons were out of sight they were being followed.

The river diggings had been unique in that they took place on the banks of a huge river, in which diggers could bathe after a hot day's work. Also, most of the diggers were colonists and not fortune hunters desperate for success at any price, so the area had almost the air of a summer work camp. One of the diggers described years later how 'The quietude of these solitary regions is now broken by the song of the happy digger as he goes forth in the morning to begin his day's labour among the huge boulders in his claim, where, throughout the day, the sound of pick and shovel is heard, or perhaps the shout of a lucky digger who has just succeeded in finding a diamond.'[5]

This friendly, almost casual atmosphere did not extend to New Rush, (later to be called Kimberley after Lord Kimberley, the British Colonial Secretary). He deliberately delayed declaring Griqualand West a Crown Colony because he said he would not have electoral divisions announced until the areas concerned had 'decent and intelligible names', and he 'declined to be in any way connected with such a vulgarism as New Rush'. There was also a third, more personal reason. He could neither spell nor pronounce Vooruitzicht and asked that districts around the mining camps should be given 'English sounding names'. New Rush therefore became Kimberley.

De Beer was a faithful member of the Dutch Reformed Church, and so zealous in his church duties that he would take a collection regularly from the diggers. Several actually received claims by paying their money directly to church funds instead of to him.

At first dozens, then hundreds, of newcomers competed furiously for claims. They hacked away at the hard earth and most found nothing but stones. It had been a waste of their time and effort. One by one they left to try their luck elsewhere.

One of the diggers who left De Beer's farm was Fleetwood Rawstorne, known for his habit of wearing a red cap; he and his group were called 'The Red Cap Party'. Rawstorne had found a few diamonds, then lost his profits gambling, and he moved away for about a mile, where he camped until he decided on his next move. He was a man of some means – his father was Colesberg's first magistrate – and he employed a Cape Coloured cook named Damon who, under the influence of drink, would sometimes disappear for days.

One evening Rawstorne ordered Damon to go away and recover from a drinking bout. Almost facetiously, he told him to go to a nearby hill, Gilfillan's Kop, and start digging for diamonds there to atone for his behaviour.

Damon did so. He returned three days later, lifted the flap of Rawstorne's tent and silently held out one hand. In his palm lay several small diamonds.

Rawstorne and his friends had been playing cards. Immediately they abandoned their game, picked up stakes and hatchets and followed Damon across the veld to the small hill, where he had dug a shallow shaft near a thorn tree. Rawstorne at once marked out his claim and the others

[5] Quoted in *Early Diamond Days*, Oswald Doughty, Longman's, London, 1963

hammered in stakes to mark theirs. In honour of the town from which Rawstorne came, this hill was re-named Colesberg Kop.

Later, the distinction of finding the first diamond here was claimed by a young mother, Sarah Ortlepp. She and her husband, with their son and daughter, were living near Rawstorne's tent. Her husband had also been unsuccessful at De Beers and, like Rawstorne, wanted to try somewhere else. But where?

One Sunday afternoon the Ortlepp family went for a walk with their dog. It was a hot day and when they reached Gilfillan's Kop they sat down thankfully under a thorn tree. Almost by force of habit Sarah put out a hand and began to sift the gravel. Among a few pebbles she found a yellow diamond.

Oddly, they did not search for any more, but returned to their tent. Why, was never explained. However, Mrs Ortlepp had definitely found a diamond, which she kept as a souvenir wrapped in a twist of paper, on which she wrote the year in which she had found it, 1871.

When Rhodes arrived all this was in the past. What mattered to him, and to thousands of others all searching furiously to find more diamonds, was the present – and their immediate future.

CHAPTER 3

'A MAN'S LIFE IS WHAT HIS THOUGHTS MAKE OF IT'

Herbert Rhodes was living in a small tent, one among hundreds in the area. Thousands of men like him, some with wives and children, who had come to New Rush from all parts of the world to search for diamonds, were living in similar tents or in little square huts of corrugated iron. A number lacked even such permanency and were still in the ox-wagons that brought them north. They reasoned that if they were lucky and made their fortunes quickly they could be away within hours, and so saw no need to buy and pitch tents or to build huts.

Stories abounded, not all fictitious, of prospectors who had arrived one morning, bought a claim cheaply from someone who was desperate for money, discovered a diamond worth thousands that afternoon and were off again before sundown. If the new arrivals had to stay here longer than they wished or intended, then their time would be better spent digging for diamonds than trying to create a permanent home. And, in any case, many did not have the money to do so.

New Rush did not possess any roads in the accepted sense of the word. People and animals moved around as best they could between wagons, tents, huts and pyramids of earth dug out of the kopje.

This was not what Cecil Rhodes had thought the end of the road from the Cape would be like. Indeed, it seemed a most unlikely place in which he could ever make enough money to pay his Oxford fees. But then he had really no clear idea what to expect and he did his best to explain the strangeness of everything in a letter to his mother.

'Imagine a small round hill at its very highest point only 30 feet above the level of the surrounding country, about 180 yards broad and 220 long; all around it, a mass of white tents, and then beyond them a flat level country for miles and miles with here and there a gentle rise.

'I should like you to have a peep at the kopje [hill] from my tent door at the present moment. It is like an immense number of antheaps covered with

40

black ants, as thick as can be, the latter represented by human beings. When you understand there are about 600 claims in the kopje and each claim is generally split into 4, and on each bit there are about 6 blacks and whites working, it gives a total of about ten thousand working each day on a piece of ground about 180 yards by 220. . . .

'All through the kopje, roads have been left to carry the stuff off in carts. . . . There are constantly mules, carts and all going head over heels into the mines below as there are no rails or anything on either side of the roads.'

This was a deliberately economical description of what Rhodes saw. He did not wish to alarm his parents with details they could find distressing, even horrifying. And it would be difficult, possibly impossible, for a country vicar in England to imagine (or believe) the harsh realities of life in New Rush.

The diggers, black men and white, worked from dawn until it was too dark to continue, every day of the week, except Saturdays when they stopped at two o'clock, and Sundays which were free. Many new arrivals had sacrificed careers as professional men to raise money for this supreme gamble. Army officers had resigned their commissions, able-bodied seamen jumped ships, lawyers and doctors abandoned their practices, along with schoolboys who simply ran away from home to join forces with innumerable gold prospectors from Canada, the United States and Australia, in a desperate search for wealth.

They lived and worked next to refugees from Russian ghettoes and tradesmen of almost every description – carpenters, grave-diggers, bakers, clerks, hod-carriers, indeed anyone who could find, beg or borrow enough money to pay the fare to this new and largely undiscovered country. Most of the diggers were powerful men who cultivated long beards. Butcher's knives or axes were stuck by their handles into their thick leather belts. African labourers wore a few ostrich feathers around their loins, or sometimes the cast-off suit of a white digger. Hundreds of Africans arrived every day, hoping for work. Their intention in the main was to make enough money to buy a musket which they could take back to their village. They would come to Kimberley barefoot and wearing loin cloths, and leave in European-style suits.

Most diggers had come only with what belongings they could carry – in many cases all they owned. Gradually the round hill was whittled away until it was level with the earth. Digging continued until what had been a hill became an ever-deepening hole.

Mules pulled carts piled with earth away from this hole to deposit it outside the claim owner's hut or tent or wagon, where it could be sifted on a table or the top of a discarded packing case.

Not every digger worked at the same pace, so the claims were at different levels. To reach them the diggers climbed down wooden ladders against the sides. Between each claim a dividing border of earth had to be left, and along these narrow tracks, often not much wider than a brick wall, men heaved wooden wheelbarrows piled high with dirt from one thin walkway to another.

It only needed a man with an overloaded barrow to meet another man without room to pass for a serious accident to occur. Spurred by the urgency to hurry, for every minute's delay was regarded as a total waste of their own time, both would argue, often with increasing vehemence and anger. One or the other, or both, could lose their balance on the precarious path and fall.

When carts dropped down the hole mules and men were often killed or fearfully mutilated, and earth that had been so laboriously removed was flung back into the bottom of the pit, to be shovelled out for a second time. Wrecked carts were hauled up to the surface at the end of ropes. Mangled corpses of men and mules were brought up in the buckets used to lift the ore to ground level.

'It needs a firm nerve to stand upon the brink alone . . . and look through the running gear – the great network of ropes that cover the face of the Kopje, as it were a spider's web spread over the whole – and, in the midst of the great buzz, to take a calm survey of the work going on,' one digger wrote. 'I have seen strong men tremble and clutch the staging whilst they looked into this great human ant-hill. . . . The giddy heights, the noise, the bustle, the elbowing, are sufficient to bewilder anyone. . . .

'Some of the men get to work in these awkward and dangerous places by means of ladders, some rope-ladders, and some the ordinary builder's ladder. Never has a native met with an accident in going to and from his work by means of holes cut in the rock; but there have been many accidents from climbing up rope and chain-ladders. . . . Men have had frightful falls without being much injured. One man fell over fifty feet, and came up only a little bruised. A man yesterday, aggravated by another, threw him down his claim, between forty and fifty feet deep. The fellow came up again as lively as a cricket; he was not even scratched.

'The greatest danger to be now apprehended is the falling in of the reef. Several pieces have fallen in, and men have been buried in the ruins. It has been predicted that the staging will yet fall in; and if that were to take place, thousands of lives must be sacrificed.'[1]

For those injured in accidents, or simply ill from a multitude of afflictions – camp fever, malaria, dysentery and typhus brought on by the insanitary

---

[1] Quoted by Brian Roberts, *Kimberley – Turbulent City*, 1976, David Philip, Cape Town.

conditions – a visit to hospital could be very little better than remaining in their tents.

The first local hospital was simply another tent at Bultfontein, known as the Dutoitspan Hospital. It lacked what many would consider the most essential item in any hospital ward – beds. Patients had to lie on the dusty floor, shielded from the heat of the sun by the canvas roof. A Roman Catholic priest, Father Anatole Hidien, a man of great compassion but without formal medical training, had built the hospital and treated the patients as best he could.

Some months after Rhodes' arrival the Diggers' Committee of Dutoitspan, Bultfontein and Vooruitzicht decided to organize a better hospital, which would be called the Diggers Central Hospital. Again, this was simply a canvas marquee, but it had the services of a doctor and a medical orderly. However, the amount of money raised by a whip-round – £400 – still did not provide for beds, and during a dust storm two months later the wind blew the marquee to pieces.

Later a more permanent hospital, two huts built of wattle and daub walls with canvas roofs, was constructed to take twenty patients. Deaths in hospital were common, so next door to the huts a tent was pitched for a mortuary. One morning the doctor visited this tent to examine a patient who had died during the night when he was off-duty. Instead of the man's body, he only found the trunk; ravenous dogs that prowled the camp had crept in and torn away the arms and legs.

Death or mutilation by illness or accidents was accepted as a risk diggers had to endure. So were other hazards, such as the searing heat, dust and storms. Above their heads the sun burned like a furnace in the sky and diggers soon learned to gauge the approach of dust storms when dust, thick as an abrasive fog, dimmed the fierce blaze of the sun.

The canvas walls of their tents would begin to flap wildly in warning and sheets of paper blew about like autumn leaves. Tent poles would creak and bend, and, as the storm came closer, people became disorientated. Tents were blown away, cooking pots lifted as though by unseen hands, and even ox-carts overturned. When the storm passed over and away from the encampment, often as fast as it had arrived, it left behind a thick coating of dust on everything. Food was ruined, clothes ripped, faces, hands and arms felt raw, as though they had been sandpapered.

Sometimes it was not worth clearing away this dust, for a rainstorm could follow with flashes of lightning. Many diggers stuck bottles upside down on top of their tent poles in an attempt to deflect the blue lightning flashes. The rain was as insidious as the dust. One moment a digger could be contemplating the ruin of his few possessions in his tent – if the tent had survived – and the next he would be standing in a pool of liquid mud.

A more constant irritation than either dust or rain storms were flies, blue and black, bloated and greedy. Because there was virtually no sanitation – latrines were simply trenches dug in the open air, perhaps screened off, perhaps not – the foul stench of sewage hung over New Rush like an evil miasma. An indication of local inertia about solving this problem is the fact that on 10 May, 1884, thirteen years after Rhodes first arrived at the diggings, the town council were still discussing tenders for removing buckets of night soil. The contract was eventually awarded to a man who said he could carry out this disagreeable work for four shillings per bucket per month.

Flies covered the unburied bodies of oxen, stray dogs and goats, and all the rubbish tips. Even the walls of cafés, known as canteens, were black with flies. Diggers ate flies with their food, drank them with brackish water, breathed them, sneezed and choked over them. Flies brought a correspondingly large amount of disease.

New Rush was clearly not a town with much to commend it. Yet, paradoxically, the discomfort, the dangers, the heat, dust and general squalor only heightened a general sense of excitement. The diggers optimistically believed that they were about to witness the birth of great individual wealth – their own. Surely any pain must be worth such a result?

Outside the immediate centre of all this frenetic activity stood tents owned by Boers, who would carry buckets of rubble, thrown away by more prosperous diggers, for their wives to sort through a second time. They were too poor to buy a claim themselves; their best hope was that they might find a few stray diamonds someone better placed had missed.

Hand-painted signs above some of the more permanent tin huts announced the nature of business being carried on inside: Rothschild's Auction Mart; Abraham & Co's Market Store (Wholesale & Retail Grocers); J.B. Bodley (Hairdresser); Ron Witch's Dispensary (Homeopathic & Patent Medicines). Above some shacks flags flew, showing their owner's nationality: Austrian, French, German, British.

The diamond dealers' huts contained desks with sets of scales protected from heat and dust under polished glass cases. The weights involved were minute, and all were polished, because the slightest amount of dust could give a false reading. To move diamonds on and off the scales the dealers used tiny shovels the size of sugar spoons. Despite this visible evidence of scrupulous accuracy – and at the diggings some buyers would shield their scales by a hat, lest even wind could interfere with their accuracy – it was generally believed that the scales were always weighted in their owners' favour, some more than others.

Buyers would sit outside their huts on wooden stools, their elbows resting on the table. They might be there for hours without a digger arriving with diamonds to spread out for their inspection and valuation. Beyond these huts were others belonging to store keepers who supplied food or digging tools, or provided goods for native labourers, blankets, mealie-meal and rifles.

Ian Colvin, the biographer of Dr Leander Starr Jameson, who would play a pivotal part in Rhodes' later career, wrote: 'Beneath and around these, [were] the disreputable trades, labour touts, liquor sellers, illicit diamond buyers, Jews and Levantines, a plausible, voluble, accommodating sub-community, so skilful in their intrigues and so powerful in the interests which united them as sometimes to threaten the very existence of the industry on which they battened.'[2]

None battened to any extent on long-headed Cecil Rhodes. Within a few months he was making a remarkable profit of £100 a week, an impressive income compared with what he could have hoped to earn in England; an unqualified clerk of his age would probably be paid 10 shillings a week. Many of the stones he found were very small but it was seldom he found a diamond that was not worth five shillings, and the number of five shillings soon added up. He wrote to his mother: 'Diamonds have only to continue at a fair price, and I think Herbert's fortune is made.'

From early morning until it was too dark to see he would sit behind his sorting table, moving debris from the diggings across it with a flat piece of iron. Sometimes his African diggers did not appear for work, usually because they had already achieved their aim, to make enough money to buy a gun. Then Rhodes would roll up his sleeves and go down the mine himself to dig. His ambition, an Oxford degree with possibly a professional qualification, was too important to be side-tracked by the failings and slackness of others. In these early days he did not appear to suffer from any heart trouble or poor health.

Such tracks as the area possessed wound around a huge and ever-increasing pyramid of earth dug out of the hole, known as Mount Ararat. This had grown from the habit of early diggers of dumping wheelbarrows of waste soil in the same place, so that, as the original kopje sank, Mount Ararat grew higher.

In the centre of the town was a flat area where ox carts were driven on arrival. Other carts waited here to leave, and still others came in from the countryside with produce to sell. Some of the houses round about had been converted into shops with cheap tin trays, pots and pans hanging on strings around the doors and windows.

Water was so short that washing was a luxury. A source that had been sufficient for a few farms was totally inadequate for thousands of manual

---

[2] *The Life of Jameson*, Ian Colvin, Vol 1, Edward Arnold, 1922.

workers. Drinking water was always suspect, and only the richer diggers could afford five shillings for a bottle of locally produced soda water. Everything they ate had to come at least 400 miles from the coast. With animals shot locally for food, a dead springbok cost a shilling (5p) in the local market, a wildebeeste half a crown (12½p). Fresh vegetables were very few and extremely expensive; an onion cost half a crown, a cabbage ten shillings (50p) and, at the height of the dry season, three times as much.

Oddly, when so much else was expensive, drink was cheap. A dozen quart bottles of champagne cost £3. Brandy was 7s. 6d.(37½p) a gallon, Cape sherry four shillings (20p) a gallon. At night there was heavy drinking in the pubs, but none of the violence associated with the gold rushes in Australia and the United States. Men drank to share the triumph of lucky colleagues, to remember their own good fortune, or to forget their bad luck, the months they'd spent here, the money they'd wasted, with no dividend, no result at all. And as they staggered back to their huts or tents, tripping over guy ropes, cursing grazing mules that got in their way, they would pass The Big Hole, dark, empty, sombre under the moon. It was a constant and silent reminder of hope won, hope lost, of despair, frustration, elation.

The continual struggle against harsh working and living conditions under a pitiless sun caused serious eye problems. Diggers had to sort all diamonds from the dirt before they could take them to dealers. Against the sunlight they wore wide-brimmed hats, and some dark glasses. Peering for hours on end, day after day, at heaps of dry earth for any tiny stones they might contain, constantly sifting and re-sifting in case they had missed one, caused fearful strain on their eyes. Married men would enlist their wives to help them with these eye-aching but absolutely essential searches.

The Big Hole was ringed with big wooden posts. These supported pulleys over which ropes stretched down inside it, already hundreds of feet deep and deepening every day. In the bottom of this pit, natives, sometimes naked, or at most wearing a loin cloth, men diminished by distance to the size of dwarves, kept hacking away at the claims, filling metal and leather buckets full of earth which others pulled up on the pulleys to take away to sort. The men down in the pit would give a warning shout when their buckets were full and ready to be hauled away. There was a constant clang of shovels on metal buckets and the hoarse cries of men shovelling in the depths of the earth.

A visitor to Kimberley in 1872 described it as 'a chaos of tents and rubbish heaps seen through a haze of dust. I had tumbled, numbed and sleepy, out of the coach that for twelve days and nights had jolted on over mountain and veld, and landed me at length amongst the rubbish heaps of Du Toit's Pan.

'Having a friend at "the Rush", I set out at once to find him, but it was a puzzling business tracking men to their camps in those days, for the whole place was a heterogeneous collection of tents, waggons, native kraals and debris heaps, each set down with cheerful irresponsibility and indifference to order.

'At length, however, after following many distracting directions, I lit upon a little cluster of tents and beehive huts, set round an old and gnarled mimosa tree: a Zulu was chopping wood and an Indian cook was coming out of the mess tent with a pile of plates: and here it was I found my friend.

'Alongside of him was a tall fair boy, blue-eyed, and with somewhat aquiline features, wearing flannels of the school playing-field, some-what shrunken with strenuous rather than effectual washings, that still left the colour of the red veld dust – a harmony in a prevailing scheme. This was my first impression of Cecil John Rhodes. As we brought our tents and set them next to his, I was destined in the following year to see much of him.

'The burly man of later years was at this time a slender stripling, showing some traces of the delicacy that had sent him to the Cape. He had not long come to the Fields, and the impression made upon such a nature as his by the novel world in which he found himself must have been particularly pene-trating. Fresh from home and school, he found himself amongst men of much experience in many walks of life; his self-reliance led him into compe-tition with them; and good fortune, and his clear head, brought him out on top.'[3]

Cecil Rhodes might tell his mother that Herbert's fortune was virtually made, but it was not being made quickly enough for Herbert. He wanted instant success, instant wealth, and soon after Rhodes' arrival he decided to leave in search of both elsewhere.

Initially he had acquired three good claims, each thirty foot by ten – three times the size of a digger's grave, as locals described these measurements, but he was not satisfied with the amount of diamonds he had found. To his chagrin he had sold what he thought was a barren claim, and within hours saw the new owner extract a 30 carat diamond.

Wherever Herbert was, whatever he was doing, he wanted to be elsewhere, doing something else. He believed that here he had missed his chance of quick wealth, because others arriving only days before him had apparently picked up diamonds worth thousands. He had only found diamonds worth hundreds.

Temperamentally, he felt unable to stay and build on the claims he already owned. Instead, Herbert decided he would go to Natal to inspect their farm and then return to England, leaving Cecil in charge of the claims.

Restless as ever, he soon came back to Kimberley, bringing with him his

[3] Michell, op. cit.

brother Frank who had left Eton to be commissioned in the First Royals. Then Herbert heard rumours of gold being found in the Transvaal and suggested to Cecil that he came along with him to see whether there was any truth in these stories.

Cecil had recently experienced what was later referred to as 'a heart attack', said to be caused by 'overwork'. It does not appear to have been serious, but it worried him, for this was the first setback to his health since he had left England. He therefore welcomed a change of scene and an escape from the pitiless heat, the clouds of dust and constantly peering at mounds of earth being sifted for diamonds. He believed that the trip would help his health, if nothing else. Frank Rhodes stayed behind to help manage the claims with Charles Rudd, a friend Rhodes had made in Kimberley, while the two brothers went north in an ox-wagon along what was called the Missionaries Road.

Charles Dunell Rudd was nine years older than Rhodes and, like him, had come to South Africa in the hope that the climate would improve his health. How they first met is vague, but it seems most likely that he and Rhodes found themselves working side by side in neighbouring claims and struck up an immediate friendship and, later, became partners.

Rudd was far more mature than Rhodes. His father had inherited an estate in Norfolk and also a ship-building business which he had greatly expanded. Rudd, like Rhodes' father, had been educated at Harrow and Cambridge. At the university he was a considerable athlete and claimed that he had damaged his health by indulging in too strenuous training for the mile race.

As a result he came to South Africa to recuperate. After various vicissitudes of fortune, including trips to Mauritius and Ceylon, he prospected for diamonds, but was unsuccessful. However, backed by a richer brother in London, he started a business to sell insurance and import from England items of equipment and clothing that diggers needed. These both proved more profitable enterprises.

Rudd's familiarity with hard times made him cautious; he knew what it was like to fail and did not wish to repeat the experience. His family background made him far more sophisticated than Rhodes; his outlook was wider and infinitely more mature. He and Rhodes had totally different abilities and qualities; together they realized they could be far more successful than working on their own.

Rudd, like Hawkins, who was also in Kimberley, understood and approved Rhodes' determination to get to Oxford. He had actually failed a scholarship examination for Balliol and had left Cambridge without a degree, so he could fully appreciate the strength of Rhodes' ambition.

In allying himself with Rudd, Rhodes showed his rare gift for recognizing the attributes of colleagues and harnessing their aims to his. Like a great newspaper editor or orchestra leader, he had the ability to bring together many talents and then use them all to his best advantage.

He became adept at manipulating, adapting and improving the experiences and skills of financiers, mining engineers, politicians and others, and then fusing together their best plans to produce an amalgam far stronger (and more useful to him) than each individual element could ever have been.

Now Cecil and his brother visited Mafeking, Bechuanaland and the Murchison Hills. On this trip he came to admire the Boer farmers at whose homes they would stay to break their journey. Land was very cheap and he bought a 3,000 acre farm. Owning land, any land, like having a recognized profession, seemed to him to be a hedge against possible poverty, and he needed such reassurance.

Accepting after this first intimation of illness that his health might not improve as he grew older, he made his first will on this trip. He left everything he possessed – not a great deal – to the Secretary of State for the Colonies, to be used to enlarge the British Empire. This will was the first intimation of what would eventually become the Rhodes Scholarships, and in making it Rhodes was following the maxim of Marcus Aurelius: 'A man's life is what his thoughts make of it'.

One of the trustees of his will he named as Sidney Godolphin Alexander Shippard, later to be the Attorney General of Griqualand West. Shippard had been admitted to Oriel College as a commoner in 1856. He transferred to Magdalen Hall as a scholar in the following year, but did not take his degree for a further seven years. He and Rhodes were neighbours in Kimberley; one of his earliest photographs showed them sitting together outside his iron-roofed house.

'For four months, I walked between earth and sky, and when I looked down I said, this earth should be English, and when I looked up I said that the English should rule this earth.' Rhodes is quoted as saying this to a Miss Flora Shaw, later Lady Lugard, but as Ian Colvin noted, 'The words do not sound like Rhodes, but the sentiment is Rhodesian.'[4]

Herbert was not interested in making a will; he simply wanted to make money. He returned to Kimberley so enthusiastic about the possibility of finding gold in great quantities that he sold his claims in the diggings to Cecil so that he could devote his time to gold-mining.

Herbert did not find much gold and abandoned this scheme to become involved in a project to sell guns, including a Portuguese cannon, to African chiefs. This plan was also unsuccessful. Later, on some other escapade, he camped near Lake Nyasa, and here he died. He kept a keg of rum in his tent

---

[4] Colvin, op. cit.

and was unwisely pouring himself a tot at the same time as he lit a cigarette. The rum caught fire and the keg exploded.

With his clothes ablaze Herbert Rhodes ran from his tent to a river nearby and plunged in to put out the flames. Fearfully burned, he crawled ashore and sent a native to a woman medical missionary some miles away with a desperate plea for help. She arrived too late to save his life.

All this lay in the future and to Cecil Rhodes the present was exciting enough. Writing to his mother, he described The Big Hole in Kimberley as being like a Stilton cheese, round and deep and divided into squares, with each owner of the claims owning at least one section. They had to dig out their claims without in any way encroaching on the squares owned by men on either side of them and behind and in front.

It was difficult for each claim owner to keep into his own square when the ground was a hill or flat, but as the hole deepened, this became increasingly hazardous and, finally, impossible. Men, black and white, worked at different paces and different levels. Someone might find a valuable diamond and pause for a few days' rest. Others, less successful, would burrow on desperately, hoping to raise sufficient money to feed their families and themselves. Thus the squares were at increasingly different levels, some near the surface, some right down, and the deeper they went the harder it became for everyone to keep rigidly to his own patch.

Despite this, Rhodes wrote home that he was being successful.

'I found a 17 five eighth carats on Saturday,' he wrote. 'It was very slightly off, and I hope to get £100 for it. . . . Yesterday I found a 3½ perfect stone, but glassy, which I sold for £30. . . . I find on average 30 carats a week.'

As the hole grew bigger so metal ropes were used in preference to hemp to lower the buckets and pull up the earth. These were safer and less likely to break. These ropes were counted at first in tens, then soon in hundreds, glistening like the threads of the web of a giant spider. As buckets constantly moved up and down, the ropes would twang with a strange resonance, like huge violin strings. On their way up and down the buckets passed various steps and stairs, ramps, terraces and parapets inside the hole, where Kaffirs were working, singing, shouting. The sound of all their frantic activities mellowed to a faint hum at ground level.

At the river diggings men had dug into the banks of the Vaal and often had to prize out huge boulders that stood in their way before they could sift the gravel and wash it. Any small diamonds they missed by sieving what they called 'the stuff' might show up when buckets of river water were sluiced over the sieve. Wet gravel remaining was emptied on to a board, known as a sorting table. The diggers, either sitting on upturned buckets if the 'table' had legs, or lying alongside it if it was on the ground, would then search avidly for any diamonds.

These conditions did not obtain in New Rush. There was little enough water to drink and less for washing human bodies or clay dug out of the hole.

The claim holders were often working with very little capital, some with no more than the money they received for any stones they found. They paid wages to the Kaffir labourers as they went along; if the diggers made no money one week, they would try to borrow it. If they could not, then they might have to sell their tools and go out of business, at least temporarily, but they always strove to honour their debts. From men totally out of money other claim holders, with some money and an eye to the future, could often buy claims for a few pounds, or even, in desperate cases, for a few shillings.

Herbert Rhodes, like many with his kind of grasshopper mentality, jumping lightly, easily and often from one plan to another, had been very popular with his contemporaries, possibly because he so clearly offered no competition to them. He was one of a group, known as The Twelve Apostles, who shared what they called a mess made from several huts joined together. This military tradition of 'messing' still lingered among better-educated prospectors.

When Herbert left to search for gold, Cecil took his place in this group, as by inheritance, but he never quite fitted in. He was the antithesis of his brother, a loner, never one to be happy in a group. The male jokes, the drinks, the back-slapping and what he considered forced bonhomie among his companions all passed him by.

Contemporaries remembered him as a dreamer, 'going silently and abstractedly to his breakfast' as one said, or else, sleeves rolled up, sitting on an upturned bucket sorting diamonds or reading a Greek text for what he felt could be a stiff entrance examination at Oxford.

He had never really appeared young and was glad to make contact again with Henry Hawkins from Natal. They would go riding together and discuss politics and plans for the future. Theirs was a meeting of minds as much as a friendship of warmth, but in time differing views and political opinions would divide them.

A less successful digger, Louis Cohen, a man with a shrewd eye for Kimberley's characters, noted Rhodes' introspective attitude: 'Practical joking at this time was exercised to such an extent that the professors of the game almost considered it a science or a fine art. Of course, there were many serious-minded men who regarded anything of the sort with indignant loathing. For example, the silent, self-contained Cecil John Rhodes. . . .

'I have many times seen him in the Main Street, dressed in his white flannels, leaning moodily with hands in his pockets against a street wall. He hardly ever had a companion, seemingly took no interest in anything but his own thoughts, and I do not believe if a flock of the most adorable women passed through the street he would go across the road to see them. Rhodes was a great and good personality, but he would have been a greater and better had he married.

'I am certain that Rhodes was never a happy man. That great brain of his was always breeding Homeric plans, the very extent of which would seem to prove their impossibility . . . . Rhodes made few friends, was a lonely man, fond of a glass or two, but could, when jolly with the bottle, talk like a Mirabeau. For the fair sex he cared nothing. He hesitated even to have Benedicts about him, and in one of his cynical moods once told a man who applied for employment that something might be done for him if only he "could forget the West End of London." A Suffragette he would have called a notoriety-seeking hussy; but, all the same, perhaps if some gentle woman's refining and composing influence had crept into this great man's life, things would have been different, and he might have been alive to-day. What was wanting in Rhodes' life was missing – the Woman and the Baby.'[5]

By November, 1871, nearly £50,000 worth of diamonds had been taken from Kimberley. The best claims, some originally bought only for a few pounds, were now fetching £4,000 each. The Big Hole was constantly deepening and becoming an increasingly unmanageable chaos of separate individual workings. Many believed that the diggers must reach bottom soon, when the supply of diamonds would be exhausted, but *was* there a bottom? Was it conceivable that they might dig down almost to the centre of the earth, or at least as deeply as the longest rope could reach, because the amount of diamonds was virtually inexhaustible?

Another more pressing question was how long this chaos could continue. It was surely in everyone's interest to amalgamate the claims instead of fighting for each on their own, to dig as a group, as a company. This was a belief that Rhodes began to hold strongly. But while this hole could be a tunnel to wealth on an almost unimaginable scale, it might also be nearly dug out, with no more diamonds still to come. While no one knew the answer, many asked the question.

At the end of 1872, just over two years since he landed in South Africa, Rhodes had acquired a capital of £5,000. By the following summer he had doubled this. Ten thousand pounds was an important sum of money, more than enough to pay his fees and dues at Oxford for the three years he would need to be there to qualify for a degree. Also, his partner, Charles Rudd, was willing to look after the claims when he was away and so Rhodes could be assured of a further income during this time.

How had Rhodes succeeded even to this limited extent when thousands had failed totally? There appear to be several reasons. First, Rhodes was not, like most out there, at best a poor digger and, at worst, penniless. He had

---

[5] *Reminiscences of Kimberley*, Louis Cohen, Bennett & Co., The Century Press, London.

arrived in South Africa with £2,000 from his aunt. If all failed he could afford to return to England or try his luck in some other enterprise elsewhere. He had not been dependent on farming cotton, nor was he any more dependent now on finding diamonds.

In this he was both rare and fortunate. Many diggers had sold everything they possessed to pay their fares to Kimberley. If they ran out of money they could either borrow at usurious rates if they had any collateral such as a gun, a tent or an ox-wagon. If such a loan was unforthcoming, they could sell their implements or just disappear, leaving quietly with no forwarding address. Always such men worked under the fear of failure and destitution.

Rhodes, on the other hand, was a man of means, possessing the inestimable confidence that comes from having money in the bank.

Secondly, he was not like his brother, rushing blindly from one new project to another without proper thought, easily put off by early failures, convinced that the man working the next claim was somehow more successful. Cecil Rhodes' team worked steadily and, equally diligently, he sorted all the earth they dug up. He did not always find large diamonds, but even small ones could be sold at a profit.

Third, he had a great advantage, often understated, in the claims that Herbert had bought before he arrived. Despite Herbert's feelings that he had arrived too late, he had actually arrived in New Rush fairly early on. His claims were as good as anyone's and better than many, so Rhodes was not reduced to hacking away at sterile ground because he could not afford to buy a better claim.

Next, he lived up to his boyhood description of being 'long-headed'. He pegged away unspectacularly, never taking undue risks, always on the look-out for means to broaden his base. When another digger might run out of money or time or health and offer his claim for sale, Rhodes was a cash buyer. He did not need to indulge in protracted negotiations about the value of his security and collateral for a loan. He did not need a loan. He had sufficient money to buy claims outright. So he and Rudd steadily increased their holdings.

Lastly, Rhodes was single-minded. He had arrived with one ambition – to go to Oxford. Everything else, all other diversions, were subordinate to this. When Rhodes felt he had to attend a local dance, or possibly cause offence if he did not accept the invitation, he would invariably choose as his partner the plainest woman on the floor. When people expressed surprise to see him dancing at all, he would blush and say he just did it for the exercise.

When others asked him about rumours that he hated women, he would parry them with a stock reply: 'Women! Of course I don't hate women. I like them, but I don't want them always fussing about.'

When he became a favourite of Queen Victoria, she also questioned him on the subject.

'I've been told, Mr Rhodes, that you're a woman-hater?'

Rhodes bowed and replied diplomatically: 'How could I possibly hate a sex to which Your Majesty belongs?'

He did not hate the feminine sex; he just had no need for them, no time for them. He regarded them as an impediment on his journey and, as his later friend, Rudyard Kipling, wrote in his poem *The Winners*:

'Down to Gehenna or up to the Throne,

He travels the fastest who travels alone.'

And Rhodes, conscious of the likely shortness of his life, and increasingly aware of what he wished to achieve within that diminishing span of years, was anxious to travel as fast as he could on his own.

The next step on this road was to return to England and somehow be accepted by an Oxford college.

CHAPTER 4

SIGNOR BARNATO AND THE GREAT BARNATO

When passenger ships approached each other in daylight hours on the South African run they usually did so as closely as their captains considered safe so that people on both vessels could rush to the rails and wave to each other as they passed. These long voyages were generally tedious and such rare encounters, with passengers finally watching each others' liner diminish in the distance, provided a topic of conversation for days.

Somewhere off West Africa the ship in which Rhodes and his brother Frank were sailing home passed a white-painted liner, *Anglian*, going south. Passengers aboard *Anglian* were in a carnival mood. Not only was this her maiden voyage, but it had become clear that the ship would almost certainly beat the record for the voyage and reach the Cape in twenty-seven days. They crowded the upper decks to cheer the other ship lustily.

Rhodes was not particularly interested in such demonstrations. He was travelling First Class and spent most days on deck reading, mostly Marcus Aurelius' *Meditations* and Plutarch's *Lives of the Greeks and Romans*. He was probably the only person travelling First who had brought only one suit, which he was wearing. His trousers gradually became so threadbare that finally he was forced to take to his bed while his cabin steward patched them up with odd pieces of sail cloth.

Aboard *Anglian*, emigrants, travelling steerage, climbed up the narrow companion-ways from their hot, cramped quarters, down near the chains that controlled the rudder, to see this homeward-bound vessel. One of them was Barney Barnato, a 20-year-old from the East End of London, short in stature but enormously strong in the shoulders, and, unusually for a Jew, with blue eyes and very fair hair. He was emigrating with his total savings of £30 in cash and forty boxes of cigars from his brother-in-law, Joel Joel.

Barney was originally known as Barnett Isaacs, but Barney was the name by which most people called him. He lived with his parents, three sisters and an elder brother Harry in a two-bedroom house in Cobbs Court on the edge of Middlesex Street and Wentworth Street, often called Petticoat Lane because of its long association with the rag trade.

The ground floor of this house was a shop where his father, Isaac Isaacs, sold second, third or fourth-hand clothes; the two brothers shared a bed in one corner. Their three sisters shared one of the two upper rooms and their parents slept in the other. Below street level was a cellar, running with rats, where their father's stock could be stored.

Since the days of Oliver Cromwell this area of London had been a refuge for Jews and foreigners, such as Huguenots, coming from Russia or Europe to escape racial or religious persecution. For some it was only a staging post. They went on to richer areas and better lives, but most stayed here, working for tailors, cutting cloth, pressing suits, making hats, buying and selling junk. It was not an environment that held out great hopes. If they needed helping hands, they had to rely on those at the ends of their own arms.

Barney was educated at the Hebrew Free School in Bell Lane nearby. Here the headmaster, Morris Angel, with a few unqualified but dedicated colleagues, taught nearly 1000 local children how to read and write Hebrew and English and the rudiments of history and geography. Like most of his contemporaries, Barney did not have pocket money. To make any, he had to begin by bartering. For this purpose he would search dustbins at the back of Truman's Brewery and pick out discarded beer bottle labels. These he would exchange for liquorice sweets, monkey nuts and anything another better-off boy might have and which Barney sensed could be a more commercial commodity.

The area attracted gangs of older boys and men who liked a fight; Irish in Whitechapel, Gentiles in Shoreditch. From the Wentworth Street Ragged School non-Jewish boys might attack Jewish boys simply because they looked different, or because they seemed suitable targets. Mr Isaacs was therefore well aware of the necessity to teach his sons how to defend themselves against such attacks.

He was a religious man and would close his shop every Saturday and observe all the formalities and rituals of his faith, but life had taught him that turning the other cheek when attacked was not always as useful as the older philosophy of an eye for an eye, a tooth for a tooth. Twice a week, in the evenings after work, he would fix up a rope square in the back yard, or when wet, inside the shop, and teach his sons the rudiments of boxing. His advice was simple and direct. Both sons were afterwards to follow it closely in business dealings as well as fist fights: 'Never let a man put his hand on you without giving him what for – and always hit him first.'

To show them how and where they could hit with most effect, for it was likely that their adversaries would be bigger than them, Isaac Isaacs told his sons stories about the legendary Portuguese-Jewish pugilist Mendoza, the

18th century champion of England, who had been brought up in Aldgate. On the door of the outside privy he pinned a sketch from an illustrated magazine of Mendoza's last bare-knuckle prize fight. His sons would see this picture going in and coming out and, hopefully, learn by it.

For these boxing sessions the two Isaacs brothers were sometimes joined by their cousin David Harris. He lived in Canonbury and was of a more studious turn of mind, cautious with money because, like the Isaacs, he did not have much. He would regularly walk the four miles to Cobbs Court and back again to save a penny fare on the horse tram.

Starting work as an office boy, and in the evenings attending a course at a local commercial college, he was now a ledger clerk in a City firm. While the two Isaacs brothers would follow sporting news in any newspaper they picked up, David Harris preferred more serious items of news and opinion.

Harry had a longer reach than his smaller brother, but Barney could land the harder punch. He suffered from being short-sighted, but made up for this by being unusually quick on his feet.

One day the Rothschilds generously paid for every child in Barney's class to spend a day by the sea at Ramsgate. They were each given an apple, a bag of sweets, a sausage and a slice of bread. The sight of sea and shore stirred Barney's imagination so much that he toyed with the idea of running away to sea as a cabin boy, but changed his mind. He did not wish to hurt his mother, because he knew that he would have to leave without saying goodbye to her.

The three Isaacs sisters married. One, Kate, married Joel Joel, landlord of The King of Prussia public house in a nearby street. Barney left school when he was 14 and took the only job available, helping his father. He and his brother trundled a barrow around the streets, crying out for old clothes and picking up what the rag trade called remnants: odd lengths of unwanted cloth which might be sold on to dressmakers or tailors.

Sometimes Barney went out on his own with a tray of collar-studs, lengths of elastic and shoe laces. He would hawk these hopefully among jewellers and clock-makers in Hatton Garden. He did not make many sales, but he had an engagingly cheerful manner and sometimes people who did not want to buy anything would give him a few coppers simply to help him.

For example, a small shop selling glass tumblers and bottles was run by a Mr H.M. Codd, on whom Barney called regularly. Codd took pity on him and, even if he bought nothing from him, he would from time to time give him sixpence, and perhaps half a crown at Christmas. Years later, as a millionaire and on one of his periodical sentimental return journeys to the East End, Barney sought out Mr Codd and repaid this kindness by presenting him with a large diamond.

When Barney became rich and famous, newspapers would attribute to him all manner of aristocratic connections. One claimed that he was 'the third son of a gentleman of Devonshire Terrace, and had been privately educated by tutors'; another that he was related to a judge, Sir George Jessel. Barney's early partner in Kimberley, Louis Cohen, half Irish, half Jewish, was caustic in his comments on such claims.

'No doubt it was something for the Isaacs dynasty to boast about, but I should like to have had Sir George's opinion on the subject. At all events, I never heard of the presence of a Jessel at any marriage, funeral or social function in which the Barnatos or Joels were interested. They are related in about the same degree as they are to the naked Moses – he of bulrush fame.'[1]

Barney's talent for financial survival later won him praise from unlikely people. In Kimberley Rhodes' secretary, Gordon Le Sueur, called Barney 'a Jewish digger, half prize fighter and half music hall artiste, [with] a peculiar faculty in one direction – and that was money-making'.

Barney would sell anything at a profit, no matter how small, for he realized very early on that no one ever goes broke by selling at a profit – any profit. For instance, he would buy lemons for five shillings for a large basket and sell them two for a penny, making a profit of 100 per cent. He sold bird seed, he plucked chickens. On Sundays he and Harry would sell bootlaces and headache powders in the street market.

Barney was a natural salesman with a gift for words and the salesman's ability to persuade people that he was genuinely offering them bargains. Harry, on the other hand, had an accountant's mind and would take care of the money their customers paid. Barney addressed the crowd who gathered round him thus: 'I am not here today and gone tomorrow. I am here today and gone today,' or 'Two packets for the price of one. Here's one free, buy another,' and so on.

Once they sold some homing pigeons which speedily flew back to their home in the loft of the Isaacs' house.

Soon the brothers realized that, despite all their efforts, they were really just running on the spot, confusing motion with progress and making barely enough money to buy stock for their next sale. In the evenings they worked in The King of Prussia as barmen, on the understanding they received a hot meal every day. When some of the labourers, prostitutes and down-the-bill artists appearing at the Cambridge Music Hall in Commercial Street had too much to drink after the last house on Saturday night they would join forces to throw them out.

The business of acting, or telling jokes and performing conjuring tricks in front of a music hall audience, attracted them both; it did not seem so very different from shouting wares in the street and could offer a better living.

[1] Cohen, op. cit.

Barney would help out now and then as a scene shifter in the Cambridge Music Hall, where he also learned how to apply make-up and how to take a fall without hurting himself. He became fascinated by the careers of the great actors like Edmund Kean and Henry Irving. When someone told him that Kean could walk on his hands and declaim at the same time, Barney practised until he could do the same, usually a soliloquy from *Hamlet*. Harry learned conjuring tricks from professionals who drank in The King of Prussia between and after shows.

It was the custom for the managements of music halls to give variety performers two free passes a week for friends or shopkeepers who displayed advertisements for the show. Barney knew that not all the audience would sit through the whole bill, and some left at the interval. They would then throw away their tickets or, if Barney approached them outside the building, would let him buy them for a penny or two. He then did his best to resell them quickly at a profit before the second part of the programme began.

One dark evening, expecting to get two pennies for half a ticket he had picked up, the buyer gave him two shillings by mistake. Years later someone asked him what he did on making this discovery.

'What did I *do*?' Barney asked, amazed at such a foolish question. 'I never stopped running until I put eight streets between me and that theatre!'

When he could not sell the tickets, he would use them himself. Of all living actors he admired Henry Irving most and learned many of his speeches by heart. Years later, rich and famous, Barney was taken backstage to meet him and told Irving how, as a boy, he had seen him in 'The Bells'.

'I sat in the pit and you were on the stage then,' he said, and added pontifically. 'Now we are both on the stage – mine being the stage of life.'

Irving recalled how he had played four characters in that play.

Barney corrected him.

'Three,' he said.

Irving looked at him with distaste.

'Excuse me, my friend,' he said icily, 'but you will perhaps admit that I ought to know what I did.'

'I don't give a continental what you *thought* you did that night,' Barney retorted. 'I'll tell you *what* you did, and every scene you played.'

And then and there he went through each scene, until Irving admitted he was right; he had indeed played three parts, not four.

Barney tried to find a permanent job in the theatre, but no manager would offer him anything more than work as a part-time scenery shifter. Mrs Isaacs knew that he would never make a living as a Shakespearean actor, any more than Harry could survive for long on what he might earn as a juggler and conjurer. However, they had to make a living somehow and both now thought that almost anything was preferable to pushing a barrow through the streets, buying and selling other people's cast-offs.

In their spare time, therefore, the brothers worked up an act between them, using old clothes they should have been selling. Harry, dressed as an upper class fop in top hat and tails, would juggle, while pretending to be drunk. Barney took the part of a clown with a taste for acrobatics, walking on his hands as he declaimed reams of Shakespearean dialogue.

They had a few bookings at local music halls, where Harry received most of the applause. One night the manager, who did not wish to offend Barney – because if he did he might lose a very cheap act – shouted out, 'And Barney, too! Barney, too!' clapping his hands vigorously to encourage the audience to applaud Barney.

Afterwards Harry decided that 'Barney, too!' could easily be condensed into Barnato, which sounded mysterious and foreign, and hence more theatrical than Isaacs. They therefore retitled their act, The Barnato Brothers. This helped their esteem, but not their takings. At this low point in their fortunes, rehearsing their act one evening in the shop, David Harris came to see them. He dumped an atlas and some newspapers on the table.

'I'm going to South Africa to find diamonds,' he announced dramatically. They looked at him in amazement, so he opened the atlas and pointed to Cape Colony and the Vaal and Orange Rivers.

'Diamonds,' he repeated. 'There are millions there. Read what the papers say about them.'

Barney and Harry read the newspaper reports, but in that squalid room, surrounded by piles of sour-smelling old jackets and trousers, the prospects of actually finding diamonds themselves seemed infinitely unlikely. But when David told them that his mother had given him her life savings of £150 to finance his trip they began to think again. Maybe there *could* be something in it?

David Harris sailed away and for several months they heard nothing from him. In fact he was having a very difficult time in South Africa and did not wish to admit this to his relatives. He had a retiring disposition and was not equipped mentally or physically for the crude and competitive conditions of the diamond diggings. Also, his progress as a digger or a dealer was hampered because he knew nothing whatever about diamonds.

At first he rented a digging claim for ten shillings a month, but this proved barren of diamonds. Once he was so hard up he had to sell his shovel and axe to pay that week's wage for his native helper.

However, David Harris was not a quitter. He doggedly learned all he could about diamonds by asking others, and would go round the diggings day after day buying small diamonds which the diggers would display on their sorting tables. This job was the lowliest form of diamond buying and was known locally as kopje-walloping.

His initial capital soon ran low, but had a boost when he made £400 in three months, working for a dealer who recognized his increasing skill in valuing diamonds. Harris now wrote home enthusiastically, saying how well his cousins would do in South Africa, because goods of all sorts were expensive and difficult to come by.

He assured them that they could make good profits by selling ribbons, toothcombs, in fact almost anything, to diggers and their wives. Their music hall act could also be successful because there was so little competition. So, even if they did not succeed in finding a fortune in diamonds, there were plenty of other ways in which they could make money. This was true, but he did not explain that a lot of other people were also trying to make it in these ways.

By the time Harris's letter reached London his own financial situation had again become precarious. Diggers were by-passing the kopje-wallopers, who had little capital and simply could not afford the prices that more established merchants could offer. One of the most successful was Julius Wernher, a former officer in the Prussian Dragoons and the son of a general. Wernher was a huge man physically and buying diamonds seemed an unlikely career for him to choose. Initially he had joined a Paris diamond merchant, Jules Porges, and he spent some time as a broker in London and Frankfurt-am-Main. Then Porges sent him to South Africa to buy diamonds for the company. He preferred to employ a German for this delicate task because he believed that French buyers could become emotionally involved, handling what were often delicate and devious negotiations.

Harry Isaacs knew nothing of his cousin's change in fortune and decided to take his advice and try his own luck in South Africa. He landed, calling himself 'Signor Barnato, The Greatest Wizard Known', bringing with him what few props he could afford for his act.

He placed an advertisement in the *Cape Argus* to announce his arrival and his first 'astounding performance of MAGIC' in the Mutual Hall. His act was successful artistically but not financially: an unexpected and prolonged storm meant that his audiences were very small. He decided to move north to Dutoitspan and try his luck there, but discovered that what an audience in the East End of London had thought amusing was not so highly appreciated by diggers of many different nationalities. Soon, in order to make a living, Harry was reduced to giving sparring exhibitions with a former policeman from Natal, also down on his luck.

He could not hope to make a career of this, so he bought a set of scales and some pliers and became another kopje-walloper. Here again he had little success. He knew virtually nothing about diamonds and had little capital to buy any that might be offered to him.

Worse, he began to realize that, in a harsh world where a stone smaller than a dried pea could fetch hundreds of pounds in the diamond fields, and possibly thousands when it reached Hatton Garden, stealing diamonds was endemic. Being known as a professional magician was therefore not the best qualification for a successful diamond dealer.

Soon after his arrival a valuable diamond was stolen and someone wrote to the local newspaper to give his opinion that 'if anybody wants to steal a parcel of diamonds, he must be as quick of hand as Signor Barnato'. This was intended as a compliment to Harry's stage skills, but the association was unhappy and Harry quickly replied, saying that the only magic he employed in his capacity as a diamond buyer was 'the astoundingly high prices I am always prepared to pay for good stones'.

Slowly his takings dwindled to virtual extinction. He had started off living in a small tin-roofed hotel, but soon even this was beyond his means and he had to move out to a tent. Finally, he was so impoverished that all he wanted was to make enough money somehow to pay his fare back to England and abandon his dreams of diamonds. Then David Harris recommended Harry to a diamond dealer named Van Praagh, who hired him to stand behind a wooden counter on which diggers would display the diamonds they were offering for sale.

So gradually, often painfully, Harry began to learn how to tell a good diamond from a dud and which colours were the most valuable. In his letters home he did not mention his hardships, but instead wrote glowing accounts of the prosperity he was enjoying and urged Barney to come out and join him. This Barney was reluctant to do.

Then, one morning, David Harris unexpectedly arrived back in London and came to see the Isaacs. He was no longer the shy, diffident youth he had been, but a young man full of confidence. To explain his good fortune, he told what seemed an almost unbelievable story. Near the diggings was a bar, Dodd's Canteen, where the owner kept a roulette table in an upstairs room. As an inducement to persuade customers to gamble, he would offer them free drinks. Sometimes men down on their luck came in simply for the free drinks.

David Harris had become so depressed with his prospects that, quite out of character, for he was not a gambler, he had gone into the bar simply for a free drink himself. The proprietor realized this and made a sarcastic remark about scroungers, which annoyed Harris. He put a coin on a number – and within seconds had won £1400.

He did not stay in Dodd's Canteen for a moment longer; he realized he could lose just as quickly as he had won. Instead, he booked the first available passage to England, repaid his mother her £150 and then announced he was going to return to Kimberley to use his new capital to finance himself as a diamond merchant.

This greatly impressed Barney. He was still working in the evenings in The King of Prussia, but the job had no prospects. As a variety act he now called himself 'The Great Barnato', but music halls would only book him for one night at a time, and even this was not on a regular basis. He decided to try his luck in South Africa; if David Harris and his brother Harry could be so successful there, so could he.

To save money for his fare, Barney stopped smoking. Regulars in the public house heard of his intention to emigrate and clubbed together to buy him a second-hand nickel watch for 25 shillings. His brother-in-law Joel Joel added a silver chain.

David Harris had told them that there were few luxuries in the diamond fields, so Joel also gave Barney forty boxes of cigars to sell until he established himself. No one ever inquired into the origin of these cigars. In more modern parlance, they might be said to have fallen off a lorry.

When Barney had saved £30 he decided that the moment of decision had arrived. Packing a set of Indian clubs for keeping himself physically fit, and his phylacteries for spiritual refreshment, with a set of flannel underwear his mother thought might come in useful, he voyaged south aboard the *Anglian*.

He had not told his brother Harry he was coming out to join him; he wanted his arrival to be a surprise. Had Harry known of his intention, it is possible that he might have warned Barney that it seemed as if all the diamonds had been dug out. Many diggers fortunate enough to find buyers for their claims were so despondent that they sold up and left, glad to go. Dealers said they were not buying diamonds for the time being because the price had fallen owing to stock market crises around the world.

Barney knew nothing of all this. Indeed, the first he heard of it was when a stranger in the Masonic Hotel in Cape Town, where he stayed on the night of his arrival, asked him where he was going.

'I'm off to the diamond fields,' Barney told him proudly.

'Too late, too late!' the other man replied mournfully, shaking his head. 'There are no diamonds left there, boy. I struck it rich, but the ground is all dry now. You'd better catch the next boat back to England.'

Barney felt depressed at this opinion, but not deflected from his aim: in any case he did not have a return ticket or the money to buy one. He could not go back, and retracing steps or retreat in any form was never an option for him. He could only go on.

Years later they met again in Johannesburg. Barney was by then immensely rich and the man was not, and did not remember that they had ever met before, but like everyone else, he had heard of Barney's phenomenal success and instantly recognized him.

'How did you do it?' he asked enviously.

'By not taking your advice,' replied Barney, or so he liked to say when he told this story.

The diggings were roughly 650 miles north from Cape Town. To travel there by coach would take thirty-five days and cost him £40. Barney moved into lodgings to save money until he could negotiate a cheaper fare.

He found one with a driver for the Transport Company taking an ox-wagon north to Kimberley. He agreed to allow Barney to put his luggage on the wagon and walk the whole way by its side for £5. Afterwards Barney would recall that the two months he spent on the journey had been the most exciting and pleasurable experience of his life.

They crossed deserts, forded flooded rivers, sometimes were stuck on rocks or in sand. At night Barney slept on the ground beneath the wagon. Nights could be bitterly cold and he was often glad of the flannel underwear his mother had given to him. His muscles ached and at first, after so much unaccustomed walking, his feet were in agony with blisters. But all hardships were bearable because he was on his way to make his fortune, or so he regularly assured himself.

When Barney saw Dutoitspan and Kimberley for the first time he was horrified. He had vaguely imagined that it would be like Cape Town, whose environs Lord Randolph Churchill would describe lyrically as being 'of surpassing beauty. Forests, groves and plantations of oak, pine, eucalyptus, owing their origin to the provident forethought of the early Dutch settlers, thickly cover the ground from the slopes of the mountain almost to the shores of the sea.

'Miles of shady lanes, extending in all directions, make riding and driving an unfailing pleasure, while on every side old-fashioned villas and country-houses, with perfect and well-kept gardens, disclose alike the cultivated taste and the love of country life which characterize the wealthier portion of the resident community.'[2]

Instead, Dutoitspan was a shambles of shabby iron huts, some with roofs painted red or green to appear tiled, and faded tents, all built between huge pits where diggers had scrabbled for diamonds and then abandoned, out of money, out of hope. Where was his brother living in all this?

He found Harry at last in a tent, ill with fever, and astounded when Barney lifted the tent flap.

'My God, Barney, you're really here,' Harry cried in amazement. They

[2] *Men, Mines and Animals in South Africa*, Lord Randolph Churchill, Sampson Low, Marston & Co. Ltd, London, 1893.

had a meal together, and the fact that they were together cheered them both. Barney felt that the moment called for some words to match its importance, but all he could think of was the line from Hamlet: 'To be or not to be, that is the question.'

Neither of them appreciated that their combined experiences of buying and selling, of acting, being cheerful and optimistic in adversity, had all been part of an apprenticeship to their future. Like pieces in a mosaic or jigsaw puzzle, each one meaningless on its own, they would now begin to fit together to form the astonishing pattern of what would eventually be their lives.

Like Rhodes, Barney had no idea what to expect, but he had never imagined he would virtually be exchanging a life of selling jumble in the East End of London to selling much the same merchandise to diggers and Boer farmers in South Africa.

Every evening auctions of such diverse items as penknives, lengths of cloth and bead necklaces, which he hoped to sell, were held at Nutzom's Hotel. A number of very sharp Jews from different parts of Europe – known locally as Peruvians – controlled these auctions. They were willing to play games of billiards or cards with Barney, but they did not welcome him as a business competitor.

Two Peruvians at an auction did promise him a commission on some sales, and then refused to pay. They were both bigger than Barney and thought he would be an easy man to swindle. He proved them wrong by knocking them both out, one after the other. They paid him, but no further commissions came his way.

Barney started work by trying to sell his brother-in-law's cigars, or at least exchange them for a more marketable commodity. When buyers complained that the cigars were explosive, Barney reassured them that any with this tendency must have suffered damage on the long sea voyage from Cuba.

He bribed one man with a free box on condition he told his friends these were genuine Havanas and the best in South Africa, but this did not significantly improve sales. He made a little money helping Boer farmers unload their carts in the market square when they brought in vegetables from their farms. Waiting for them to arrive, he would juggle with eggs, and soon became known as a 'card', a character. People waved to him and wished him good day, but what he desperately needed were not good wishes but deals.

Gradually the price of diamonds recovered as news from stock exchanges round the world improved, but this was only of academic interest to Barney because he knew nothing about diamonds. For this reason David Harris did not want to employ him any more than when he had wanted Harry to join him. Harry, still working for Van Praagh, had also nothing to offer his younger brother; his own future was by no means secure.

Barney's boxing skills earned him a little money. When a travelling circus arrived in town, one of its attractions was a boxer advertised as 'The Champion of Angola'. This enormous bruiser announced he would take on anyone for the prize of a gold medal and a return of the shilling entrance fee his challenger would have to pay for the honour of fighting him.

Barney, who barely came up to the champion's chest, decided to use the skills his father had taught him and announced that he would fight this giant. When word of this went round, bets were laid as to how soon he would be defeated – within 30 seconds, one minute, and so on. Barney placed his own bets with the local bookmakers – on himself to win. He was given big odds because it was widely believed that, in such an obviously unequal contest, he would be lucky to survive even one round.

This would be a David and Goliath match and on the night of the fight the fairground booth was crowded with diggers hoping to see a massacre. The champion disposed of a few other contenders easily enough, and then came Barney's turn.

He realized the value of publicity and climbed nonchalantly into the ring wearing a bowler hat and his wire-rimmed glasses. Not knowing what to make of him, the crowd cheered and booed him in roughly equal proportions. Barney bowed to them all gravely, then carefully removed his hat. As the Champion of Angola came out of his corner, Barney bent over, so that his spectacles fell off his nose. Bent double, he groped for them short-sightedly in the dust.

Anxious to get on with what he believed was a ridiculous contest, the champion bent down near Barney and pointed them out to him. Instantly, up went Barney's right, straight into the man's solar plexus, then a left to his chin. The champion fell like a tree under a woodman's axe.

Barney celebrated his win by juggling his bowler hat, three beer bottles and a sponge from his corner. He received back his shilling, but the gold medal turned out to be made of thick cardboard painted gold. Not that Barney was particularly concerned; he had money to collect from the book-makers.

The circus owner dismissed the defeated champion and engaged Barney in the unusual dual role of boxer and clown, paying him five shillings a day and what he could eat. This arrangement lasted only for five days, however, and Barney, having been billed briefly as 'The Greatest Conjuror in the World', went back to buying and selling – and in between times appearing in plays at the Theatre Royal in Kimberley.

Barney was something of a ventriloquist and managed to persuade a gullible customer to buy what he assured the man was a hen with the gift of speech. With this money he bought several sets of braces, which he tried to sell to diggers at their claims. In return for running errands for some of them, they would occasionally allow him to re-sift gravel they had already discarded and to keep any stones he found. He found very few, but David Harris bought these from him for rather more than he would pay to someone who was not such a close relation.

David Harris had been attracted to a girl he met aboard ship on the voyage. When she landed in South Africa he believed that they would never see each other again, and since he had no definite prospects to offer a wife, he felt it would be impossible for him to propose marriage. However, to his great delight, she arrived in Kimberley and they were married in the local synagogue that had just opened.

Every Friday night they would lay a place for Barney at their table. They were both generous people, but they could not approve of Barney's choice of companions. David Harris was obviously going to be prosperous, while Barney seemed to be attracted to a low class of person. This was partly because he lacked money to choose better companions than the habitués of seedy bars, where he would recite Shakespearean speeches standing on his head for the price of a drink or a one-course meal, and also because he found their raffishness attractive.

Barney's sharp eye would pay dividends, though, even with David Harris. This was shown when they asked him to dinner to celebrate the festival of Chanukah, which marked the victories of Judas Maccabeus over the Syrians, commemorating the re-dedication of the Temple in 165 BC, after its desecration by the Syrian king.

For the occasion Harris and his wife had brought out all their best cutlery. Barney was impressed – and annoyed to see one of the guests surreptitiously pick up a silver spoon and slide it down the side of his boot, obviously meaning to take it away with him. This sort of behaviour, by a guest in his cousin's house, was not to Barney's liking and, after the meal, he offered to do some conjuring tricks. In one of these he picked up a soup spoon and, with Harry as his straight man, made it disappear. A search in the room for the spoon proved unsuccessful, so Barney asked another guest to look inside the boot of the man sitting in the corner. Miraculously, the spoon was discovered.

'And,' said Barney afterwards, 'I went home with the other one . . .'

Barney Barnato met his first friend and partner in Kimberley soon after his arrival. This was Louis Cohen, son of a Jewish father and an Irish mother. He was an egregious character who kept a boisterous record of his early days in Kimberley. Not always successfully he bought diamonds and alternated this by writing articles for the local newspaper. Cohen was 17 – the same age as Rhodes – when he went to South Africa. For his journey his father gave him some clothes, a revolver, a tent and 25 golden sovereigns, and paid for his second-class passage to Cape Town aboard the *European*.

Cohen was working in Kimberley with a cousin, Lewis Woolf, and, like the Barnatos, living in a tent. Their only furniture was an empty packing-case on which stood a kettle, three tin cups, a few pans, a loaf of bread and pots of sugar and coffee. They each used a portmanteau to store their clothes. After paying for their diamond-dealing licences and, like most newcomers knowing nothing about diamonds, they offered £3 10s, nearly half their total capital, for their first diamond. This turned out to be a stone without any value whatever.

Around the same time Barney had a similar humiliating experience. Standing at the sorting table of a burly Boer digger, he had seen one stone glitter in a mass of worthless gravel. He at once offered the Boer £5 for it. Barney would have offered more, but this was all he had on him. The Boer appeared not to want to sell, but Barney used all his efforts to persuade him, and then discovered that the stone was not a diamond, but a worthless sliver of crystal.

Cohen had been much impressed by the feeling of optimism in Kimberley he noticed on his arrival. He had watched what he called 'troops of dusty naked natives singing Kaffir songs of glee, and following their white masters who walked ahead of them as would a leader of a regiment. They were a splendid stamp of men, these early claim-holders, big, brawny, fine made fellows and in many instances highly educated. They did honour to England, Ireland, Scotland and Wales.'[3]

Cohen made his first successful deal by tentatively offering £130 to a Dutchman for a diamond the man had just discovered. At that time Cohen's total capital amounted to 35 shillings in the back pocket of his trousers, so when the Dutchman showed interest in his offer, Cohen told him hurriedly that he would need to examine the diamond in what he called his office. He took it into the first real diamond merchant's hut he could see and told the merchant he wanted £300 for it.

After the usual criticisms of buyers to sellers – the diamond was cracked, smoky and off-colour and of minimal resale value – Cohen sold it to him for £210, part in notes, part in gold. Then he went back and paid the Dutchman.

After this initial deal Cohen's luck improved slightly and he moved to a cheap hotel called The Scarlet Bar, kept by a former policeman and a friend. From time to time these two proprietors would argue over the division of their profits and always settled the dispute with their fists. The hotel was really only a large tent, with smaller tents, the bedrooms, each lined with green flannel, leading off from it.

One day Cohen was eating a meal in the main tent when someone pointed

[3] Cohen, op. cit.

to a small young man who had just come in. This newcomer threw his soft-peaked cap up on to the hat-rack and then sat down between two older men who were engaged in conversation. Without any apology or paying the slightest attention to their curses and black looks, he pushed them apart to get in himself. The newcomer had very fair hair, his face was dusty and he wore spectacles.

'Do you know who that is?' someone asked Cohen, who shook his head.

'He's Barney Barnato, Harry Barnato's brother. He's just come out.'

Cohen knew Harry, so looked at the younger brother with interest. Barney had ordered a plate of soup and was now blowing his nose loudly. Suddenly he choked on a spoonful of soup which splattered over the table and the clothes of diggers all around. He blew his nose again and, seeing Cohen looking at him disapprovingly, explained ingenuously, 'A fly flew up my nose'.

A couple of days later the two men ran into each other again. Cohen was going round diggings hoping to buy diamonds and saw Barney with a satchel in which he was carrying a set of diamond-weighing scales. Barney had already bought about £10 worth of diamonds and they spent the next two or three hours visiting sorters looking for more. They walked back together to The Scarlet Bar.

Cohen showed Barney the tent where he lived and they weighed out the diamonds they had bought and calculated the potential profit. Barney told him that he was going off to Dutoitspan, three miles away, to see what he could pick up there. It had been a hard day for him, peering at piles of gravel, his weak eyes watering in the blinding glare of the sun. Now he had another three miles to walk to save a fare of a few coppers.

'You'll find we'll have some mozel [luck] tomorrow,' Barney assured Cohen cheerfully. 'See if we don't.'

They shook hands. They were in partnership.

Cohen put in £60 on his side and Barney his £30, plus all the cigars he could not sell, on the other. A local lawyer drew up an agreement and they started business in a shed, six feet by eight.

Initially Cohen had been dubious about taking the cigars as collateral, but Barney assured him seriously that they were the best Cuban cigars procurable, only available through the brilliance of his brother-in-law who was a connoisseur of fine cigars.

Cohen complained that, when he tried to smoke one, it made him feel ill. Barney explained that this must be because he was not used to really good cigars, which, like rich food and vintage wines, were an acquired taste.

Barney trudged doggedly round the diggings every day, while Cohen stayed in the office to deal with any buyers. Dozens of other kopje-wallopers were competing with Barney, but not all had his apparent cheerfulness in the face of any rebuffs – or the bottle of South African brandy, known as 'Cape Smoke', from which he offered a drink to seal any business he could do.

Cohen's job was far more pleasant, but even so he began to resent Barney's generosity with the bottle. He was not a natural entrepreneur like Barney and could not understand that much of their turnover was due to Barney's outgoing personality. Cohen believed that a guinea saved was a guinea 'earned'. Barney knew that first they had actually to earn a guinea before they could save one.

They started work every morning at seven o'clock and kept on working until dusk, except for half an hour they allowed themselves for lunch – a plate of soup. Supper was usually curry and rice, or mealies cooked behind the tent.

Barney was always very short of money. Every time he spent £20 buying diamonds, he would visit the nearest diamond dealer to sell what he had bought to raise cash to bid for others.

After some weeks they both took time off to drink two lemon syrups in a corrugated iron canteen run by an Irishman named Maloney near The Big Hole. Next door to this cheap bar was a vacant space. Barney suggested that it would be a good idea to build an office here, where diggers could come to sell to them rather than always visiting the diggers at their claims. It would also appear more businesslike than operating from his tent in The Scarlet Bar.

They put the proposition to Maloney. Would he rent them a space and put up a corrugated iron shack they could use? He agreed, for a guinea a day. This was beyond Cohen's means.

'That's a bit too stiff, isn't it?' he said to Barney.

'I don't know,' replied Barney thoughtfully. 'If we can make two pounds a day out of that, it isn't dear for a guinea, *and* we've an office into the bargain.'

There was little violence in Kimberley – the diggers worked too hard and for such long hours – but it was not a particularly virtuous town. It was said that there was a bar, liquor-booth or public house for every forty people. They had names such as 'The Hard Times', 'First and Last', 'The Digger's Retreat', 'The Crystal Palace' – so many, in fact, that a temperance organization, known as 'Good Templars', proposed to open what they called Lodges to sell non-alcoholic drinks.

Some barmaids were also part-time prostitutes. Initially, professional prostitutes were black girls, working in huts and tents off the main streets.

One day Barney discovered that two new white girls had arrived from Cape Town and were staying in The White House, known to be a brothel. He asked Cohen to accompany him on a visit of exploration.

The White House was unprepossessing; it simply contained two small rooms without windows. Each was lit by a single candle to add an atmosphere of mystery and muted light to what was basically an unromantic financial transaction.

Barney got into conversation with the girls, discussing a price. When Cohen heard the sum of £5 mentioned, he decided that such expenditure was quite out of his league. He therefore told Barney disapprovingly that, if he wished to spend so much capital so unwisely, he would wait for him outside. Before Cohen left the house he saw Barney walking towards one of the rooms with a girl and take a £5 note out of his pocket as they went inside.

Cohen walked about outside the house for a short time and then Barney rushed out and grabbed his arm.

'Run!' he cried excitedly. 'Run!'

'Why? Where?'

'Never mind! *Run*!'

'But I saw you give that girl a £5 note?'

'No,' Barney corrected him. 'You saw me *show* her a £5 note. I had a piece of paper in my other hand, and when she blew out the candle, I gave her that instead.'

One white prostitute, with dyed hair and calling herself 'The Blonde Venus', arrived from Cape Town. She realized that Kimberley contained a number of young men who had far more money than most of their age and decided to increase her fee accordingly. An auction was therefore announced, the prize for the highest bidder being one night with her.

Long before bidding began, the canteen where the auction was to be held was packed. Some diggers had actually put on evening dress as though this was to be a high-class social occasion.

The Blonde Venus stood on a beer crate where all could see her and bids were called. The first was for £5, but then enthusiasm increased. Top bid was £25 and three boxes of champagne.

The successful bidder led his prize triumphantly to his tent, not imagining that unsuccessful bidders would take their revenge. In silence, they ringed his tent and, when they judged the moment right, they whipped up the canvas sides so that everyone could have a good view of the couple inside.

Gradually competition to buy diamonds became increasingly difficult for small operators like Barney and Cohen, so Barney tried to persuade his partner that they should move out to some of the smaller diggings on the outskirts of Kimberley where competition would be less. These claims were too far away to walk to regularly and Cohen disliked the idea. He wished to continue as they were.

Barney knew that they had to expand or go out of business, and this seemed the only course to take. Cohen replied that the diggers were Boers, suspicious of the British, who they believed would short-change them whenever they could. How would they ever be able to find men prepared to sell when they were so distrustful?

No amount of argument seemed likely to persuade Cohen to change his mind, until another small-time buyer, Jack Saunders, who drank heavily, and who regularly visited these outlying claims riding a lame old pony, told Barney he was leaving for England and wanted to sell his pony and all his equipment.

Barney knew that Saunders was often too drunk to guide the pony, which, like a horse pulling a milk cart on a London round, would stop out of habit at each of his customer's houses.

Barney told Saunders he would like to buy the pony, not for himself, because this might arouse Saunders' suspicions that he planned to take over his round, but for an unnamed Boer friend. Barney paid £27 10s, a transaction very reluctantly agreed by Cohen. He could not appreciate how useful this animal would be, not only for transporting them to and from outlying claims, but, much more important, because it would stop at every point where Saunders already had a client. For their money they were buying much more than Saunders' pony; they were buying his list of customers.

Barney and Cohen ended their partnership shortly after this in the same casual way in which it had begun. Cohen did not give the purchase of the pony as a reason for his disenchantment, but said he objected to the number of Barney's relatives who, as he put it, 'continually haunted' their office. He found them 'particularly obnoxious'.

Also, he believed that Barney was not doing his fair share of the work. He stayed out late each night, going from bar to bar, picking up news, meeting diggers. Barney was surprised at Cohen's attitude.

'You do as you like in the business, you have full control of all our funds,' he told him. 'We're doing well. What more do you want?'

Cohen said he wanted to be on his own.

'So,' said Barney. 'You wish to have a settle up?'

'I do.'

'All right, governor. It's no use being pardners if you don't want to.'

Then he paused, and suddenly asked, 'Who's to have the office?'

'The one who pays most for it,' said Cohen.

'I'll give £100,' Barney replied.

'A hundred and five,' countered Cohen.

'It's yours,' said Barney at once. 'And cheap at that. But I couldn't sit in an office all day long.'

The books were produced, but Barney did not bother to examine them.

'If you'd wanted to rob me you had plenty of time to do it,' he said simply. 'We've trusted each other. Give me what you reckon is my due.'

After Barnato and Cohen parted company, Barney worked temporarily with another man, who promptly set out to swindle him. But as Cohen wrote later, 'B.B. was at all times a bad man to beat, and to get over him one would have to rise very early in the morning. And, if you tried that, you would find that "pug" had not gone to bed at all.'

The swindle was simple, but could have been effective, and was based on the fact that often the scales used by diamond buyers were weighted, even if only slightly, in their favour. When each day's purchases were weighed, therefore, the aggregate weight declared would not be the weight of all the individual diamonds, but one in the merchant's favour. In a two-man business, this difference might be four or five carats at the end of each day.

Barney and his new partner were working and sleeping in the same room. Barney was a heavy sleeper, but once he suspected treachery, he became determined to keep awake to see what his partner might be doing.

For several nights nothing happened; then one night his partner suddenly cried out, as though in a nightmare, that he heard burglars. He lay still, as though asleep, but all the time cautiously watching Barney, not suspecting that, through half-closed eyes, Barney was also watching him.

When he assured himself that Barney was still safely asleep, he climbed out of bed very stealthily and went to a corner of the room. Here he scratched the earth floor and pulled out a small bag. He slipped some small stones into this bag, replaced it, smoothed the earth over it and went back to bed.

Next morning, when he went for breakfast, leaving Barney in the hut on his own, Barney immediately dug up the bag. As he suspected, it contained diamonds, worth possibly £150. Barney replaced the bag carefully and, every morning for the next three weeks, while his partner was out, he unearthed it and checked that it was steadily growing heavier.

A couple of days before they were due to dissolve their partnership – Barney had decided to join his brother Harry – Barney dug up the bag when he was on his own and put it in a pocket in his body-belt. The two men settled up what was owing from their association and Barney went off for breakfast. His former partner at once dug in the corner of the hut, but of course could find nothing. When Barney returned, the man looked distraught and Barney asked him whether he was feeling well.

'My head is bad,' the man admitted. 'You can see that. My eyes are watery.'

Barney agreed.

'They shine like *diamonds*,' he said pointedly.

At this word, the other man looked at him sharply and Barney went on innocently, 'I thought you might have lost something?'

'No, no, I haven't.'

'I'm glad of that. A headache can be cured. Go to the *corner—*'

At this word the man looked shocked again.

'Go to the *corner,*' repeated Barney, 'and see the chemist. He'll fix you. But you are *sure* you've not lost anything?'

'No. Have you *found* something?' the other man asked him belligerently.

'Nothing that isn't mine,' Barney replied. 'But to cure that headache, buy an ounce of mustard, put it in *a little black bag* – and . . .'

The man interrupted Barney with abuse before he could finish speaking. So, once more, Barney Barnato was in business on his own.

CHAPTER 5

'EVERY MAN HAS HIS PRICE'

When Cecil and Frank Rhodes landed in England they travelled to Bishop's Stortford to visit their parents. From his father's vicarage Cecil wrote to Dr Sutherland in Natal, asking him to invest some money that a colleague in Kimberley would send to him for this purpose.

'I prefer railway shares,' Rhodes wrote. 'And £18 or even £19 would not be too much, but if you will be kind enough to take the trouble for one of your old immigrants, I feel I cannot do better than leave it to your discretion.'

He added, 'I am rather sorry now all the money I made I brought home to England; one puts it out at such low interest, as high interest here is another name for "smash".'

This prudent investment arranged, Rhodes took the train to Oxford. He was 20 years old, only two years older than most undergraduates coming up to Oxford straight from school, but in these extra two years he had faced extraordinary conditions and problems in a strange land 7,000 miles away. As a result he had little in common with most other young men of his class and generation, nor did he have their qualifications for entry to the university, not even a letter of recommendation from a headmaster. And although Rhodes had used much of his spare time reading Latin texts, his Latin was still not of a very high academic standard.

At Oxford he booked a room at The Mitre Hotel in the High Street and applied to University College to be admitted as an undergraduate. He never explained why he chose this particular college, but since he was actually in the university, it is possible that the name 'University College' struck him as being the easiest to approach. This college is also in the High Street, only a few hundred yards away from the hotel, so it could well have been pointed out to him.

University College did not accept him. Two possible reasons have since been given for their rejection. First, his Latin was not up to the required standard. Second, he wished to read for a Pass degree and not for an Honours degree, which was more usual. This second reason seems unlikely, because a number of undergraduates were already reading for Pass degrees in University College at that time.

Next, Rhodes tried Oriel College. According to some accounts, this was because the Master of University said he would give him an introduction to the Provost of Oriel, 'where they are less particular in this respect', but in what respect is not clear. Again, this is quite possible, but it is more likely that Rhodes, having been rebuffed once, decided to consider the situation more objectively, following the advice of Periander of Corinth, one of the seven Greek philosophers whose sayings were inscribed in the temple of Apollo at Delphi, and whose precept usually guided his actions: 'Exercise forethought in everything.'

Rhodes had been friendly with Henry Caesar Hawkins in Natal and in Kimberley; Hawkins' uncle, Dr Edward Hawkins, was the Provost of Oriel. Rhodes had often discussed with Hawkins his wish to go to Oxford and it seems very possible that Hawkins gave his uncle's name to Rhodes as someone in Oxford who might help him.

Another reason why Rhodes chose Oriel could be that he is also likely to have discussed his wish to go to Oxford with Sidney Shippard. He and Rhodes were friends and he had appointed Shippard to be one of the executors of the will he made when he accompanied his brother Herbert on their trip north. But, in either case, or in both, why did Rhodes not select that college first of all?

For whatever reason he selected the college, he wrote to Dr Hawkins asking for an appointment to discuss his wish to enter Oriel. Edward Hawkins had by then been Provost for 42 years, having previously been vicar of St Mary's, Oxford. Earlier, he had been private tutor to Viscount Caulfeild on the continent and had left Paris in 1815 on the day Napoleon entered the city.

At the meeting with Rhodes, Hawkins read his letter of application and then, according to one account, 'stared down at his table in hostile silence'. He then broke this silence to remark, 'All the colleges send me their failures'.

This seems an unlikely claim for the head of a college to make to a potential candidate for admission. And whatever the lack of Rhodes' academic qualifications, he was clearly a remarkable young man and manifestly not a failure. Rhodes protested, or so it was said, and then the Provost replied, 'I think you will do'. Whatever was or was not said at their meeting, Hawkins accepted Rhodes as an undergraduate.

Rhodes' father, by then in poor health, still hoped that his son would either enter the church or the army, but Rhodes was of a different mind.

'I go up to Oxford next week,' he wrote to Dr Sutherland. 'Whether I become the village parson, which you sometimes imagined me as, remains to be proved. I am afraid my constitution received rather too much of what they call the lusts of the flesh at the diamond fields to render that result possible!'

On 13 October, 1873, Rhodes arrived at Oriel and became a pupil of the Dean, the Rev W.M. Collett, who noted that when Rhodes signed the admissions book his signature was 'clumsy, boyish and unformed'.

He had to pass an examination called Responsions, which in those days he could sit as a member of the university; later this became an entrance examination. He took rooms at 18 High Street and passed Responsions in December, a month after the death of his mother.

He felt her loss desperately. She was one of the very few people in whom he could confide, knowing that she would understand his motives, whatever he did and whatever the result, and the only woman in his whole life with whom he would ever enjoy such closeness and affinity of spirit. It was tragic that she died just as his career was beginning to blossom. After her death Rhodes exchanged very few letters with his father. He had lost more than a mother; he had lost his best and closest friend.

Rhodes was remembered in Oriel as going down to the river to row only once, where another member of the college coached him, although others have said he was a keen oarsman. Within months of arriving in Oxford, however, he returned to South Africa. It was said that he caught a severe chill while rowing on the Isis. A specialist then warned him he had only six months to live unless he returned to a warmer, kinder climate. A later Provost of Oriel, Sir George Clark, thought that a more likely reason for Rhodes leaving was that he was running out of money.

'It is certainly untrue that he was unable to live in England in the winter because of some affection of the lungs,' he wrote.[1]

Indeed, when Rhodes returned to Oxford three years later, he kept all three terms of each academic year, going back to South Africa in the summer vacations, but not missing a single term until the end of the academic year in June, 1878. The college tutorial register, however, has a note: 'In the Lent term, 1874, he went out of residence owing to ill-health.'

Before Rhodes left Oxford, he bought ten newly built houses in Hampstead for £6,200. He put down a deposit of £1,800 and mortgaged the rest at 4% a year. His income from this investment was around £12 a week. Within three years the houses were worth £7,000. Rhodes thought of selling them and offered a half-share to Rudd, but Rudd was not interested. The investment was speculative and his previous experience made him reluctant to take any risks if he could avoid them. From Rhodes' point of view, the investment was an attempt to bolster his capital against any drastic

[1] In the *Oriel College Record*, 1953.

fall in the value of diamonds. The rents from these houses could then help pay his fees and living costs at Oxford.

Just as he had landed in South Africa at a decisive moment in that country's history, so he was at Oxford at a time when Britain became suddenly more conscious of imperial possibilities, but always at the least possible financial cost to the Treasury. This feeling probably reached its climax when Queen Victoria, to her great delight, was proclaimed Empress of India. Possibly the greatest influences on Rhodes at this time were Gibbon's *Decline and Fall*, which he read and reread many times, and the lectures of John Ruskin, the Slade Professor of Fine Art at the University. Reading Gibbon brought home to him the responsibilities, opportunities and privileges of the old Roman Empire, which he believed were paralleled by the British Empire.

Ruskin was lecturing to receptive audiences of undergraduates on the value of dedicating their lives to public service. His lectures were part sermons, part homilies, often illustrated with drawings and exhibits, and always delivered with a vivid emotional and personal appeal. There is no evidence that Rhodes attended Ruskin's lectures, but he could hardly have remained unaware of their popularity and influence.

In one lecture, for instance, Ruskin declared passionately: 'There is a destiny now possible to us, the highest ever set before a nation, to be accepted or refused. We are still undegenerate in race; a race mingled of the best northern blood. We are not yet dissolute in temper, but still have the firmness to govern and the grace to obey. . . .

'Will you, youth of England, make your country again a royal throne of kings, a sceptred isle, for all the world a source of light, a centre of peace; mistress of learning and the Arts, faithful guardian of time-tried principles, under temptation from fond experiments and licentious desires; and amid the cruel and clamorous jealousies of the nations, worshipped in her strange valour, of goodwill towards men? . . .

'This is what England must either do or perish: she must found colonies as far and as fast as she is able, formed of her most energetic and worthiest men; seizing every piece of fruitful waste ground she can set her foot on, and there teaching these her colonists that their chief virtue is to be fidelity to their country, and their first aim is to be to advance the power of England by land and sea: and that, though they live on a distant plot of land, they are no more to consider themselves disenfranchised from their native land than the sailors of her fleets do, because they float on distant seas.

'If we can get men, for little pay, to cast themselves against cannon-mouths for love of England, we may find men also who will plough and sow for her, who will behave kindly and righteously for her, and who will bring up their children to love her. . . .

'You think that an impossible ideal? Be it so; refuse to accept it if you will; but see that you form your own in its stead.'

This outlook corresponds very closely to Rhodes' own views, and on 2 June, 1877, during one of his later sojourns in Oriel, he wrote what he called his Declaration of Faith, outlining what he felt he could, and should, do with his life, how he would focus all his energies on advancing the interests of his country.

He was still an undergraduate, but also by 1877 growing rich. He knew that he would soon be even richer, but he was not making money simply to acquire grand houses, steam yachts and other expensive possessions: he wanted money – needed it desperately – to carry out the plan that was developing in his mind.

'It often strikes a man to inquire what is the chief good in life,' he wrote, employing unusual punctuation. 'To one, the thought comes that it is a happy marriage, to another great wealth, and as each seizes on his idea, for that he more or less works for the rest of his existence. To myself thinking over the same question the wish came to render myself useful to my country. . . .

'I contend that we are the finest race in the world and that the more of the world we inhabit the better it is for the human race. Just fancy those parts that are at present inhabited by the most despicable specimens of human beings what an alteration there would be if they were brought under Anglo-Saxon influence, look again at the extra employment a new country added to our dominions gives.

'I contend that every acre added to our territory means in the future birth to some more of the English race who otherwise would not be brought into existence. Added to this the absorption of the greater portion of the world under our rule simply means the end of all wars. . . .

'I look into history and read the story of the Jesuits what they were able to do in a bad cause and I might say under bad leaders.

'In the present day I become a member in the Masonic order I see the wealth and power they possess the influence they hold and I think over their ceremonies and I wonder that a large body of men can devote themselves to what at times appear the most ridiculous and absurd rites without an object and without an end.

'The idea gleaming and dancing before one's eyes like a will-of-the-wisp at last frames itself into a plan. Why should we not form a secret society with but one object the furtherance of the British Empire and the bringing of the whole uncivilised world under British rule for the recovery of the States for the making the Anglo-Saxon race but one Empire.

'What a dream, but yet it is probable, it is possible. . . . Just picture what they have lost, look at their government, are not the frauds that yearly come before the public view a disgrace to any country and especially theirs which is the finest in the world?

'Would they have occurred had they remained under English rule great as they have become how infinitely greater they would have been with the softening and elevating influences of English rule, think of those countless 000's of Englishmen that during the last 100 years would have crossed the Atlantic and settled and populated the United States. Would they have not made without any prejudice a finer country of it than the low class Irish and German emigrants? . . .

'Put your mind into another train of thought. Fancy Australia discovered and colonised under the French flag, what would it mean merely several millions of English unborn that at present exist we learn from the past and to form our future. We learn from having lost to cling to what we possess. We know the size of the world we know the total extent.

'Africa is still lying ready for us it is our duty to take it. It is our duty to seize every opportunity of acquiring more territory and we should keep this one idea steadily before our eyes that more territory simply means more of the Anglo-Saxon race more of the best the most human, most honourable race the world possesses.

'To forward such a scheme what a splendid help a secret society would be a society not openly acknowledged but who would work in secret for such an object. . . .

'For fear that death might cut me off before the time for attempting its development I leave all my worldly goods in trust to S.G. Shippard and the Secretary for the Colonies at the time of my death to try to form such a Society with such an object.'

Rhodes' first biographer and his former banker, Sir Lewis Michell, wrote: 'It is easy to laugh at the high-stepping political ambitions of the young digger "sitting on the edge of the Kimberley mine"; it is easy to disparage the light that irradiates his day-dreams as a "light that never was on land or sea", but the document for all that is worth analysis'.[2]

Subsequent critics and writers on Rhodes, some who he might possibly have classified as 'loafers', have poured ridicule on his dreams, and certainly all were impossible to achieve. But in former colonies, where British rule, British law and British justice once were paramount, can anyone honestly claim that life has since changed for the better for the ordinary people of these countries, as opposed to their present rulers?

Later, in 1877, Rhodes adapted his Confession of Faith into his second will. He left his entire estate to Lord Carnarvon, then Secretary of State for the Colonies, and his successors in office, and to his friend Sidney Shippard

[2] Michell, op. cit.

'of the Inner Temple', as Trustees. He described himself as being 'of Oriel College, Oxford, but presently of Kimberley in the Province of Griqualand, Esquire'.

'To and for the establishment, promotion and development of a Secret Society, the true aim and object whereof shall be the extension of British rule throughout the world, the perfecting of a system of emigration from the Kingdom, and of colonisation by British subjects of all lands where the means of livelihood are attainable by energy, labour and enterprise, and especially the occupation by British settlers of the entire Continent of Africa, the Holy Land, the Valley of the Euphrates, the Islands of Cyprus and Candia [Crete], the whole of South America, the Islands of the Pacific not heretofore possessed by Great Britain, the whole of the Malay Archipelago, the seaboard of China and Japan, the ultimate recovery of the United States of America as an integral part of the British Empire, the inauguration of a system of Colonial representation in the Imperial Parliament which may tend to weld together the dispersed Members of the Empire, and, finally, the foundation of so great a Power as to hereafter render war impossible and promote the best interests of humanity.'

When Rhodes arrived back in Kimberley after his first stay in Oxford he consulted a local doctor about his health. The doctor told him that he must not think of returning to England with its colder climate. This depressed Rhodes, but when two friends who were going by ox-wagon to Hebron on the Vaal River invited him to accompany them, his spirits – and his health – revived. The open air life, exercise, plain living and early hours cheered him greatly, and he returned to Kimberley apparently fit.

Whether Rhodes initially had to return to South Africa because of ill health or because he was short of money, there was in fact a much more urgent reason for his going back to Kimberley and he may have been informed of its importance.

Earlier that year the Austrian bourse had collapsed, which led to a worldwide fall in prices and interest rates. Banks and stockbrokers in London, Glasgow, Edinburgh, New York and Chicago went out of business. This fall in financial confidence had, in turn, a very serious effect on diggers in Kimberley, who might never have heard of the Austrian bourse. They were vulnerable individuals, working without much capital, with little bargaining power, hoping to get the best prices they could in the open market. If that suffered, so did they. As one anonymous digger wrote on a daguerreotype of the original kopje which hung on the wall of his hut:

'Of course I thought that once on the field
Every load a stone would yield.

But I owned, after many a weary day,
That gravel is gravel and clay is clay.'

The whole diamond mining industry had, from the beginning, proceeded in a casual, haphazard way. Roads regularly collapsed in the mines; there was frequent flooding, hazards which everyone accepted. But more alarming to the diggers, and less easy to accept, was the fact that the soft earth, which they called yellow ground, and which had given up its diamonds relatively easily, seemed nearly dug out.

Below this lay hard, rocky 'blue ground'. It was widely believed that this held no diamonds whatever, and in any case the rock was so unyielding that picks and hammers could barely chip pieces from it.

The diggers, for the most part, had never been particularly interested in discovering where diamonds actually originated. Many thought vaguely that somehow they had arrived in rivers, which had then carried them along on their currents, or they were somehow buried in this soft yellow ground. Perhaps, by now, they had all been discovered? If so, what would the future hold for thousands and thousands of hopefuls who had sold everything to come here? The answer was too sombre for many to contemplate.

Some months before Rhodes left Kimberley for his first visit to Oxford, Richard Southey, the Cape's Colonial Secretary, had been appointed Lieutenant Governor of Griqualand. When he arrived in Kimberley virtually the entire town turned out to welcome him and accompany him to Government House – not a mansion, but a corrugated iron shack with two windows and a wooden verandah.

The diggers hoped that somehow Southey could rescue them from ever-increasing despondency and, in many cases, ruin. Claims were being exhausted and, although diamonds were more difficult to dig, prices for those they found grew less and less.

In addition, Cape Colony kept all customs dues paid on goods that went in and out of the area, and direct taxation, which had been £3 per head in 1872, had risen to £10. It could not be increased because it simply could not be collected. Southey knew that a survey should be carried out to bring an end to the constant disputes about who owned what. Proper facilities for pumping out the pits should also be provided and an efficient police force organized. But there was no government money for any of these amenities, let alone all of them.

Southey advocated the amalgamation of claims into large syndicates or companies and ended the regulation that prevented any individual from owning more than one claim. He sensed that the day of the individual digger, working on his own, and for himself, was all but over. This many diggers refused to accept. His attempts to gain their support were further sabotaged when it became clear that he wished to allow Africans to be eligible to vote and to hold claims.

Southey pointed out the indisputable fact that, until the whites had arrived, nearly all the land in Africa had been owned by coloured people, and that this should always be remembered. But diggers of many nationalities, educated and uneducated alike, did not subscribe to his more liberal proposals. They formed what they called a Committee of Public Safety, which was led by a gifted agitator, Alfred Aylward, who was also, surprisingly, the local correspondent for the London *Daily Telegraph*. Aylward's vehement cries to resist Southey's proposals were wildly cheered at every meeting he addressed.

Southey, considerably alarmed at this rising political tension, issued a proclamation warning everyone against 'taking illegal oaths or assembling in arms'. In response Aylward ran up the black flag of rebellion and organized his supporters so well that they were drilling openly, presumably for armed insurrection. Southey appealed to the Governor of the Cape, Sir Henry Barkly, to send troops to Kimberley in case of violence.

When the troops arrived tension eased, but Southey had been humiliated. He had attempted the impossible. Authorities in London and Cape Town wanted general prosperity and peace, but would not pay the essential outgoings that these desirable results demanded. Southey was recalled.

Now that men could legally own more than a single claim, many diggers did join with colleagues to buy as many as they could afford, and so spread their costs. Cecil Rhodes and Barney Barnato realized the wisdom of this, but both faced problems about raising money to buy the claims they wanted.

Rhodes had the idea of selecting people to work for him, a system called working claims on 'halves'. The owner would take half the profit and the lessee the other half, out of which he paid his working expenses and any repairs to his gear. Flooding continued and became exceptionally serious. The sides fell in regularly and, after each fall, hundreds of tons of shale had to be laboriously removed before work could restart. In these circumstances banks became nervous about advancing money for consolidation and refused loans. As a result many operators became bankrupt; others abandoned their claims and disappeared.

'Rhodes was often hard up,' one friend recalled afterwards, 'as we all were.'

Because of this shortage of money, Rhodes decided to realize his investment in the railways, about which he had earlier written to Dr Sutherland. It appears that Sutherland had asked for a subscription to church work in Natal, which Rhodes was reluctant to give, and possibly he could not afford.

May 28/74
Kimberley Diamond Fields.

'Dear Dr Sutherland, – Many thanks for your letter. I have a bill to meet of £150, so would like to know if you could sell those shares for what they were bought, or (what I would prefer) could you get me £150 on them at the Natal Bank and remit to me?

'I am not a great believer in Churches or Church purposes, in fact, am afraid life at college and at the Diamond Fields has not tended to strengthen my religious principles.

'There was a man who came out with me named Williams, a second-class passenger in the *Asiatic*. He went on to Natal very bad with consumption and hard up; no friends; packed off from England to die abroad. If he is not dead, please give him the balance. If he is dead, take it for the Church. I fear he is dead by this time. If you could manage any means to send him to the Free State, I would pay the further expense . . .
Yrs,
C. Rhodes

'P.S. – Just now the Kopje is full of water, no money coming in from ground, all going out. In about six months I will repay the Bank. Please remit, if you can, by return.'

Rhodes was not a regular churchgoer. Possibly as a boy he had heard too many Sunday sermons from his father to make him enthusiastic to hear more, but he believed in doing good and, as with Barney Barnato, no one who approached him with a genuine case for help ever went away empty-handed.

When Rhodes returned to Oriel after his long stay in South Africa, Dr Hawkins, although still nominally Provost, had left Oxford to spend his last years elsewhere. The new Dean, the Rev Arthur Gray Butler, was living in the Provost's lodgings in college.

Butler and Rhodes became friends. As a boy, Butler had been a notable scholar and sportsman, and later was headmaster of Haileybury. Once, when he criticized Rhodes for not attending lectures, Rhodes replied, 'Oh! I promise you I shall manage it. Leave me alone and I shall pass through.'

During his time at Oxford Rhodes joined Vincent's Club and was elected to the Bullingdon Club in 1877. He was also initiated into Freemasonry in the Apollo University Lodge, and scandalized other Masons when he revealed details of the initiation ceremony at a dinner some time afterwards. But the strength and discipline of the Freemasons nevertheless impressed him greatly, as did the solidarity of the Jesuits.

He was also Master of the Drag, ('a quaint appointment, bearing in mind that he rode with a loose rein and had an eminently unsafe seat in the saddle').[3] His neighbours had to suffer many late nights when he was practising on the horn in order to acquit himself well with this instrument. He also played polo, but took little part in other aspects of Oxford life.

A friend arriving from South Africa sent a wire to Rhodes at Oriel saying that he would soon be in London.

'He at once came up to town and fetched me down, and I stayed as his guest at the Mitre. He was at that time out of college. I remember he was keen on polo, which was not so common in those days.

'I went with him to a wine, and was amused to notice how much older in manner the other undergraduates were than Cecil. They were full of that spurious wisdom assumed by many young men as a defensive armour, an armour he did not require.'

Butler, recalling Rhodes' time there, wrote later: 'He belonged to a set of men like himself, not caring for distinction in the schools and not working for them, but of refined tastes, dining and living for the most part together, and doubtless discussing passing events in life and politics with interest and ability.

'Such a set is not very common at Oxford, living, as it does, a good deal apart from both games and work, but it does exist and, somehow, includes men of much intellectual power which bears fruit later.'[4]

Rhodes was still considering whether he should become a barrister. As a barrister, he believed he would command authority which he believed was lacking in anyone without a professional qualification. His thoughts were sharply divided between his two centres of interest, Oxford and Kimberley.

On 1 June, 1876, he wrote from Oxford to Charles Rudd in Kimberley about equipment they needed to pump out the deep mine shafts which flooded from underground streams.

'My dear Rudd,

'I must tell you that I have ordered an engine one of the Roley and Co. patents with gear under boiler. . . .

'With reference to myself, I am just through two terms more on the 20th of this month and have entered at Inner Temple. I can get through in two years from now and have determined to do it. On calmly reviewing last year I find we lost £3,000 owing to my having no profession. I lacked pluck on three occasions through fearing that

[3] Michell, op. cit.
[4] Quoted in Rhodes' obituary in the *Westminster Gazette* in 1902.

one might lose and I had nothing to fall back on in the shape of profession.

'I refer to caving in at Dutoitspan, abandoning claims there, and letting Graham in at De Beers and E J Gray also, none of which things would have occurred if I had not funked collapse. You will find me a most perfect speculator if I have two years and obtain a profession. I am slightly too cautious now.

'My dons and I have had some tremendous skirmishes. I was nearly caught going to Epsom, but still I do not think I shall be sent down. The change at first was rather odd. I would in conclusion say do not plunge for much more at the fields.

'We have a sufficient block at De Beers to make a fortune if diamonds last and have enough property in Kimberley. If we make more money I would sooner say lend it or go in for a nest egg here at home, and by all means try and spare me for two years. You will find I shall be twice as good a speculator with a profession at my back. I will be reading here all the summer. . . .
Yrs
C.J. Rhodes.'

Rhodes' lack of any interest in his dress or appearance was as much in evidence in Oxford as it had been in Kimberley. Undergraduates shared the services of a scout, a manservant who would look after their needs when they were in residence. Like many college servants at that time, Rhodes' scout, William Hodge, was not particularly well paid. He was therefore grateful for any tips in cash or kind which undergraduates might care to give him.

Rhodes had originally arrived at Oriel with only one suit, which he was wearing, patched with a piece of cloth by the steward on the Union Castle ship bringing him to England. In Hodge's opinion, Rhodes needed, as the absolute minimum, at least one other suit. Rhodes agreed and went to Hookhams, the tailors, and ordered a suit to be made exactly like the one he wore. Hodges hoped that, when it arrived, Rhodes might then pass on the old suit to him. But no. Rhodes said he had already promised it to the cabin steward on the ship.

Hodge admired Rhodes; he was what he called 'a good payer', but he had a habit that worried him. Rhodes disliked and distrusted banks, and at Oxford he did not use a cheque book. Instead, he carried in the pockets of his waistcoat and his jacket odd uncut diamonds wrapped in twists of tissue paper, after the manner of diamond traders in Hatton Garden. When he needed money, he cashed a diamond.

This casual attitude caused Hodge much concern. He was worried in case Rhodes should lose any of these diamonds, which he left about in his rooms without any thought of security, and then he might be blamed. He therefore pleaded with Rhodes to abandon this custom. Rhodes refused to do so.

Another contemporary at Oriel was also surprised by Rhodes' habit of carrying diamonds about with him. He recalled that 'on one occasion, when he condescended to attend a lecture which proved uninteresting to him,' he took out a small box from his waistcoat pocket, opened it and passed it round his colleagues to right and left.

The box was full of small diamonds. Someone reached out to have a closer look at them and upset the box. Diamonds scattered all over the lecture-room floor. The lecturer was surprised to see members of his audience suddenly leave their seats and crawl about on the floorboards and asked the reason for this behaviour.

'It is only Rhodes and his diamonds,' was the reply.

In Kimberley, meanwhile, a Royal Commissioner had been appointed, a Colonel Crossman, with the brief to examine the whole situation in the mining community. This marked the end of Southey's wish for a more liberal policy towards African workers. From then on they would not be allowed to hold claims or even to wash débris that might contain diamonds. Their status was fixed as labourers.

Such was the atmosphere of unease in Kimberley, a genuine fear for the future, when Rhodes returned after his first term at Oriel. Conditions there did nothing to improve matters. Anthony Trollope, the novelist, paid a visit to the town (now with about 18,000 inhabitants, black and white) and was horrified by 'dust so thick that the sufferer fears to remove it lest the raising of it may aggravate the evil, and of flies so numerous that one hardly dares to slaughter them by ordinary means lest their dead bodies should be noisome.'[5] An average temperature of 100 degrees Fahrenheit in the shade was also conducive to short temper and displays of anger.

Certainly diggers felt they had much to be angry about. One of their gravest day-to-day concerns was endemic flooding in the mines. Men could not work under water and, while the level rose and sometimes fell, the water was nearly always there, making digging impossible.

Rhodes and Rudd, with an Australian engineer, William Alderson, bought second-hand pumps in Cape Town, to pump out the mines. Their engines had originally powered agricultural machinery and were old and not much better than scrap. As a result they frequently broke down and their boilers needed huge amounts of wood. Rhodes owned a shaggy Basuto pony and a yellow cart and he would ride around the countryside before sun-up hoping to waylay Boers who were taking wagon-loads of wood to Kimberley market

[5] *South Africa*, Anthony Trollope, London, 1878.

and persuade them to sell to him to ensure his pumping engines had enough fuel.

One day, when Alderson was elsewhere and Rudd was working on the edge of the mineshaft, Rhodes had promised to keep the boiler supplied with wood and water. Rudd happened to look up and was surprised to see Rhodes walking up and down, obviously deep in thought over some other problem, while the safety valve on the boiler hissed dangerously. Before Rudd could shout a warning to him the boiler burst. Rhodes had forgotten to see that it was filled with water.

Rhodes and Rudd ordered new pumping equipment from Cape Town. While waiting for it to arrive, a Mauritian engineer, in charge of the existing pump at the De Beers mine, claimed that someone had offered him a bribe of £300 to sabotage the mechanism. When the case came to court, he would not name this person, but instead wrote on a piece of paper 'Mr Cecil Rhodes'.

Other witnesses said that this engineer had told them how Rhodes was not the person who tried to bribe him. Because Rhodes' name was only written down, lawyers ruled that the court had no evidence that Rhodes had actually been named. The engineer was therefore sent for trial himself on a charge of perjury. For reasons never revealed, this curious case was dropped. In fact, when the new pumping equipment did eventually arrive, it required far less supervision, and so the engineer faced being out of a job. This prospect could have influenced his claim.

The diggers, never backward in making complaints or allegations, angrily demanded that Rhodes get this new equipment installed quickly. This was impossible to do because heavy rain had flooded all roads and tracks and the railway ended 400 miles out of Kimberley. No ox-wagon or mule-cart could haul such heavy, cumbersome machinery through thick mud and across flooded rivers. An urgent meeting was called to discuss the matter and Rhodes was instructed to attend and explain reasons for the delay.

Diggers packed the hall where the meeting was being held, all vociferous in their complaints. Hawkins accompanied Rhodes and was greatly impressed by the way in which he handled the extremely hostile meeting.

'I have never forgotten the way in which he, still quite a youth, handled that body of angry men and gained his point – an extension of time.'

Rhodes gained time by giving the meeting his personal guarantee to have another pump in position within 30 days – or lose £100. After some discussion and argument, this proposal was reluctantly accepted. Now Rhodes had to find a stop-gap pump, and quickly.

He had heard that a farmer many miles away owned a pump capable of pumping out the mine and had been using it for pumping water to irrigate his crops. There was no means of communicating with the farmer except by going to see him, so Rhodes took a Cape cart and drove south to his farm, a journey that took eight days. When he arrived and explained the reason for his visit, the farmer told him bluntly that he was not interested in selling his pump.

'I bought it for certain work,' he explained. 'I want it.'

'Yes,' Rhodes agreed. 'But you are not using it at the moment and you are not going to for some time. So sell it to me at a fair profit and send for another.'

The farmer refused.

'I might want it before another got here,' he said cannily. 'I absolutely refuse to sell.'

Rhodes was not content with this reply. He went away, but was back again that afternoon to make a higher offer. Again the answer was no. But the farmer did not know how desperately important it was for Rhodes to acquire this pump, nor did he realize his tenacity.

Every morning, every afternoon, for several days Rhodes appeared at the farm, each time increasing his offer. Finally the farmer decided to send him on his way for ever. He said he would sell the equipment for the enormous sum of £1000, much more than far superior new machinery would have cost, and not far short of the price of a farm. Rhodes did not demur.

'Very well,' he said immediately. 'I'll buy it. Let's get it on the wagon at once.'

Within hours he was on the way back to Kimberley. He had taken more than two weeks to find the pump and buy it, and the rains meant that the roads were still flooded, and consequently the wagon could only make very slow progress. At last the driver, a Boer, said he could not go any further until the weather eased off. If he did not stop and rest his oxen he would kill them.

Rhodes appealed to him.

'It will ruin me if you are not there on time,' he explained.

'It will ruin me if I try,' the Boer retorted. 'My oxen are my only means of livelihood.'

'I will buy them at a good price and you can get others,' Rhodes told him.

As he spoke, he realized that he did not have sufficient money with him to pay the man in cash, but the Boer recognized a good offer when he heard one and agreed to accept it.

'It is right,' he said. 'As you are a good sort of fellow, I will sell.'

They shook hands on this arrangement. Rhodes took out his cheque book, but found he had neither pen nor ink, so he borrowed a pencil from the Boer and wrote out the cheque in pencil. They reached Kimberley on time.

The Boer's confidence greatly impressed Rhodes. He knew that Boers distrusted cheques just as much as he disliked banks, and a cheque written in pencil was not legal if it should be challenged. But the man had taken him at his word and from that day on Rhodes' respect for Boers, already high since his trip north with his brother Herbert, increased immeasurably.

He had also learned something else about human nature. When the farmer finally decided to sell his pump and the driver agreed to continue his journey, both against their own wishes, he had been able to persuade both to do as *he* wanted, by offering them a price they simply could not refuse.

'Every man has his price,' Rhodes would say. Some might question this realistic (or cynical) assessment, but those who did so often assumed that the price was being reckoned in money. If the price is not in cash, but in some other currency of greater value to the recipient, then fewer would disagree with Rhodes' claim.

Thus the price could mean unexpected (or even undeserved) promotion; an honour, an award, entry into a school, a university, a club when all the lists were closed. The secret was in finding each man's price, and for the rest of his life this was something that Rhodes invariably managed to discover.

He and Rudd had negotiated lucrative contracts for pumping water from the mines; De Beers mine paid them £400 a month and Dutoitspan £500. Rhodes, like Barney Barnato, fully realized the necessity of diversification to keep solvent.

He and Rudd also bought a machine for making ice to cool drinks and one for producing ice-cream. Rhodes would stand, shielded from the sun by a white cotton blanket hanging from the side of a tent, as he turned the handle of the churn. Rudd sold the ice-creams from a packing case, sixpence for a wine-glass full, and another sixpence if the buyer also wanted a slice of cake. After the first summer they sold the machine for £1500 and used the money to purchase more claims. All their efforts were directed to acquiring as many claims as they could. So far as Rhodes was concerned, everything else was subordinate to this imperative aim, because on its achievement depended the realization of his dream.

CHAPTER 6

'TIMES HAVE CHANGED AND NOW THE SUN IS SHINING FOR ME.'

The Barnato Brothers' journey from penury to wealth seemed incredibly short and swift to those who only saw their arrival, but to the Barnatos it had been a long slow march, with no guarantee of how or when it would end. Survival in Kimberley, as Barney had discovered very early on, was not only a matter of the fittest, but of the shrewdest and, sometimes, the most courageous.

When he was left on his own for the second time, his financial situation became so desperate that he was forced to sell his silver watch chain, and then the works of his nickel watch, for which he received five shillings.

He kept the empty case for two reasons. First, he thought that it would come in useful for holding diamonds – it was much more solid than a matchbox – and also he felt that it was in the nature of a mascot and might bring him good luck. In fact, his own efforts brought him his good luck and, as many other successful entrepreneurs have proved, in Kimberley and elsewhere, the harder he worked the better his luck became.

In those early months Barney sold shaving brushes and necklaces, anything he could buy for a few pennies and sell for a few more. Years later he would say, 'There is nothing that this country [South Africa] produces that I have not traded in, from diamonds and gold, right the way through wool, feathers and mealies to garden vegetables. I have always found that I was as good a hand at buying and selling as most people I came across.'

Some people have a gift with words. Others can paint, or compose, or carry an audience; a few can even sway nations with their eloquence. Barney had the gift of selling, plus a rarer and more valuable ability: he could somehow make money in the most upromising circumstances.

Gardner Williams, an American mining engineer who became general manager of De Beers, said admiringly of him, 'One could scarcely have cast him in any society or any place on earth where his nimble wits would not have won him a living.'[1]

His first partner, Louis Cohen, summed up another aspect of his remarkable character.

'Barney knew me better than any man,' he said, 'and would have done anything for me in the world – bar give me a sixpence.'

Barney, for his part, talking about Cohen later on, said, 'Lou, I'd forgive you anything, except one thing.'

'What's that?'

'Pulling your blanket off me when we slept in the shed in Kimberley at the beginning.'

They had been so poor then that they slept on a straw mattress under a single green blanket which Cohen owned. As its owner, he kept most of this blanket for himself on cold nights. Barney, uncharacteristically, was too much in awe of the older man to complain and would wake up shivering and thankful for the long flannel underwear his mother had so wisely given to him.

Barney bought a watch-maker's glass and screwed this into his eye when he had a diamond to examine. This not only helped his short sight but, like a theatrical prop, made him look the part of a professional diamond buyer, as though he had actually served his apprenticeship in Hatton Garden or Antwerp. He picked up knowledge from anyone and everyone and quickly learned to detect flaws in stones, to distinguish their different colours, and so assess their value, and also to spot any stone that had been doctored to increase its value.

Some diamonds had a dull, yellow colour not due to nature, but to man. Louis Cohen was an expert at discovering these doctored diamonds. Soon after his arrival he was sold several, believing them to be genuine. When he found he could not pass them on at a profit, he decided to find out why.

He was advised to put one in a glass of acid, then clean it with a chamois leather. The diamond's original creamy tint vanished and the stone appeared yellow and insipid, which, in practical terms, meant that it was worth at least 30 shillings a carat less than he had paid for it.

Such stones, he discovered, had been altered in a complex way. First of all, a mixture of borax, salt, chloride of lime and arsenic was formed into a sticky paste. The poor-quality diamond was rubbed into this and then held by pliers over an oil lamp. The man who was hoping to increase the value of the stone would put a tube in his mouth and blow air on the flame to increase the heat. When the stone glowed crimson he dropped it into a bottle

---

[1] Le Sueur, op. cit.

of sulphuric ether. It was then removed and quickly sold before the colour had time to change.

The best way to keep it looking expensive was for the seller to hold it in his mouth under his tongue until he could dispose of it. Sometimes, because of this, diamond fakers were discovered when merchants offered to buy them a drink in a canteen. Drinks were very rarely refused in Kimberley and the fact that someone might decline one could in itself arouse suspicion.

Every morning Barney would be out early, trying to buy diamonds. Sometimes he would make as much as £20 before breakfast, on a few occasions even £30. He and Harry discovered that the best day to buy, from their point of view, was Saturday, because banks closed early and cheques could not be cashed until the following Monday.

During the weekend the Barnatos would endeavour to sell diamonds they had bought on Saturday and deposit their profits in the bank as soon as it opened on Monday. There would thus be sufficient money in their account to honour the cheques they had given to the men from whom they had bought the diamonds. Some of the more devout Jews in Kimberley were averse to working on the Sabbath, but Barney and Harry were willing to work any day if they could show a profit. After all, that was why they were there.

Shrewd diamond buyers might make several hundred pounds on one stone. Sometimes diamonds changed hands several times, each man making a profit on the deal. But such occasions were rare and did not often come Barney's way.

Once, when he did make a quite unexpectedly large profit, he decided to celebrate. The Kimberley Hotel advertised dances 'for merchants and their ladies'. Because these dances could easily become a rough-house if everyone was allowed in, evening dress was stipulated.

Barney did not own evening dress, but Harry had a number of clothes he used for his act and Barney borrowed a suit from him, altered the trousers to fit and went to the dance. Within the hour he was back in the bar of the London Hotel where Harry was helping out as a barman.

'Those geezers wouldn't have anything to do with me after I'd had a couple of goes round the dance floor,' Barney explained sadly.

His brother was not surprised.

'Well, you can't dance, can you?' he said practically.

'But I was learning, wasn't I?'

Individual diggers were now facing very strong competition. Many grouped together to form syndicates when the law allowed. They realized that the day of the individual entrepreneur was passing; life was becoming more complex, and more and more feared for their future. Many thought that it might be wiser to leave now, when they had some chance of selling their claims, than to stay on and probably not find a buyer. The actual business of digging was also becoming more difficult and more dangerous, because, out of sheer desperation, diggers were going down too fast and too deep for their own safety.

Harry had left Van Praagh and was in charge of all the money that came in from Barney's daily journeys. When their total resources reached around £200 they had a wooden sign painted which they nailed above their door: 'Barnato Brothers, Dealers in Diamonds and Brokers in Mining Property'.

At night Barney would still tour the bars and billiard saloons. This was the best way to discover who had money and who had not, who was buying, who was selling. Barney was a good billiards player and he usually won. If he lost he would promise to settle up the next day, which he always did. He was a man of his word and people trusted him. He never carried money with him in case the coins rattled.

Harry did not appreciate the potential commercial value of Barney's nightly visits. He could not bear to see money trickling away in such places, just as Louis Cohen had been concerned and alarmed for exactly the same reason when Barney kept late hours.

To reduce outgoings, Harry cut down what he allowed his brother to spend, so that when Barney played billiards or dominoes he simply had to win, in order to have enough money to pay for his drinks and cigarettes. In case there might be any money over and above these basic running costs, Harry would often come with him to collect it. Gradually, by living with the utmost economy, their savings grew, while the savings of many others in Kimberley dwindled quickly. Diggers tended to live for the day. The habit for many was to spend lavishly when they found a good diamond; to drink champagne, often, literally, from a bucket.

Living and working conditions in Kimberley were steadily deteriorating. In addition to what was known as 'camp fever' and other illnesses caused by bad food, water and poor sanitation, there were growing concerns about safety in the mines. The Kimberley and De Beers mines had become huge holes, so that the miners were continually forced to go deeper to find fewer diamonds and take greatly increased risks while doing so.

Roadways would now cave in more frequently; water would seep in more quickly, the sides of the mine might suddenly collapse, known as the reef falling in. This convinced more diggers and buyers that the yellow ground in the mines was all but exhausted. Barney, like Rhodes and Rudd, took a different view. The day of the individual might indeed be ending, but the day of the large group, the amalgamation of many claims, with a consequent reduction of overheads, was about to begin.

Diamonds so far had been found mainly on river beds or dug out in mines.

Many diggers knew that river water had washed them down – but from where? No one seemed much concerned. It was enough that diamonds had appeared, and now their number was dwindling.

Barney was impressed by one visitor to Kimberley, who he called 'a man with eyes he could use'. This was Dr Atherstone, who had identified the first diamond, Eureka. He came to see the situation in Kimberley for himself and he explained to anyone interested how diamonds had been formed thousands of feet beneath the ground near the heart of the earth. When the heat and the pressure at such enormous depth became too great a molten mass was forced upwards, to spew out across the earth's surface.

Diamonds had not somehow 'grown' in the beds of rivers. They had been forced up from the centre of the earth by volcanic eruption. Some had then been carried along by river currents.

The shape of a diamond pipe, as these channels to the surface were called, was like a funnel, with the diameter growing steadily smaller the deeper down it went. This shape arose from the fact that, as the molten diamond-bearing mass of earth and rocks was driven upwards by immeasurable heat and pressure, the further it travelled from the centre of the earth the less resistance it encountered. When it finally burst out on the surface to form a small mound or hill, like Colesberg Kopje, there was little pressure left behind it.

Barney listened to Atherstone's theory and calculated that, because of the forces that drove diamonds upwards, there must still be more buried deep in the earth than remained close to its surface.

This made sense at a time when more and more diggers were leaving, because the yellow ground had apparently yielded up nearly all its diamonds. Beneath this yellow ground lay hard rock, the so-called blue ground, too solid to be cut by axes. Explosives were needed, and more sophisticated equipment. Individual diggers were daunted by the prospect of such heavy investment without any guaranteed return.

Thus, when the diggers packed their bags to leave because they could not make any worthwhile impression on the blue ground, Barney and Harry Barnato bought up their claims, sometimes very cheaply.

Barney was convinced that if Atherstone was right – and his instinct told him he must be – then the biggest diamonds were still waiting to be found. By far the best was sure to be, not in the yellow ground, but in the blue ground, embedded in rock so hard that it blunted axes and broke the shafts of the heaviest hammers.

In early 1876, three years after they arrived in South Africa, the Barnatos learned that two brothers named Kerr wished to sell four adjoining claims in the Kimberley mine. They had decided to leave and try their luck panning for gold in the Transvaal. At first the Kerrs were asking more for their claims than Barney and Harry could afford, but eventually, after long negotiations, they agreed to accept £3,000.

This was virtually all the Barnatos had saved by then, and a bank loan was absolutely out of the question, as Rhodes and Rudd had discovered when they lacked £6,000 with which they could have bought the entire De Beers mine.

Harry and Barney had now virtually no money left in reserve in case anything went wrong. A sudden fall of rock, a flood, the caving in of a path, any of these hazards could ruin them. They were out on their own, backing their faith in Atherstone's theory against the scepticism of the majority. This was an enormous gamble, all or nothing, and without any hope of a second chance.

Bucket after bucket of hard blue rock was hauled up from their new claims and not one contained the smallest diamond. Later a few tiny stones appeared in one bucket. Barney exhorted his workers to dig even harder. He promised them bribes and urged them to take short cuts and ignore the risks. The prize was too great to allow any avoidable delay. He not only encouraged them verbally to greater efforts, he went down into the pit himself and helped them dig.

His enthusiasm and determination were infectious, but as bucket after bucket came up with only a few minute diamonds in ground so hard it had to be soaked with water and then hammered into small pieces before it could be sifted, Harry shook his head over what seemed a most pitiful return for so much money and effort. Barney, outwardly at least, remained supremely confident.

They were working every day now from six each morning until dark. Barney would still be up at dawn, exercising with his Indian clubs. Then he would pour a bucket of cold water over his head and shoulders and indulge in shadow boxing to loosen his muscles. He was very fit, and needed to be, because his schedule was punishing. He still toured the saloons and canteens each night, finding out what other people were doing, what they thought of the chances. Always, and to everyone, he appeared confident, whatever his private feelings.

Then, suddenly, most unexpectedly, everything changed. Their buckets began to disgorge rocks that, amazingly, contained diamonds of 10, 15, 25 carats each. In one week the Barnatos sold enough diamonds to repay the entire cost of the Kerr brothers' claims. In a single hour in the following week Barney found thirty diamonds, and sold them for £10,000 – actually about half their real worth, as he discovered later. No matter. No one ever went broke taking a profit, and soon the Barnatos' claims were yielding on average £2,000-worth of diamonds every week. At the end of twelve months in the blue ground they had sold around £90,000-worth of diamonds. The days of poverty were behind them for ever.

'Since I was certain that the diamonds came from below, it followed that there must be more lower down, if not in the blue, then the other side of it,' Barney said later.

'I determined to go on until it broke me, and I was right. It didn't break me. We soon found that the blue itself was the true home of the diamonds. We found in it, as I expected, more and better diamonds than all the yellow contained.'

Success did not change him. He still appeared on stage at the local theatre, simply because he loved acting. Once, in the unlikely role of Othello, when he spoke the line, 'Haply that I am black,' some wag in the audience shouted up to him, 'Go and wash your face then, Barney.'

When a rival diamond merchant, who also had theatrical pretensions, was in the audience and jeered Barney's performance, Barney turned aside and warned the interrupter that if he did not shut up he would make him laugh on the other side of his face. The man went on baiting him, so Barney jumped over the footlights, knocked him on the jaw, vaulted back and continued with the scene.

In the local dramatic society he met a young girl, Fanny Bees, who acted when she was not working as a barmaid. She was taller than Barney and some years younger. Her family were originally Huguenots; her father had been a tailor in Simonstown, the naval base, but, when business fell off, he came north with his wife and eight small children, to try his luck as a diamond digger. He did not have much luck, nor did he initially have a very high opinion of Barney as a suitor for his daughter. She became friendly with Barney when she was a prompter to him during rehearsals. Soon they fell in love.

Barney said later that they went through a civil marriage, but to avoid offending his parents he did not make this public until Fanny could be converted to Judaism in England. Anyhow, they set up house together. When they were married later in London, Barney was described on the marriage certificate as a bachelor and his bride as a spinster.

Fanny had a pleasant and agreeable personality and proved to be a very tolerant and understanding wife. Without any complaint, she put up with what some wives would have found most unusual behaviour. Simply out of exuberance Barney would box anyone willing to risk several rounds with him. He was out late most nights, drinking, playing cards or dominoes or billiards, and would rarely sit through a meal she had cooked. He was restless, would jump up and walk round the room, or leave half-way through, unable to stay still for more than minutes at a time.

He was totally unpredictable. One day, for example, tired of paying money to bookies at local horse races which were not infrequently rigged in their favour, he appeared as a bookmaker himself – and made a profit of £400 on the day. Again, some card-sharpers, new to Kimberley, thought they would fleece this small, harmless-looking man who wore thick spectacles. Barney readily agreed to a game – and won all their money from them. They were astounded – not least when he gave each of them a pound to buy themselves a drink, with the advice: 'Never mark Barney Barnato down for a mug again'.

Neither they nor anyone else ever made that mistake twice.

Barney meanwhile had told his sister, Kate Joel, of the great opportunities her three sons, Jack, then known as Isaac, Woolf and Solly would have in South Africa. She was unenthusiastic, but allowed Woolf to come out to Kimberley. He was then 16 and Fanny made much of him. Both she and Barney were impressed by Woolf's common sense and natural ability with figures. He learned all he could about diamonds, and he learned quickly. Barney, only 11 years his senior, was soon more like a brother than an uncle to him. Woolf read widely, and while Barney tended to run his increasingly prosperous business in a most casual way, Woolf kept a restraining hand on him. As Stanley Jackson wrote in his biography of Barney, 'He developed an acute perception of high finance, while Barney was still in the abacus stage and over-inclined to rely on his memory.'

Barney paid Woolf £50 a week, a huge salary at a time when in London he would be fortunate at his age to earn that in a year. On Barney's next trip back to London he persuaded his sister to allow her other two sons to come out to South Africa with him.

Fanny tried to give Barney another interest, apart from making money, and persuaded him to stand for Kimberley council. This he did, but he had a fear of making a fool of himself before men of greater education. It was one thing to act the fool with friends, or on a stage, but quite another to appear a fool in front of people who might regard him as being out of his depth.

The astonishing success Barney and Harry Barnato enjoyed, in what seemed so short a time, understandably aroused great envy from others less successful. To diggers, hard-pressed to scratch a bare living from hacking day after day from sun-up to dusk, in fearful conditions of dust and heat, such sudden and prodigious wealth seemed unbelievable. Yet it was true. So how did two young strangers succeed so amazingly when many more mature diggers of far longer experience manifestly did not?

Rivals could not understand how, when the sides of other men's claims caved in, when mines flooded, such setbacks seemingly did nothing to diminish the number of diamonds that the Barnatos could still place on sale. Rumours spread that they must be dealing illegally in stolen diamonds. These whispers gained strength when Harry Barnato took over a bar and rooming house known as The London Hotel, which had a dubious reputation as the meeting place for people involved in illegally buying and selling diamonds.

In this hotel, as in other bars and canteens and elsewhere, Kimberley police maintained teams of informers and natives known as 'trap-boys'. Detectives supplied them with diamonds to offer to men suspected of being involved with illicit diamond buying, known as I.D.B.

If the trap-boy could persuade a suspect to buy a diamond from him and pay over the money for it, the man would be arrested before he could be rid of the diamond and while his money was still in the trap-boy's pocket. Sometimes such clumsy police plans misfired and trap-boys were badly beaten up.

They accepted these risks because they seemed a quicker way to make enough money to achieve their ambition of owning a gun and ammunition than by working for months in the mines. Hundreds of obsolete military muskets were openly for sale in Kimberley shops at between £5 and £6 each. Shopkeepers displayed them attractively in piles four or five high, along with bayonets, powder flasks and boxes of percussion caps, so that Africans passing along the streets could examine them.

On Saturdays work stopped in the mines at two o'clock in the afternoon and diggers paid the Kaffirs their wages. Obviously most could not afford to pay outright for the gun of their choice, but each would put down as much money as he could afford to reserve a gun. The shopkeeper then put that particular gun away in a corner of his shop. Every Saturday afternoon thereafter the African buyer would come to admire it and pay a little more, until he had paid the full price and the gun was his. Then he could take off to his home village with this trophy, the mark of a man's success.

The Barnatos once bought a claim from a Polish Jew who was later caught receiving stolen diamonds and sentenced to a session working on the breakwater being built in Cape Town harbour. There was no evidence whatever that Barney and Harry had any involvement with this man's activities, but their association with him was enough to cause heads to nod.

'Envy, hatred, malice and all uncharitableness were made manifest, for amongst those who had not gained wealth and amongst those who had not been able to keep it when gained, the whisper went round that such continued richness was unnatural,' wrote Harry Raymond, their friend and biographer.

Of this time of envy and suspicion, Barney later said sadly, 'How many times . . . I felt inclined, almost determined, to quit Kimberley and South Africa for ever. I was making a pile and gathering power; but I had enough to live on and should have been free from those never-ceasing rumours because of my good fortune. No one knew or ever can know how hard I worked for it all. If I have made millions I have worked for them as few men ever can have worked. But how I have been blackguarded by men who could neither gain nor work.'

To remind himself that he was not alone as a target for the envy of others, Barney carried in his jacket pocket a newspaper report of a speech made by another successful diamond man, Joe Mylchreest, at a banquet given in his honour before he retired to England.

'Times have changed and now the sun is shining for me,' Mylchreest said. 'Yet I cannot but recall the cruel days, when from a certain clique of my fellow citizens, every form of slander and insinuation was heaped upon me.

'They compassed me round about and laid snares for me. Men of the diamond fields, you can never know the bitterness they caused me. And why? Because, as my friend C.J. Rhodes stated the other day, I had, by dint of energy, integrity, and perseverance, done better than my neighbours and paid my way. I was successful and becoming rich and so they cried, "Down with him!"'

Barney would read this cutting every time some other insinuation of illegality or financial chicanery was made about him or his brother.

'As for the money men on the fields, is it a libel to say that most of them owe their wealth either to Illicit Diamond Buying or to taking advantage of the necessities or inexperience of unfortunate diggers?' wrote Lady Florence Dixie, a journalist who visited Kimberley around this time.

'Some of the most prominent men . . . were yesterday selling umbrellas on the streets of London, or catching birds on Hampstead Heath. And yet, although everybody knows all this, everybody winks at it.'[2]

Barney, so Rhodes' secretary Gordon Le Sueur claimed, 'was supposed to represent the illicit diamond buyers of the community'.[3]

Stanley Jackson reported that Barney and his brother 'were linked by rumour with I.D.B. or peddling stones smuggled out of the mines. Less fortunate diggers envied the Barnatos and whispered that their output was too phenomenal to be entirely legitimate.

'It was hinted that they bought their first claims from the proceeds of I.D.B. and were merely using them as a cover for continued operations. The very fact that they sold all their own diamonds, usually of far-above average size and quality, was another ground for suspicion.'[4]

'Poor Barney!' said Harry Raymond. 'He was successful in his great end of money getting and yet, as appears from his life, he was not altogether happy. He had money, but he had not reputation, and there perhaps lay his sorrows. Why Kimberley refused to entertain a high opinion of him we can

[2] *In the Land of Misfortune*, Lady Florence Dixie, Bentley, London, 1882.
[3] Le Sueur, op. cit.
[4] *The Great Barnato*, Stanley Jackson, Heinemann, 1970.

only guess. Upon the evidence, as already hinted, we must acquit him of any share in the "common crime" for a man is innocent until he is proved guilty. But it came near to him – near enough for the censorious.'[5]

Ian Colvin, the biographer of Dr Jameson, described Barney as: 'An Oriental, cunning, quick, emotional, mercurial, unabashed, and yet by all accounts good-natured, with an art to turn all things to gold – and yet with a scruple to turn all gold to dross – for in the end poor Barney drowned himself.'[6]

When Barney had first arrived in Kimberley and people asked who he was, the answer was invariably, 'That is Harry Barnato's brother'. A few years later the reply to the same question would be: 'That is Barney Barnato. Harry Barnato, the diamond expert, is his brother.'

When profits of £2,000 a week that he and Harry were making are compared with the annual sum of £12,000 proposed by Colonel Crossman as being necessary to maintain 'a minimal administration under a civil commissioner with a few mining inspectors, police and magistrates,'[7] the magnitude of Barney's achievement comes into perspective.

In the early days it was estimated that as much as 50% of all diamonds dug out were going missing. If this continued unchecked, or worse, if this huge loss were allowed to increase, the value of all diamonds could diminish sharply, and so would hope of improvement in the Cape's often wavering economy.

In an attempt to stop this financial haemorrhage action was announced against the lowly kopje-wallopers, who were thought to play a big part in this illegal traffic.

In 1876 the *Government Gazette* carried the following announcement: 'His Excellency the Administrator directs to be notified for general information that from and after this date the practice known as "kopje-walloping", or otherwise the purchasing of diamonds in places other than the offices of Licensed Bankers or Diamond Dealers, will be strictly prosecuted by the police who have received orders etc. Offenders under the section relating thereto are liable to a penalty upon conviction of not less than £100 and the forfeiture of the Licence.'[8]

The Kimberley police became increasingly active in attempting to track down people suspected of handling stolen diamonds or diamonds otherwise illegally acquired, but several factors continually hindered their efforts.

First, rich and influential people suspected of being involved, and indeed

[5] *Barnato: A Memoir*, Harry Raymond, Isbister & Co. Ltd., London, 1897.
[6] Colvin, op. cit.
[7] *Cecil Rhodes*, John Flint, Hutchinson, London, 1976.
[8] Quoted in *In the Early Days; pioneer life on the South African diamond fields*, John Angove, Handel House, Kimberley & Johannesburg, 1910.

faced with seemingly overwhelming evidence, could often succeed in bribing their way out of trouble. This would not necessarily mean bribing policemen directly, but they could come to some discreet accommodation with men who might otherwise have borne witness against them.

Secondly, the sheer extent of I.D.B. made it very difficult to trap more than minor operatives. Men and women found guilty were usually sentenced to hard labour; these sentences could be for many years and involve working on the breakwater being built in Cape Town harbour. Natives could face death. Punishments were so high because pilfering and selling diamonds privately was not only damaging to the company which legally owned the diamonds and often employed the pilferers, but also to Cape Colony, which was becoming increasingly reliant on the sale of diamonds overseas. Diamonds could only keep their value if they remained relatively scarce, and so exclusive. If markets were flooded with them, their desirability would rapidly decline.

Natives were heavily implicated in I.D.B. because they had the most opportunities; they did most of the actual digging and so were best placed to abstract a diamond before the dirt was sifted. But without facilities for selling such diamonds, they would have had no reason to steal them, so the whites were at least as guilty – and their profits immeasurably larger.

Kaffirs concealed stolen stones in their noses and mouths. They swallowed them, put them in their ears, and in what searchers delicately called 'other bodily orifices'. A strong dose of Epsom salts could usually reveal swallowed diamonds, but a variation was to wrap them in a ball of mealies and feed this to a horse. The fence or his accomplice could then ride the horse over the border to the Orange Free State and out of the jurisdiction of Cape Colony. Some Africans gashed their legs or arms, pushed stolen diamonds into the wounds and bound them up with a bandage. Such diamonds were sometimes discovered when the cuts went septic.

An ingenious means of secreting stolen diamonds was used successfully by a man with a glass eye. He hollowed out this eye, filled it with diamonds and walked away with a fortune.

Several large consignments of diamonds disappeared through a house deliberately sited so that it straddled the border. One part of the house was in Cape Colony, the other in the Orange Free State. People could be illegally holding stolen diamonds in the kitchen, but had only to move them to a bedroom to be safe from prosecution.

Suspects carrying diamonds were frequently chased to the border by police on foot or horseback, sometimes with onlookers cheering ironically as they raced through Kimberley. The popular feeling was often with the hunted rather than with the hunter, as had been the case a century before in the West of England when smuggling from France was at a peak.

One rider, making such a journey to the border with several very valuable diamonds, realized that his pursuers were rapidly closing on him. The diamonds were too big to swallow, and if he threw them away in the veld he could never hope to find them again. Yet, if he kept them, he would inevitably lose them and face years of hard labour. As he rode, he managed to wrap the stones in a piece of tin-foil that had been round an ounce of tobacco. He threw this into a bush, guessing that the dust kicked up by his horse's hooves would shield his action from the detectives a hundred yards behind him. He then slowed to a trot and stopped. The detectives searched him vigorously. Then they searched his saddle, the horse's bridle and every part of the horse's equipment, but of course nothing was concealed. Finally, and with great reluctance, they had to let him go. When they had ridden away he gave them an hour to be well out of sight and then rode back slowly along the trail until he could see sunlight glint on the twist of silvery paper that contained a fortune.

The wife of another suspected dealer was warned by a contact in the detective force that her house was about to be searched. She told her husband to get out of town quickly and leave her to handle the matter. When the detectives arrived, she expressed surprise that they should wish to search the house, but offered them every assistance. Meanwhile, since the afternoon was hot and they had had a long ride, would they care for tea and bread and butter and jam? She explained she had just baked a loaf, which she put on the table, still warm, and made as though to slice it. The detectives thanked her politely, but explained that they were on duty, and to accept her hospitality in the circumstances would not be right or proper. They searched the house thoroughly and found nothing incriminating. Before they left, she again offered them tea, which once more they refused. She watched them out of sight – and then cut open the loaf to remove the diamonds she had hidden inside it.

One diamond dealer involved with I.D.B. aroused much local sympathy because he suffered from a deformity; one leg was shorter than the other. To compensate, he wore a surgical boot with a thick heel. But events proved that he was not deformed at all; he simply used this heel, hollowed out, to carry diamonds when he limped out of Kimberley to board a coach to Cape Town.

The men who bought from the thieves, who made fortunes and who were never caught, might indeed have once been selling umbrellas on the streets of London or catching birds on Hampstead Heath, as Lady Florence Dixie declared, but that was then and this was now. And now they were extremely wealthy with strong political muscle.

Anyone who found a diamond illegally, either by digging it out of the mine and concealing the discovery or buying from someone else who had done so, could either try to take it out of Kimberley himself to sell elsewhere, or sell it in Kimberley to a go-between, of whom there were many.

Not a few were strongly suspected by the police, but they lacked firm evidence. A valuable stolen diamond could change hands several times and show a profit on each transfer. What might only bring a few pounds to its original discoverer could eventually make thousands for a dealer in Antwerp, Amsterdam or Hatton Garden.

To move the diamond either over the border to the Orange Free State, or out of Kimberley to Cape Town to board a ship, required someone willing to take serious and often totally unexpected risks. For example, one smuggler carried 2,700 diamonds to Cape Town concealed in the barrel of a rifle he was taking back to England. His ship was due to sail in a few hours and, knowing he faced several weeks cooped up aboard, he decided to spend these last hours ashore. By an extraordinary coincidence, someone he had swindled over another matter in England happened to be in Cape Town and recognized him. At once this man called the police and laid a charge against the smuggler. His cabin and belongings were searched and the diamonds found.

Another man, needing to be rid of a number of illicit diamonds, gave them to his wife and a woman friend. They sewed the diamonds into their dresses and left Kimberley for Cape Town. Here their ship's departure was unexpectedly delayed for some days and so they booked into a small hotel. They were both elated by the fact that they had left Kimberley without apparently arousing any suspicion, although the woman's husband had been under surveillance for some time. They could not keep the secret of their success to themselves and, in a private dining room, they removed the diamonds from the dresses to show to the landlady. They spread them out on a tablecloth for her to admire. She appeared very impressed indeed when they whispered the huge sum the stones would fetch in London. At that moment they heard a knock on the door of the room. To their horror two policemen entered with a woman searcher. As they came in, the landlady scooped up the tablecloth with the diamonds on it and took it out, as though to get rid of crumbs. The two women were thoroughly searched, but of course nothing was found. Afterwards, much relieved at their narrow escape, they congratulated the landlady on her presence of mind. Now could they please have back their diamonds?

'What diamonds?' she asked them innocently. 'I saw no diamonds. I only swept up the crumbs.'

Some time afterwards, when the railway had reached Kimberley, the police learned that a large and extremely valuable diamond had been stolen. Clearly the guilty party would want to get this out of the country very quickly. It was believed that the man suspected was going to take the train to Cape Town with it and then board a ship for England. Detectives were at Kimberley station when he left, but for some reason decided not to search the suspect in front of his friends. A crowd cheered him on his way. He stood in silence until the train drew into the station. Then he opened his mouth to thank his friends for their wonderful send-off – and the police pounced. There in his mouth lay the missing diamond.

Barney's critics, and they were many and vociferous, who hinted at his involvement with I.D.B., but on a far more successful level, totally ignored his early years of poverty and struggle, and either dismissed, or did not know or admit, the slow but steady steps with which he and his brother had advanced to their remarkable success.

One of the men in Kimberley most strongly against illicit diamond buying was Joseph Benjamin Robinson, a character remarkable for three things. First, as one of the first diamond hunters in Kimberley, he was one of the most consistently successful. Second, he was a man of almost unbelievable meanness. He would never enter a bar until he could make certain no one he knew was already inside in case he had to buy him a drink. Third, he was universally disliked, for his harsh business methods as much as his parsimony, and when he finally died, knighted and a multi-millionaire, the usually decorous *Cape Times* published a remarkable editorial about his life and character.

'His immunity against any impulse of generosity, private or public, was so notorious that the name of J.B. Robinson became during his lifetime proverbial for stinginess, not only in South Africa but wherever men of the world congregate together. . . .

'The evil which this dead man thus speaks of himself is terrible to contemplate. . . . Those who in future may acquire great wealth in this country will shudder lest their memories should come within possible risk of rivalling the loathsomeness of the thing that is the memory of Sir Joseph Robinson.'

But in Kimberley, while being actively disliked, Robinson was also greatly respected because of his success. His parents, who came out to South Africa as immigrants from England, had been very poor. Robinson's main boast as a youth was not of any academic or sporting achievement, but the fact that by his sixteenth birthday he had beaten every boy of his age in the neighbourhood.

He learned the language of the Boers and, when he left home, he travelled from farm to farm, making a meagre and precarious living buying and selling wool, crops, and eventually small farms.

After the discovery of the Eureka diamond, Robinson began to look for diamonds as an easier way of making money. He was 28 by then, and totally out of luck, when he noticed some glittering pebbles on the bed of a river he was fording. He picked up a handful and went on to spend the night at a Boer farmhouse.

He did not know what a diamond looked like, but he knew that it could cut glass and would glow in the dark. He rubbed each stone against a windowpane near his bed. The first six stones made no mark. The seventh scratched the glass deeply.

He then rubbed the side of a tumbler with this stone, which glowed faintly. He knew he had found a diamond. He gave such a shout of triumph at this discovery that the farmer came running to his room to ask whether he was all right. Robinson explained that he had had a dream. This was only partly true: he had dreamed of the wealth that could so soon be his – if he found more diamonds.

Next day he headed for the Vaal River, where he knew other diamonds had been found. He asked around to find out whether anyone had seen any unusual stones. An African told him he knew of an old man who had found one which might interest him.

Robinson went to see this man, in his eighties, and guessed the stone was a diamond. He offered him £12 for it. The old man would not accept money, but Robinson persuaded him to accept 20 goats at 7s. 6d. (37½p) each – which worked out rather less. Robinson sold the stone and was in business as a diamond dealer.

Another local suggested he tried a certain part of the river where unusual stones had been seen. Robinson brought in labourers and set them to work sifting sand and pebbles from the river bed. Within six weeks they found thirty diamonds which he sold for £10,000.

Robinson was tall, thin, abstemious, and without any sense of humour. He wore a white pith helmet of unusual shape. Contemporary photographs show him in this strange hat, a tall, macabre, ghostly figure, with the crowd, but somehow never of them. To cut out any middle-men, Robinson dealt direct with buyers in London. In addition to being mean, he was a bully. Once he publicly horsewhipped a slightly built Jewish dentist, a foot shorter than himself, because he thought the dentist had sold him a dud diamond. In later life his hobby was litigation; he simply loved going to law, a foible which he found lawyers very ready to indulge.

Robinson was vehemently against illicit diamond buying, which might affect his own profits, which were huge.

He disliked Rhodes because he felt inferior to him, socially and culturally. He disliked Barnato because Barney was richer, and he suspected he might be involved with I.D.B.

In 1882 the Diamond Trade Act was passed with his strong support. This gave the police power to examine the books of any diamond dealer. They chose to look at Isaac Joel's books. He could not explain satisfactorily how he came to own a 16½ carat diamond which he had sold some days earlier, and entries did not seem to have been made for this stone and for three 10 carat diamonds. They invited Joel to come to their office and discuss this discrepancy with the chief detective, John Larkin Fry.

Joel had no explanation immediately acceptable to Fry and so was arrested. The following day he appeared before the resident magistrate over two alleged offences under the Diamond Trade Act. The first charge involved selling the 16½ carat stone. The second dealt with the three other stones. Joel was given bail to appear before a special court.

Now various delays arose, not unusual in I.D.B. cases. Witnesses belatedly decided that it might not be in their best interests to testify, or they suddenly went absent or fell ill.

When Joel's case came up, he was acquitted on a legal technicality: the first charge had not stated specifically that the 16½ carat stone was not his property when he sold it. He stepped down from the dock a free man – and was immediately re-arrested on the charge of illegally possessing the three 10 carat stones. Again he was given bail, £2,000 being paid by his brother Woolf, and £2,000 promised by him.

Barney Barnato had been in England for eighteen months, but as soon as he heard of this outcome, he took passage on the first ship back to the Cape. Later, in court, he would claim that he was about to return in any case, and that this rush to do so was totally coincidental and not in any way related to his nephew's problem.

In Kimberley Barney went to see Robinson, as chairman of the Diamond Mining Protection Society, and appealed to him to use his influence to stop the case. Robinson declined. He said afterwards that Barney 'looked upon this action against his nephew as a kind of persecution against himself or his firm and that there was a conspiracy against him. . . . Barnato was crying most bitterly most of the time.'

He told Robinson that worry over the matter had actually given him a skin rash. He ripped open his shirt to show its extent. He then said he would give five or ten thousand pounds to clear his nephew.

'My nephew is worth £30,000,' he said, 'and he can well afford £10,000 to get free.'

Robinson asked whether he was offering him money to help Joel. Barnato denied this, but begged him to do what he could to have the charge dropped. Robinson went to see Fry, who told him that this was the strongest case he had ever brought to court. He could not possibly abandon it. Obviously, as one of the most vociferous movers against I.D.B., Robinson could not, in these circumstances, persuade him to do so.

Since Robinson would not square Fry, Barney attempted to do this himself. He invited him for a drink and, when Fry accepted, Barney complimented him on a fine diamond pin he had heard that Fry owned. Fry said that it was in his office. Barney went there with him to look at it.

'I showed him the diamond pin,' said Fry later, when he had to appear in court. 'I asked him what he thought was the value of it and he said: "If I were you I would not take £1000 for it".'[9]

Fry knew that the stone was only a 2 carat diamond and would fetch £100 at the most. Indeed, he later sold it for this sum.

Barney hedged around, and then said he wished to talk to Fry about the whole business of illicit diamond buying, but did not want to do so in his office.

'He told me to look around the office. It was a very insecure place and people might hear next door. Would I meet him that evening elsewhere?'

Fry agreed, then changed his mind. 'Something occurred to rouse my suspicion,' he said, although he did not reveal what this had been. A couple of days later Fry was passing Barney's office when Barney called him in. He explained that he was certain Isaac Joel was innocent. The family would suffer great disgrace if the case came up.

Barney said, 'If you knew how ill and distressed the poor boy's mother is, you would have mercy on him.' He was very distressed himself and he rolled up his sleeve to show Fry eruptions on the skin which he said had been caused by this distress.

Fry explained to Barney that he could not help him. Barney should see the Crown Prosecutor himself if he felt so strongly about it.

'He proposed to give me £5,000 for the diamond pin on condition that I obtained the release of his nephew, Isaac Joel, or withdrew the charge against him,' said Fry. 'I refused. I reported the matter to the Crown Prosecutor.'

Three days after this Isaac Joel's case was due for hearing in a special court. But Isaac Joel was not in court. He had jumped bail and, seemingly, had totally disappeared.

Woolf Joel paid the £2,000 bail he had agreed, but only £346 of the £2,000 promised by Isaac Joel was ever recovered.

Barney Barnato liked to cultivate the image of a nineteenth century cheeky chappy, the little irrepressible Cockney who could endure all manner of set-backs and insults, but somehow in the end would always come up smiling, generous, cheerful, philosophical.

This was indeed one side of his character, but not the only side, and possibly not the most important one. Although Barney had left school at 14, and some critics claimed he was illiterate, this was simply not so. He was well read, especially in Shakespeare's plays. He was an avid theatre-goer and an actor and stage comic of no mean ability. When he became a diamond

---

[9] Reports of the case in *The Argus*, Cape Town, 5 & 6 May, 1885.

magnate and a councillor and later a member of the Cape parliament, his public speeches, whether to shareholders or to parliament, were never the ramblings of someone intent on playing to the gallery, but cogent and well-expressed views of an extremely shrewd and very intelligent man.

Barney played down his abilities because it suited him to do so. People would rather deal with a person to whom they could feel superior than a man who was obviously far cleverer than they would ever be.

There was also a third side to his character, a darker side. He had a rooted inferiority complex, possibly based on his background, his lack of further education, his physical size. He was belligerent and, true to his father's teaching, always got his blow in first. If he did not succeed, he could become vindictive. He was a good and generous winner, but not a good loser.

This side of Barney Barnato's character now came into sharp prominence. He considered that Fry had bested him and he reacted in the only way he knew, by attacking the detective. This would be as unequal a contest as when Barney had agreed to fight the Champion of Angola. The champion had not expected Barney's ruse to beat him so quickly and Fry did not expect the stream of vitriolic attacks on him that now appeared in a new newspaper, *The Diamond Fields Times*.

In a number of articles Fry's methods of securing convictions for I.D.B. were strongly criticized. He was said to be quite unfit for his post and, indeed, in September, 1884, Fry was suspended from his duties.

Just before *The Diamond Fields Times* published this unexpected news Barney happened to see Fry in the Queen's Hotel. He took him into a private room and said he wanted to shake hands. Fry asked him why. Barney replied, 'I'm a good friend but a bitter enemy.'

Fry said, 'I suppose I have to thank that scurrilous print which you support for the position I'm placed in at present?'

He considered that *The Diamond Fields Times*, which he knew Barney owned, had maligned him greatly. He asked Barney whether he would have started the newspaper if the prosecution of his nephew had been withdrawn. Barney agreed he would never have done so.

There indeed the matter might have ended, with Barney victorious, Fry dismissed and soon to fall ill with cancer and die. But there was a strange twist to the story. Fry had taken a few days' holiday away from Kimberley, after his totally unwarranted suspension, and travelled back to Kimberley with Francis Joseph Dormer, the proprietor and editor of the *Cape Argus*.

In the course of the journey Fry explained what had happened and how Barney had used his money and influence to manipulate his suspension. Dormer was very interested. First, as a journalist, he recognized an intriguing story that would attract readers. Secondly, it was not generally known that Cecil Rhodes had given Dormer £6,000 to buy the newspaper, so that he could have an apparently independent paper to take his side in any controversial issue. It was, of course, essential that this arrangement would never be made public.

Dormer sensed that Rhodes might also be intrigued by Barney's harsh treatment of a very efficient and incorrupt police officer, and decided to print an account in his paper. But, as sometimes happens with even the best of journalists, Dormer got wrong one basic and vital fact. He confused Isaac Joel with Woolf Joel, and published the story mentioning Woolf instead of Isaac.

Dormer started his article by saying that, 'If Mr Fry has been guilty of irregularities, by all means let him be sent about his business; but even then, give him a fair trial and shut the mouths of those who say that he has been sacrificed on the altar of friendship, reared by the loving hands of the Attorney General of this colony and a certain resident of Kimberley, not wholly unknown to fame.

'If the jade rumour does not lie, this gentleman, one of the Barnato Brothers, Barney of that ilk, told Mr Fry he would not have lost his situation if he had accepted the £5,000 which he offered him for a worthless diamond which he wore when proceedings commenced against one Woolf Joel.' He explained that Woolf had jumped bail and absconded 'in order to evade his trial and defeat the ends of justice'.

This news appeared on 27 December, 1884. In the next issue Dormer printed an apology, admitting that the real name of the offender was Isaac Joel. He took 'the earliest opportunity of tendering to Mr Wolf Joel the sincere apology to which he is entitled, and can only assure him his name was mentioned instead of that of Isaac Joel without any malice or intent to do him injury, in fact by inadvertence.'

Curiously, just as Dormer had made a mistake confusing Woolf with Isaac, he now misspelt Woolf's name as 'Wolf'.

Both Woolf and Barney immediately sued for libel. In court Francis Dormer readily admitted his mistake and on the recommendation of the judge was only fined £10. More importantly, the jury also found Dormer not guilty of libelling Barnato.

Mr Fry had to explain to the Chief Justice: 'Your Lordship is aware that the Diamond-fields is divided into cliques. The party that Mr Barnato belongs to is not the respectable party. They were people who objected to the Diamond Trade Act and not the party that wished it continued.'

Chief Justice: 'But people might object to the Diamond Trade Act and yet be honest. Would they belong to the wrong set?'

Mr Fry: 'Socially, they don't hold the same social position.'

There was a hint that Barney's own methods of business were sometimes open to question, and his appearance as a witness lacked conviction.

However, he had won part of his case against Dormer. This was, however, a Pyrrhic victory; the case only served to arouse old envies and accusations that otherwise might have died.

Isaac Joel returned to England by what was said to be a circuitous route. Thereafter he was not referred to as Isaac Joel, but as Jack Joel.

In 1898 he became a director of the Johannesburg Consolidated Investment Company and, after the death of his elder brother Solly in 1931, was chairman until his own death nine years later. He was also a director of several other important South African companies involved with diamonds and gold. His personal fortune was said to be in excess of £4,000,000.

Jack Joel had an estate in Hertfordshire and a London house in Grosvenor Square. He was a most successful racehorse owner. He won the Derby twice and for three seasons headed the list of winning owners. But he did not go back to Kimberley.

CHAPTER 7

'A VERY USEFUL CHEQUE'

'I dare say you may think I am keen about money,' Rhodes once remarked to an acquaintance. 'I assure you, I wouldn't greatly care if I lost all I have tomorrow. It's the game I like.'

The game for Cecil Rhodes, from his Oxford days, was to put all Africa under the British flag. In this aim he fully recognized the claims and contributions of the Dutch, who he admired, and who he went to great pains to praise and not to antagonize. His ideal was a union between British and Dutch, to run the whole country in both their best interests.

To achieve such a grandiose aim he needed to have enough money to finance it. Money meant power. He knew that the British Treasury was notoriously parsimonious and British politicians, most of whom lived on inherited wealth, had no wish to become involved with any task that could involve either personal or political risk, least of all high endeavour.

In his Declaration of Faith, Rhodes had expressed his low opinion of politicians:

'What thought strikes a man entering the House of Commons, the assembly that rules the whole world?' he asked. 'I think it is the mediocrity of the men . . . whose lives have been spent in the accumulation of money and whose time has been too much engaged to be able to spare any for the study of past history. And yet in the hands of such men rest our destinies.'

Rhodes knew that, if he were to achieve his dream, or even a part of it, his destiny must rest in his own hands, not in theirs, or, indeed, in anyone else's. It was useless to have great plans without money to carry them out – or the muscle to overcome political obstacles.

Very few British politicians had ever been to Africa and could not possibly know the problems from first-hand experience, or what could be achieved if his plan worked, or what he believed could be lost if it failed.

All his life Rhodes was unusually conscious of working against time. He felt he had only limited time to achieve his ambitions, because of his health problems, and he knew he was also working against time to build a road to the north while this was still possible, before other European countries thwarted the entire scheme.

The best and easiest way north from Griqualand West was north-west through what was known to the British as Bechuanaland. As a country, this had little intrinsic value. It contained the huge Kalahari desert, and trade between the Tswana tribesmen, who lived in Bechuanaland, and Europeans was largely restricted to ivory and ostrich feathers, used for fans and to decorate women's hats and dresses.

From Bechuanaland the route could continue to the centre of Africa and the Zambesi basin. The Boers were in the Transvaal to its east and the Germans to the south and west. Rhodes recognized the importance of Bechuanaland and frequently referred to it as 'the road to the north', 'the neck of the bottle', 'the Suez Canal into the interior', the key 'of this country's road to the interior'.

This was true, but the mood in Britain was much less favourable to the aspirations of British settlers in the south of Africa than it had been, because of an unhappy episode that sharply diminished public confidence in overseas engagements.

In April, 1877, when the Boers would not agree to what the British called 'a federation' with their colonies, the British government sent a token force of twenty-five soldiers to hoist the Union Jack with the claim that the Transvaal was now annexed.

The President of the Boers was Paul Kruger, who, as a boy, had taken part in the Great Trek from the Cape when the British arrived. He never drank any alcoholic beverage and to the end of his days believed that the earth was flat. He declared that every Boer should be 'fearless, ruthlessly virtuous . . . a man who struck when he was angry, but who, with a hunter's wisdom and a farmer's patience, was able to wait, certain of divine protection'.

Now the Boers waited until they could decide on their response. Then in December, 1880, they attacked, drove the British from the Transvaal and invaded Natal. The matter ended on 27 February, 1881, in what was later called the Battle of Majuba Hill in north-west Natal. This was hardly a battle. In brief, a British force, led by General Sir George Colley, was ambushed when Boers, hidden in the bushes in foothills on either side of their column, unexpectedly opened fire.

The Boers were excellent marksmen. They had to be: in the veld they often lived by what game they could shoot. Now each man aimed at one specific officer or soldier. They did not miss. The Battle of Majuba ended within minutes with three results: victory for the Boers, a consequent surge of nationalism among Afrikaners in the Cape and a desire by the British there to revenge such a military defeat in which even the General was killed. It was not lost on them, either, that most of the arms and ammunition the Boers used had been supplied by Germany.

The danger now was that European quarrels and rivalries could spill over into the Dark Continent and, once other nations achieved seriously sized colonies, it could prove almost impossible to carve a way through them to the north. Rhodes believed he had a means to prevent this influx of European rivals, but to have any hope of success he would need to finance his ambition himself, and the only way of making sufficient money lay in Kimberley. Here a great deal of money was being made, but his present earnings were only a fraction of the profits that could result if he could control the whole diamond industry.

While Rhodes had never lost sight of the imperative need to acquire sufficient wealth for his dream, he knew he also needed political muscle if he wished to carry it out successfully. In 1880 six seats in the Cape Town legislative assembly were allocated for representatives from Griqualand West. Ideally, Rhodes would have liked to stand for Kimberley, where he lived and where he was making his career. But Joseph B. Robinson was of the same mind and he was richer than Rhodes. There was no question of having a secret ballot, so the man with the most to offer electors was usually elected. Robinson won that seat and Rhodes stood for Barkly West, which had a preponderance of Dutch farmers. He was elected.

Rhodes was not a very good public speaker, although he had won a prize for elocution as a schoolboy. But he was clearly sincere in everything he said, or so audiences believed, and he had the rare ability to sway a hostile audience to his arguments – and to be loudly applauded by them.

Germany was now becoming increasingly interested in acquiring African colonies and cultivated the Boers, stressing their European links. They called the Afrikaners 'the low German brothers' because they had originally come from the Netherlands, and so had been neighbours of Germany. There was talk of a 'German-African empire', even a 'second India', that would come under Germany's control.

France was also anxious to acquire African colonies, and Germany, partly in order to assuage French feelings about the loss of Alsace and Lorraine, which Germany had seized in 1870, encouraged French aspirations. In addition, King Leopold of the Belgians had plans for a huge Belgian colony in the Congo.

Despite all these clear warning signs of European countries becoming eager to establish themselves on a huge scale in Africa, and consequently become serious rivals to Britain, the British Government still vacillated over Bechuanaland. They did not wish to incur any extra expense; Britain already had a large enough empire; the Government could not see any immediate profit to them, whether morally, politically or commercially by annexing this vast and arid area.

Lord Derby, the British Colonial Secretary, actually said in Parliament: 'Bechuanaland is of no value to us . . . for any imperial purposes. . . . It is of no consequence to us whether Boers or native chiefs are in possession.' Then, after years of hesitation and indecision, the British Government sent General Sir Charles Warren with 4,000 troops to assert British supremacy and so secure the route to the north.

This sudden and uncharacteristic spur into action had been the result of Germany's actions in South-West Africa. For a long time Germans had operated trading posts on that coast. Then a German trader, F.A.E. Lüderitz, asked for his country's support as he planned to operate a chartered company to control the area covered by his trading activities.

The British were perturbed at this proposal, a response that infuriated Bismarck, the German Chancellor. He had supported Britain over the occupation of Egypt in 1882 and thought that Britain should now, as a *quid pro quo*, support Germany. When she did not, he simply declared that the area would become a German protectorate. It soon would grow into the colony of German South-West Africa.

Had the Germans been content with their original trading posts Britain would probably have done nothing, because that was the easiest and least expensive response. But now action of some kind was necessary while it could be confined in its scope and extent.

A Russian corvette, the *Skobelev*, was returning from the Pacific in 1884 when the Captain received orders from the Russian Chief of Naval Staff to advise on this new colony in South-West Africa. Why was it there?

The officer reported: 'The truth is that Germany, in all probability, does not mean to confine itself to the territory of Lüderitz, and hopes either by purchasing land or by some other method to penetrate into central Africa which has long been the object of the attention and aspirations of other European states, and there to establish a colony.'[1]

That same year Germany signed a trade agreement with the Transvaal. When the Afrikaners established what they called their 'new republic' in Zululand, German agents were given 60,000 acres by the Zulu ruler and his permission to build a railway line from the Transvaal to the Ocean.

When Britain had recognized the Transvaal as an independent state, after the Battle of Majuba, one of the conditions of the agreement was that the Transvaal would not extend west into Bechuanaland or east into Zululand.

---

[1] Quoted in *Cecil Rhodes and his Time*, Apollon Davidson, Progress Publishers, Moscow, 1984.

Britain was too powerful for the Boers to flout this agreement openly, hence their reliance on the Germans.

In September, 1885, the southern part of Bechuanaland was declared to be a British crown colony and the north a protectorate. Rhodes' road to the north, which he so badly wanted, could now be started. But while he had the will, and was gaining political influence, he lacked the most essential ingredient for his task – money.

Rhodes had become friendly with Jan Hofmeyr, who had formed the Farmers Defence Union, less nationalistic than the newly formed Afrikaner Bond, which had the rallying cry of 'Africa for the Afrikaners' and the aim of an independent South African republic outside the British Empire.

Hofmeyr's attitude was more reasonable, and Rhodes' friendship with him was another example of his ability to cultivate people who could prove useful. Actually he liked Hofmeyr as a man, but the fact that he was of great value to him politically was an added bonus to their association.

Hofmeyr amalgamated his Defence Union with the Bond, which meant that he could control the Afrikaner vote in the Cape Parliament. Rhodes, looking ahead as always, saw that, if he could make alliance with Hofmeyr, this could, in the end, provide him with the votes he needed to enable him to become Prime Minister of Cape Colony. As Alfred Beit advised Rhodes in his financial dealings and steered him through its complex maze, so Hofmeyr was now at his elbow in the world of South African politics.

The Cape Government became concerned about the activities of the Sotho tribe in Basutoland. They had sturdily maintained their independence against attempts by Zulus and Boers, and now they were resisting the Cape's efforts to bring them to order. Large numbers of Sotho men had worked in Kimberley mines and bought muskets with their pay. Back home, they represented a very strong armed force, which was increasing. It was proposed that they should be disarmed to minimize any threat they posed.

Rhodes said in the Cape Parliament that, in his opinion, the Sotho had every right to their guns, which they had bought with their own earnings, and that it would be impossible to disarm them. The Cape Government put the matter to a vote and was defeated. The new cabinet included John Xavier Merriman, who Rhodes had known in Kimberley, a son of the Bishop of Grahamstown, and Jan Hofmeyr. Rhodes was increasing his own influence without appearing to do so.

In the summer parliamentary recess he went back to Oxford to finish his final term and take his degree. On his return he discovered that the Cape's new prime minister, Thomas Scanlen, had engaged General Gordon, a charismatic soldier with a remarkable military career in China and the Sudan, to sort out the Basutoland problem. Gordon did not do so. Like

Rhodes, he admired the Sotho and felt that the plan to disarm them was not only morally wrong, it was unworkable.

Rhodes and Gordon got on well together. Gordon told him, 'Stay with me and we will work together'.

Rhodes declined the offer; he had his own work to do. Gordon was surprised at this refusal.

'There are very few men in the world to whom I would make such an offer, but of course you *will* have your way,' he pointed out. 'I have never met a man so strong for his own opinion. You think your views are always right and everyone else's wrong.'

'I have studied my subject from all sides,' Rhodes replied.

'But not from mine,' Gordon retorted.

Gordon told Rhodes how, in China, the government there, out of gratitude for what he had done, had offered him a room full of gold as a gift. He had refused it.

'I'd have taken it and as many more roomfuls as they offered me,' said Rhodes shortly. 'It is no use having big ideas if you have not the cash to carry them out.'

Gordon went north to the Sudan. When news came of his death at Khartoum Rhodes kept repeating, 'I am sorry I was not with him. He was cranky in many ways. . . . But he was a *doer*, a man who would move mountains and gain the objective he had set himself.'

Gordon looked remarkably like Rhodes, with a big moustache, a brooding face. He was also a bachelor and had a similar fixation about death. King Leopold of the Belgians invited him to be his agent in the Congo. To most people, one of the main drawbacks of such an assignment would be the Congo's lethal malarial climate. To Gordon this was a special attraction.

'There is, then, a good chance of the end of one's pilgrimage,' he said, 'which I incessantly long for.'

Rhodes' income at this time was £50,000 a year. Barney Barnato was making four times as much. While Barney had arrived in Kimberley long after Rhodes, he was a born dealer, whereas Rhodes was not. Rhodes could manipulate people brilliantly and did so on every level, always with his main aim in view, but to him making money was not an end in itself, simply a means to an end.

Barney Barnato's early apprenticeship in buying and selling from a cart or a market stall in the East End of London was now translated into buying more claims which, in turn, could produce more diamonds. Barney wanted to make more money simply for the sake of making it. Rhodes wanted wealth because it was the only way to finance his patriotic dream.

Rhodes and Rudd steadily bought all the claims they could afford and by 1879 they held the majority in the De Beers mine. They also knew that they could control it entirely if only they could raise another £6,000. But this they could not do. They simply did not have the money, and, despite the very considerable sums coming in, the banks would not advance any more.

Rhodes had postponed going back to Oxford for the one final term he needed because he believed that what was happening in Kimberley was far more important. He therefore followed the advice of Marcus Aurelius: 'When things about you give cause for alarm, return to your own pace at once, and do not depart from it more than necsessity ordains'.

Working at their own steady pace, he and Rudd bought out the remaining claims of any size in the following year, and then floated the partnership as the De Beers Mining Company with a capital of £200,000.

Rhodes had spent so much of his own money to achieve this that he had to draw £5 on account from the company towards his own salary as secretary. Indeed, he rarely had money to pay for his day-to-day expenses and was habitually overdrawn at the bank. When he travelled by train he often did not carry enough money on him to pay for his ticket. Frequently a colleague had to do this for him.

Within five years De Beers' capital had increased to £841,550. Now Rhodes was rich, but he could be richer. He was powerful, but he could exercise infinitely more power if only he could take over the entire diamond mining industry. Concerns about how to finance his dream would then all be behind him. But, as always, the clock was ticking away against him.

Others in Kimberley had also seen the enormous opportunities that awaited whoever could control more and more claims, but the stronger De Beers became, the more difficult it was for others to challenge Rhodes and Rudd. Some who might have done so backed off at the last moment, lacking the nerve for the final thrust. Others, without capital themselves, could not raise sufficient credit. The risks were great and banks were not disposed to take them.

Rhodes and Rudd did not succeed entirely on their own, but were helped immeasurably by a third man, Alfred Beit, whose gift was as rare as Barney's talent for selling anything and Rhodes' total dedication. Quite simply, Beit was a genius in valuing diamonds.

In appearance he was small and slightly built, with a very large head. His kindness and generosity were remarkable in a harsh and acquisitive world. In later life, whenever he heard of a former Kimberley worker down on his luck, Beit would always give him at least £100 to help him.

He had been born in Hamburg in 1853, so was the same age as Cecil Rhodes. His father and mother were of Sephardic families, but anti-Semitism was growing in Germany and no unbaptized Jew was eligible to enter the civil service or to hold an army commission.

Knowing this, Siegfried Beit and his wife brought up their children as

Lutherans, although, in fact, neither of their two sons went into the army or the civil service. Siegfried Beit imported French silk from Lyons. At this he was moderately successful, although other members of his family had become extremely rich through founding engineering and scientific companies.

As a boy Alfred Beit appeared to have no particular inclination for any career. After discussions with relatives, it was decided to see how he shaped with Lippert & Co. in Hamburg, with whom they had close contacts. This firm imported wool from the Cape. Three of Daniel Lippert's sons had emigrated to South Africa, running branches in Port Elizabeth, Cape Town and Durban, and soon they were dealing in diamonds among other ventures.

Alfred showed remarkable ability, with an extraordinary aptitude for figures. Colleagues said admiringly that he had a mind like a calculating machine. He only needed to glance at columns of figures to be able to memorize them completely. Relatives helped him to find another job in Amsterdam, the world's centre of diamond cutting, where he became absorbed in the world of diamonds. At the age of 22 he decided to go to South Africa, where diamonds were being dug out in increasing quantities.

Alfred Beit had very little money of his own, but before he left he visited a rich uncle and explained his intentions and his present lack of funds. His uncle heard him out and said he would give him 20,000 marks (£1,000) on one condition: 'I don't want to hear any more from you. From now on, you no longer exist as far as I am concerned, so I don't want you to rely on me and imagine that you can get any more help and support. Now, goodbye and God bless you.'

Years later Beit returned to Hamburg and called on his uncle to explain that he had since made his fortune in South Africa and had now returned to pay his debt. His uncle was amazed.

'I've heard of cases where a rich uncle has come to the help of a nephew,' he said, 'but this is the first time I've heard of a nephew coming to the aid of his uncle!'[2]

When Beit landed at Port Elizabeth he took the first coach to Kimberley, where a cousin and various other friends from Hamburg were living. Here he also met Julius Wernher, who had been joined by Julius Porges, an extremely successful diamond dealer. Porges had come to Kimberley from his original home in Bohemia by way of Vienna and Paris, where he had changed his first name to Jules. Beit and Porges became friends, and eventually Porges, realizing the potential of this young man, took Beit into

[2] *Le Gaulois*, Paris, 17 July, 1906. Quoted in *The Will and The Way*, Sir Alfred Beit, Longmans, London, 1957.

partnership – an important step-up from the £15 a month retainer the Lipperts had been paying him.

'When I reached Kimberley,' Beit said afterwards, 'I found that very few people knew anything about diamonds. They bought and sold at haphazard. And a great many of them really believed that the Cape diamonds were of a very inferior quality. Of course, I saw at once that some of the Cape stones were as good as any in the world. And I saw, too, that the buyers protected themselves against their own ignorance by offering generally one tenth part of what each stone was worth in Europe. It was plain that if one had a little money, there was a fortune to be made.'

Beit made that fortune – quickly. Because he knew the value of diamonds, he offered much higher prices to the diggers who produced them. This meant that his business increased enormously. It is not known exactly when Rhodes and Beit met, but they were bound to do so eventually in a town the size of Kimberley.

One night Rhodes was passing Beit's office and saw a light burning. Out of curiosity, he went in to see who could be working there so late – and found Beit.

'Do you never take a rest?' Rhodes asked him.

'Not often,' Beit admitted.

'Well, what's your game?'

'I'm going to control the whole diamond output before I'm much older,' said Beit simply.

'That's funny,' said Rhodes. 'I've made up my mind to do the same. We'd better join hands.'

And so they did.

'Rhodes could never have achieved what he did in Kimberley nor in Rhodesia without Beit, and Beit in turn might have landed himself in terrible financial trouble but for the wise head, the cool judgement and the clear vision of Wernher,' said Lionel Phillips, who had originally been in charge of a printing works which Robinson established to produce a newspaper, *The Independent*, and later worked for his mining company. 'If . . . Rhodes was the commander-in-chief, Beit was his chief of staff.'[3]

Beit was a brilliant speculator and, later, in gold mining, an innovator, while Wernher remained in the background, urging caution, ready to warn of possible dangers. He was the less well known of the two men, and indeed once complained that people thought that Wernher was simply Beit's Christian name.

Beit, like Rhodes and Barnato, knew the value of having a second or third string to support him if the diamond boom faded. Soon after arriving in

[3] *Some Reminiscences*, Lionel Phillips, Hutchinson, London, 1924.

1. Cecil Rhodes as a boy. 'He always had an unusually serious outlook and was nicknamed "Long-headed Cecil"' (p.24).

2. Cecil Rhodes when Prime Minister of Cape Colony.

3. Barney Barnato: 'born into a two-room shanty above a shop where his father sold cast-off clothes' (p.3).

4. 'New Rush did not possess any roads in the accepted sense of the word' (p.40). This is the earliest known photograph, taken in 1871. On the left is the London Hotel (!) and Billiard Room, later owned by Harry Barnato.

5. 'The great network of ropes that come from the face of the Kopje, as it were a spider's web spread over the face of the whole' (p.42).

6. 'African labourers wore a few ostrich feathers around their loins' (p.41).

7. Hauling gear at the Kimberley mines in 1873.

Kimberley he bought a piece of land and put up twelve buildings on it. These he let out to diamond buyers and merchants for the then enormous rent of £1,800 a month, and eventually sold them off for £260,000.

He also had the ability to recognize diamonds he might have handled years previously. Once someone tried to sell him some stolen diamonds. Beit recognized then instantly as some he had sold seven years earlier and he challenged the thief, who admitted they were stolen. Beit did not prosecute the man. Instead, he paid for his passage back to England.

Like Rhodes and Barnato, Beit was up early and worked until midnight. Like Rhodes, too, he never married, but whereas Rhodes would like to go off for a couple of weeks from time to time shooting for the pot, Beit had little interest in such activities. Rhodes used to say that all Beit really wanted was to become wealthy enough to give his mother a pension of £1,000 a year. Again, like Rhodes and Barnato, he was totally devoted to his mother.

On his first visit home Beit took her out for a drive in a fine new coach with two horses. On their return he asked her how she had liked this. When she replied that the experience had been very agreeable, Beit replied, 'They're yours,' and gave the whole equipage to her, explaining, 'As a child, I used to say that one day I would buy you a carriage and a pair of horses.' Now, he had done so.

Rhodes' De Beers company and Barnato's Kimberley Central company were the two most important diamond mining concerns. As the world's greatest suppliers, they could influence the price of diamonds internationally.

They were both using more sophisticated mechanical apparatus in the mines. For instance, when the hard blue ground was hauled out, instead of beating it with hammers and soaking it with water to soften it, they used steam rollers with spikes on their metal wheels to go backwards and forwards to crush it. Rhodes had also cut down on the thefts of diamonds by having African workers kept in compounds during their period of contract labour. Here they were given food and shelter and kept away from the sellers of liquor.

Barney was the stronger financially and could arguably have pushed Rhodes out of the race, but he saw no reason to do so. He actually sold some claims he owned in De Beers, so that by 1887 Rhodes and Rudd owned all the claims in their mine. Barnato, meanwhile, was quite content with his Kimberley Central Mining Company, because he believed it to be at least three times as rich in diamonds as De Beers. In this situation, he calculated, he had only to wait until Rhodes would have to come to an agreement with him to fix the world price of the diamonds they produced. If Rhodes was unwilling to do this, Barney could produce far more diamonds for much less than De Beers, and eventually this could even drive De Beers out of business.

Rhodes, taking as always the long view, looked beyond this purely commercial possibility. He wanted to control all the sources of both their mines, but he was not interested in simply having an enormously powerful mining company. He wanted the money for his political purposes and he tried to persuade Barney to join with him under De Beers' banner. Barney saw no need for this. As the richer of the two, he reckoned that it was for Rhodes to come to an agreement with him on the price they would charge, not the other way round.

Finally, Rhodes realized he would have to put this constant skirmishing to the ultimate test before De Beers became seriously concerned by Barney's competition.

While Barney had been making more and more money, Rhodes had gone out of his way not to antagonize the Boers. He knew that they wished to have a united South Africa, quite outside the British Empire, but there was no need to attack them for that. He gave the impression that he understood fully their claims, their fears, their aspirations. This was essential if he was to secure their co-operation for his drive to the north. It would be difficult enough to do it with them; he could not conceivably do it without them.

Rhodes knew that, while Barney was the majority shareholder in Kimberley Central, two blocks of claims in the company were actually owned by others. The Compagnie Française des Mines de Diamant du Cap de Bon Espérance, which everyone called 'the French Company', owned the largest amount. The other organization, owning a far smaller number of claims in Kimberley Central, was the firm W.A. Hall & Company.

Rhodes thought it would be easiest to take over their claims first, and this he attempted to do. He then found to his annoyance that the founder of the Castle Line of ocean steamships, one Sir Donald Currie, who Rhodes called 'The Scots fox', was also interested in the possibilities of amalgamation and had bought £110,000 worth of shares from the Cape of Good Hope Bank.

Currie was about to leave for England in one of his own steamships. Rhodes wanted these shares, but because he could not spare the time to sail to England with Currie, he sent two agents to travel aboard the same ship. They approached Currie and offered him a price which would give Currie a profit. When the ship called at Lisbon Currie was able to study current Stock Exchange prices for the first time since leaving Cape Town and saw that the value of these shares had risen above the price he had been offered. He was furious and called Rhodes' agents 'young thieves'.

'Had I listened to you, I would have sold at a loss,' he told them angrily, ignoring the fact that they could not know the price had risen because there was no communication between ship and shore.

The two unsuccessful agents telegraphed Rhodes, explaining that Currie had decided not to sell. Rhodes was not a man to be thwarted so easily when so much was at stake. He immediately sold some shares he had already acquired in the company, which brought down their value sharply. When Currie did come to sell his, he had to accept a much lower price than Rhodes had offered.

Rhodes now turned his attentions to the French Company, founded by Jules Porges. Here Beit was Rhodes' contact.

Rhodes also looked to Gardner Williams to help him. Williams was an American consulting engineer with a degree from the College of California, later the University of California. He was then general manager of De Beers and had previously worked as a mining engineer in Germany, had prospected for gold in Nevada and originally came to South Africa on behalf of a British company which Nathan Rothschild, the financier, had formed with two other American engineers to prospect for gold.

Not only was Williams an excellent and innovative mining engineer, but he was very valuable to Rhodes now because he had the ear of Nathan Rothschild, whose banking company was the richest and most prestigious in Europe. It had earlier arranged a £5,000,000 loan to the British government during the Crimean War, and then produced another £4,000,000 so that Disraeli, as Prime Minister, could purchase the Suez Canal for Britain. Rothschild had the highest personal regard for Williams and, since he also admired Rhodes by reputation, he was willing to meet him and discuss whatever proposal he had to make.

Rhodes also found Jules Porges very helpful. Porges was related by marriage to Rodolphe Kann, head of one of France's most successful investment companies, with offices in Paris and London, and he also used his influence to help Rhodes with continental financiers.

Therefore, when Rhodes sailed for England to meet Rothschild, he had already arranged to go on to Paris to see other possible backers – some of whom Beit, through his own extensive associations on the continent, had already suggested.

Rothschild heard what Rhodes proposed and then advised him to go and discover what the reaction of these overseas financiers might be.

'In the meantime,' he said, 'I will see if I can raise the £1,000,000 which you desire.'

Hardly had Rhodes left his office before Rothschild told a colleague to follow him and tell him that, if he could buy the French Company, Rothschilds would provide £1,000,000 to help him.

After some discussion, the French Company's directors agreed to sell for £1,400,000. Within weeks the shares rose from £15 to £22. Everyone seemed to have made a profit and Rhodes had gained full control of the company – or so he thought.

But here he had reckoned without Barney Barnato, then on his way from

England to Cape Town. When he heard the news, Barney announced that he would pay £1,700,000 for the company – £300,000 more than Rhodes. He already owned a fifth of the shares and claimed that Rhodes was buying the company too cheaply. He called a shareholders' meeting in Kimberley to explain his views.

Later Rhodes met Barnato and told him bluntly, 'You can go and offer £300,000 more than we do for the French, but we will offer another £300,000 on that. You can go on and bid for the benefit of the French holders *ad infinitum* . . . because we shall have it in the end.'

Not wishing to antagonize Barney totally, Rhodes softened this frank – and accurate – prophecy by saying that he was prepared to sell to Barney's company the French Company shares (for which he had paid £1,400,000) for only £300,000 in cash, plus an agreed number of deferred Central shares.

Barney, as someone who had come up the hardest way of all, was doubtful; this seemed too good an offer to be genuine. But his nephews, Woolf and Solly, were in favour of Rhodes' proposal. Acceptance would give Rhodes' company a holding of one-fifth of their shares, but their holdings would still be far greater and worth much more. Although Barney, who virtually owned what he called 'the richest hole on earth', did not feel too sanguine about Rhodes' offer, he did not appreciate that Rhodes was only making it to gain a toe-hold in his company. Jack [formerly Isaac] Joel was in London watching these developments with Harry Barnato, while Woolf and Barney stayed in Kimberley.

Barney began to consider floating his Kimberley company on the London Stock Exchange. This would bring him enormous personal prestige in the City and then he would hear no more gibes and sneers and innuendoes about once being involved with I.D.B.

The possibility that his company might go public alarmed the Rothschilds; once that happened, it would be too late for Rhodes to buy it. Rhodes warned Barney, that although Barney's company was producing far more diamonds than De Beers, a battle between them could ruin the market for both. The demand for diamonds was not immeasurable and their price had to be kept up by rationing the amount produced.

Rhodes asked Barney to come to his office in De Beers to discuss the matter personally. Barney knew the psychological advantage of fighting such a battle on his own ground, not on one of his adversary's choice. He therefore replied coolly that he might be available for a meeting in *his* office if they could arrange a mutually convenient time. Rhodes was in a hurry for an agreement. His impatience had caused him to misjudge his opponent; he had not realized how prickly Barney could become if he suspected he was being patronized – or how much he felt the need to stay in his own place, surrounded by people and objects he knew well.

Rhodes therefore went to see Barney. They sat facing each other over Barney's desk, drinking black velvet, a mixture of stout and champagne. Both smoked continually. Their mutual irritation increased with every puff of smoke.

Rhodes tried to explain how, if they amalgamated their two companies, a unified diamond business could look forward to a time of absolutely unparalleled prosperity. In support, he quoted Latin tags from Marcus Aurelius. Barney was unimpressed.

'When he talked Greek,' he told his nephew Woolf afterwards, 'I knew he was dotty. He thinks he's Kimberley's bloody Messiah.'

Rhodes then offered to write Barney a cheque for anything he might lose in agreeing to his offer. Barney replied piously that he owed it to his shareholders, not to himself, to get the best possible deal. They parted without reaching any agreement.

'Rhodes looks down on me because I've never been to college like him,' Barney complained to Woolf. 'If I'd had his education, there would have been no Cecil Rhodes.'

Actually Barney was overestimating the strength of his position. He remembered very clearly, and with all the warmth of nostalgia, how he and others in his class at school had spent a day at the seaside through the generosity of the Rothschilds. He imagined, without any cause whatever, that the Rothschilds would also remember him as warmly, and so would back him. Nor did he realize the strength and extent of Beit's influence and standing in the world of international finance.

As Barney's biographer, Stanley Jackson, wrote: 'His values had remained static. Rhodes had emerged from his dreamy youth as both man of action and visionary. . . . Money became no more to him than an instrument of power for discharging his ambitions. Kimberley's diamonds had simply transformed Barney from an East End barrow boy into a huckster with a protean flair for speculation. . . . He needed only to gratify his gambling urge by constantly increasing the stakes.'[4]

Rhodes pointed out to Barney that, while he was being loyal to his shareholders, they were in fact selling their shares behind his back as the price rose. He was, in effect, fighting himself. Barney knew this, but still he held out against selling the company he had founded.

Rhodes rarely took 'No' for an answer. If he could not achieve his objective in one way, he would try another. He therefore arranged for a number of parcels of diamonds to be laid out in his office for Barney to see and admire, and then draw his own conclusions as to the prodigious potential of De Beers.

[4] Jackson, op. cit.

'Just a small part of our reserve stock,' Rhodes assured him with delib-erate casualness. 'Gathered like mushrooms in a field. Only one day's workings. Twelve thousand carats.'

Barney was impressed, but not over-impressed. Rhodes then laid out more diamonds, worth 200,000 carats, in De Beers' boardroom. They had all been meticulously graded according to size and value, in 160 small piles on squares of tissue paper, and placed on a long plank of wood. This had raised sides so that the stones could not fall to the floor. Rhodes then invited various diamond merchants to come and inspect them, but of course this ploy was aimed at Barney and no one else.

Barney arrived with Solly Joel and his cousin, David Harris. Rhodes had previously had the stones valued at £500,000. Allowing for the possibility of some bargaining, he now put a price of £700,000 the lot, to give himself a margin if he was not offered his asking price.

He explained that he wanted to sell all the diamonds to one dealer, not in small amounts to several, and then left the room, leaving David Harris and the Barnatos to discuss the matter. Finally they agreed to meet Rhodes' asking price. Rhodes professed his pleasure at their decision and urged them not to sell too soon, because putting so many diamonds on the market at the same time could only depress their price. Then, before anyone could stop him, he raised one end of the trough. All the diamonds slid forward into a bucket at the other end.

'I've always wanted to see a bucketful of diamonds,' he said casually. 'Now, let's walk down to your office with it and show it to the others.'

So, between them holding the bucket containing a fortune, Cecil Rhodes and Barney Barnato walked through Kimberley. Too late, Barney realized what Rhodes had done – and why. It would take at least six weeks to sort so many diamonds again, according to their various values. During that time they could not be sold. De Beers, through Rhodes' strategem, had main-tained the price of diamonds. Later, Barney would tell this story against himself.

'Rhodes only beat me once, over those diamonds in that bucket. But I didn't mind. It pleased him. Just a bit of sugar for the birds.'

Still Barney would not agree to allow De Beers to absorb his company, so Rhodes played on what he guessed were Barney's personal weak points, working on his own frequently quoted maxim when someone proved obdurate: 'Can they be squared?'

Barney believed, correctly, that he was not highly regarded socially. He had been snubbed for membership of the Kimberley Club because, despite his wealth, some of the members did not consider him to be a suitable candidate.

Rhodes now invited him to lunch at the club and kept on inviting him so frequently that the committee raked up a rule, or invented one, which declared that non-members could not be invited as guests more than once a month. Rhodes challenged this and proposed Barney's membership to the committee. He was too powerful for anyone to risk blackballing his candidate, so Barney was elected, a fact that also demonstrated Rhodes' power and influence. Rhodes had found Barney's price: 'social acceptance'.

'I'll make a gentleman of you yet,' Rhodes promised him.

Barney also had a second ambition, to be a Member of Parliament in Cape Town.

'God knows why,' Rhodes said to Beit, 'but if he wants it, let him have it.'

Rhodes therefore nominated Barney as a candidate at an election about to be held. He said that diggers and everyone else involved with diamonds would support him because he knew about their problems first hand. They did so. Barney now agreed that his company should join with De Beers.

From Barney's point of view, he realized that the amalgamation would be a huge step forward in controlling the world's supply of diamonds, which meant far more profits for smaller expenses. But he could not understand Rhodes' wish that their joint company should be able to acquire 'tracts of country anywhere, make treaties, trade, manufacture, build roads, railways, canals,' indeed anything Rhodes felt necessary in order to carry out his plan. Even so, Barney reluctantly admired Rhodes.

'It is a mighty scheme,' he admitted to Woolf. 'And Rhodes is the only man to pull the thing through.'

Arguments about some details of the amalgamation continued for weeks, day by day, often night by night. Finally, both men knew they had to decide. They went to the Kimberley Club for lunch, where Alfred Beit and Woolf Barnato joined them, and then they sat down in Rhodes' tin-roofed bungalow to work out the final details.

Rhodes tried to explain to the two East Enders exactly what he had in mind when he wished to acquire tracts of country and do so many other things not usually within the remit of ordinary commercial firms.

'Aren't these just dreams?' said Woolf. 'Dreams don't pay dividends.'

'No, my young friend,' Rhodes replied. 'They are not *dreams* but *plans*. That's the difference.'

They went on talking, four remarkably successful men, all in their early thirties; Barney, at 35, was the oldest. Finally, at four o'clock the following morning, eighteen hours after they first started the discussion, Barney wearily agreed with Rhodes' wishes.

'Some people have a fancy for one thing, some for another,' he said. 'You want the means to go north. Well, I suppose I must give it to you.'

But there was still one last point to discuss, very important to him. Barney knew that directors could be dismissed as easily and quickly as they were elected. He therefore proposed that there should be a higher tier of life governors, above the directors. ('Just to guard against the adoption of any unwise policy.') In this way, if he accepted office, Barney knew he could never be sacked. He would be one of four life governors. Rhodes was another, Beit a third, and the fourth, a lawyer, Frederick Philipson-Stow.

So De Beers Consolidated Mines Ltd was born with a nominal capital of £100,000 in £5 shares. Barney held more than 6,000 and the three other life directors 4,000 each.

Some shareholders of the old Kimberley Central had expected more generous terms for themselves. They therefore brought a charge in the Supreme Court claiming that the amalgamation was illegal because, under the terms of the trust deed, De Beers was not what they called 'a similar company' – that is to say, one solely engaged in mining diamonds. Counsel representing the shareholders of the Central company addressed the judge on this point.

'They can do anything and everything, my lord. I suppose, since the time of the East India Company, no company has had such power as this. They are not confined to Africa and they are even authorized to take steps for the good government of any territory, so that if they obtain a charter in accordance with the trust deed from the Secretary of State, they would be empowered to annexe a portion of territory in Central Africa, raise and maintain a standing army, and undertake warlike operations.'

The court ruled in favour of the plaintiffs. But, inevitably, Rhodes had the last word. He was not to be beaten at the last legal fence.

He now controlled Kimberley Central and he could do what he liked with it. What he did was to liquidate the whole company and sell its assets to De Beers Consolidated Mines for £5,338,650 – what Rhodes' secretary, Gordon Le Sueur, rather wryly called 'a very useful cheque'.

CHAPTER 8

'WHAT A DEVIL OF A FIGHT THERE'LL BE OVER THE CHIPS'

In considering the careers of Cecil Rhodes and Barney Barnato, it is too easy to assume from this distance of time that the major events in their lives followed on in strict chronological order. But, as with many people, this was simply not the case. Often their projects and plans ran concurrently; then, some a little ahead, others behind.

For example, while Barney Barnato was making a fortune in Kimberley he was also becoming widely known as a member of the Cape Town Assembly. With his nephews, he founded a bank, and during prolonged stays in London, where Fanny gave birth to two children, he rented a magnificent 18th century house in St James's Place and began to build one of London's largest private mansions in Park Lane.

When Cecil Rhodes had amalgamated De Beers with Barney's Central Mining Company he was elected Prime Minister of Cape Colony, while still endeavouring to secure what he called 'the road to the north'.

The groundwork for this now involved sending an expedition to obtain concessions from Lobengula, King of the Matabele, for that country's mineral rights. This would eventually, and inevitably, lead to taking over his entire country.

Both Rhodes and Barnato were at the same time investigating gold deposits in the Transvaal. Barnato was also buying properties and sites in and around the rough camp that speedily metamorphosed into the city of Johannesburg. And all through their various vicissitudes of fortune, their characters remained basically as they had always been: Rhodes the manipulator, the puller of strings behind the scenes, who never lost sight of his eventual goals; and Barney, effervescent, outwardly the little Cockney comic, an appearance that cloaked his ruthless ability and a genius for making a deal against any odds.

Their characters and characteristics did not change with wealth and power, but became more pronounced, larger, sometimes almost to the point of parody. Rhodes, ever serious, grew more dogmatic, more certain of himself, sure that his decisions were always right. Barney flitted from one deal to another, one bar to another, glass of champagne rarely out of his hand, smoking, eating, joking, sometimes it seemed all at the same time, as though day and night were one and his energies would never end.

Both men made huge fortunes from gold, but Rhodes could have made much more and far more quickly – and so would have had infinitely more capital with which to fund his plans – had he listened to the shrewd advice of Dr Hans Sauer, a Kimberley physician and amateur mineralogist.

Hans Sauer, of Boer background, had been brought up on the boundary between Cape Colony and the Orange Free State, where his father owned several farms. Sauer left South Africa to qualify in medicine in Edinburgh and returned to the Cape to practise.

A friend advised him against becoming a country practitioner. He considered it would be difficult for him to make a reasonable living and suggested that, instead, Sauer should go to Kimberley – 'The only place in the country where there is any liquid cash about'.

He arrived about four years before the amalgamation of Rhodes' and Barnato's mining interests and, while Rhodes was already a member of the Cape Parliament, he was by no means so widely known and respected as he would become after this amalgamation.

Sauer's sister had married a Kimberley lawyer, Harry Stratford Caldecott, who was Charles Rudd's brother-in-law. When Sauer arrived, he stayed with them, and the town's Sanitary Inspector called to see him. He had heard that Sauer was a medical practitioner and, since none of the doctors already established in Kimberley would undertake the important task he was about to propose, in case it should affect their private practices, he hoped that, since Sauer had not yet begun to practise in Kimberley, he might be more amenable.

The Inspector explained that he urgently needed a doctor who could stop and monitor travellers coming into Griqualand from the Cape, where there was an outbreak of smallpox. This doctor would require them to produce medical certificates showing they were not suffering from smallpox, and had been vaccinated, before they could be allowed to cross the border.

If smallpox spread to Kimberley thousands of African workers in the mines could panic and desert. The mines might then have to close, and so not only Kimberley but all South Africa could be brought to the edge of economic ruin.

Sauer instantly agreed to help. He was given an escort of mounted police and, when he asked under what law he could stop people on the Queen's highway and order them to be fumigated and, if necessary, quarantined, the inspector pointed to these policemen.

'There is your law,' he said simply. 'And behind them is Kimberley Town Council.'

Later Sauer wrote, 'He might have added, but did not, and behind the Town Council is a certain Mr Cecil Rhodes'.[1] At that time Sauer had never heard of Cecil Rhodes.

Over the next fourteen months Sauer estimated that he stopped, vaccinated or quarantined literally thousands of travellers. At one time he held 1,800 people in quarantine without any legal authority whatever. As a result he faced nineteen actions from the more important of them for assault, battery and interference on the Queen's highway.

'It was Rhodes, and Rhodes alone, who conceived the plan and persuaded all the important factors . . . to back the adventure. As always, Rhodes displayed his extraordinary ability for pulling the strings and keeping entirely out of sight.'

After Sauer had concluded this assignment successfully, he spent some time shooting and being shown over the first successful gold mine in South Africa.

'This little expedition awakened in me a desire for a more adventurous life than that of a doctor. . . . The gamble of searching for gold reefs appealed to me strongly.'

In June, 1886, walking to his consulting room in Kimberley, Sauer met a friend who knew of his new interest in gold mining. He asked Sauer whether he had seen what appeared to be samples of gold bearing ore, which a local shopkeeper, a Mr Sheasby, had brought back from the Transvaal, where he had been hunting.

By coincidence, that same morning Sauer had received a letter from a doctor who had recently left Kimberley, telling him that gold had been discovered on a farm 30 miles south of Pretoria in an area called the Witwatersrand (White Waters Ridge). Sauer was interested and called into Mr Sheasby's shop across the Market Square to see the ore. A couple of pounds of it were pounded in a pestle and mortar for him and they could see what Sauer described as a 'long rich tail of gold'.

Sauer went on to his consulting room, but when he found he had no patients at all that day he decided to go with two friends to the Transvaal and investigate for himself the possibilities of finding gold.

In the coach he was surprised to see Joseph B. Robinson already occupying a corner seat. Robinson claimed that he was actually going on to Pretoria. Sauer did the same, but when they should have changed coaches for Pretoria, they found they were in fact both bound for the Witwatersrand area, but had not wished to admit this in case of arousing competition.

[1] *Ex Africa*, Hans Sauer, Geoffrey Bles, London, 1937.

Robinson, who had made a fortune from diamonds, was actually desperately short of money. He had a huge overdraft at the Cape of Good Hope Bank, which was threatening legal action to recover. Profits from Robinson's diamond dealing had been squeezed by the activities of Rhodes and Barnato, and, hearing rumours of gold being found in the Witwatersrand, he had decided to go there in the hope of recouping his losses.

Lacking finance for this, Robinson had asked Alfred Beit for backing, claiming that Beit owed him a favour. The mild-mannered and kind-hearted Beit advanced him money on the understanding that they would go 50/50 in any profits. So much money was changing hands in Kimberley then that afterwards Beit simply could not remember whether he gave Robinson £20,000 or £25,000 to help him out.

Sauer and his friends stayed with Robinson in the house of a widow who owned a small farm. Robinson decided that this would be a good base in which to start mining, but the widow was reluctant to sell. Robinson simply seduced her, and then persuaded her to sell the farm to him for £1,500, including all rights for anything he might discover in the earth or on it.

The widow showed Robinson a plan of the area, which gave its acreage. Robinson immediately had the whole farm surveyed and found that this plan was optimistic by two or three acres. He therefore deducted some money from the price.

'At a guess,' wrote Sauer later, 'I should say that the mines on this farm have produced anything from £100,000,000 to £200,000,000 sterling. This action of Robinson cannot exactly be called generous.'[2] It was, however, in keeping with his character.

Sauer examined the area closely and decided that the amount of gold it contained must be almost beyond belief. He could not afford to invest in any claims himself, so he collected a bag of ore specimens and returned to Kimberley to ask his brother-in-law for advice about raising money to finance mining. Caldecott suggested that Sauer should go to see Rhodes the following morning.

Sauer called so early that Rhodes was still in bed. He asked Sauer to sit on the edge of his bed and tell him why he had come to see him. When Sauer explained about the gold, Rhodes told him to return at one o'clock with his samples. Sauer did so and found Rhodes, Rudd and two Australian engineers waiting for him with a pestle and mortar, a gold panning dish and a bucket of water. They immediately crushed several of his specimens; each showed rich strains of gold. Rhodes asked Sauer to meet him at four o'clock that afternoon in his office at De Beers to discuss future action.

[2] Sauer, op. cit.

'Are you willing to go back to the Witwatersrand and acquire an interest for me?' Rhodes asked him then, adding that he could catch a coach due to leave early on the following morning. Sauer replied that he had his medical practice to consider. Rhodes told him brusquely that another doctor could take that over. After further discussion, Sauer agreed to go.

'What interest do you want in the venture?' Rhodes asked him.

'Twenty per cent.'

'Fifteen,' replied Rhodes quickly.

They agreed. Rhodes took up a sheet of notepaper, scribbled an agreement to this effect, signed it and handed it across the desk to Sauer.

The doctor said that he would like some money on account. Rhodes immediately gave him a cheque for £200 and told him to approach him for any more he might need.

'That cheque for £200 was the most remunerative Rhodes ever signed, as it led to the making of millions,' Sauer later recalled. 'He amassed a far greater fortune within the gold mines than he ever got out of diamonds.'

Next morning Rhodes told Sauer it would be wiser if he did not join the coach in Kimberley in case anyone saw him leave. They would know he had only recently returned from the Transvaal and might draw the conclusion that he had found gold and was returning quickly to develop it.

'It is better not to excite curiosity,' Rhodes explained, and Sauer agreed.

He therefore walked twelve miles to the next place where the coach would stop, and was astonished to see Rhodes and Rudd already sitting in the best seats, backs to the driver. They offered no explanation and he did not ask for one.

Their destination resembled Kimberley in its very early days. The market square of a shanty town was surrounded by tents, ox-wagons, huts. At night camp fires burned as men cooked their evening meals. Their claims were marked by wooden pegs hammered into the hard red earth. The nights were cold; Johannesburg stands at roughly the same latitude as St Moritz and its climate is similar.

At first there was no sanitation. Diseases spread. Many diggers, who had been unsuccessful in Kimberley and had come here in the hope of better results, died in their first winter. The area was controlled by the Boer government in Pretoria, who organized a police force and regulated the registration of the hundreds of claims and their marking out on the ground. Within ten years this bare site of Johannesburg would have spread across six square miles, with a population of 8,000 Boers, 34,000 British and 43,000 Africans.

Rudd was unimpressed by talk of huge veins of gold. He believed strongly that any gold the diggers found was not indigenous, but had been deliberately placed there – 'salted' – to push up the prices asked for claims. Of course some claims were salted, often very crudely. For example, one

133

prospector found fragments of gold in his claim, which had cost him more than he could easily afford. He was furious when he discovered that the gold had been stolen from his own dental plate which he had lost a few days earlier.

Sauer acquired an option to buy twenty-one claims for £500 outright purchase, but Rhodes and Rudd simply let them go. Sauer was certain that the reef contained gold of almost immeasurable value and hired two white miners to blast holes with dynamite and pan the ore in an attempt to prove to Rudd and Rhodes how rich it was. But still Rudd would not believe it. Sauer simply could not understand the indifference Rhodes and Rudd were both showing to the opportunity of amassing a huge fortune from such a tiny outlay.

'So the opportunity of securing one of the richest gold mines the world has ever seen was missed,' he wrote later.

Now Beit arrived to see how Robinson was faring. Beit bought these same claims for £750 and, meeting Sauer by chance, asked him to tell Rhodes that he could have a half interest at cost price. Sauer explained that Rhodes had already refused to buy them for £500.

'Never mind. Give him my message,' said Beit. Sauer delivered it that evening, but still Rhodes would not buy.

When these claims, with a few others became the Robinson Gold Mining Company with £500,000 capital, the £1 shares quickly soared to £80 – and its capital to £2,750,000.

For £250 Sauer had the opportunity to buy part of a farm next to land which it was known the Transvaal Government planned to develop shortly as a new residential area. Within two years this patch of farmland was worth £3,000,000.

Rhodes and Rudd knew nothing about gold mining and both suspected, against all evidence to the contrary, that this gold rush could simply be an immense confidence trick. Sauer did his best to explain how this impression was totally false, but he could not convince them.

Rhodes explained his reasoning.

'When I am in Kimberley, and I have nothing to do, I often go and sit on the edge of the De Beers mine, and I look at the diamondiferous ground, reaching from the surface a thousand feet down the open workings of the mine, and I reckon up the value of the diamonds in the "blue" and the power conferred by them. In fact, every foot of blue ground means so much power. This I cannot do with your gold reefs.'[3]

In the middle of these arguments, discussions and Sauer's mounting incomprehension of such extraordinary reluctance to venture small sums for

[3] Sauer, op. cit.

the near certainty of gigantic returns, news came that Rhodes' secretary, Neville Pickering, was on the point of death in Kimberley.

Pickering was the son of a Port Elizabeth clergyman. He had been working in Kimberley for a branch of a Port Elizabeth firm when Rhodes hired him as secretary to the De Beers company. He was ten years younger than Rhodes and his opposite in character and outlook: cheerful, happy, not over-ambitious, and, unlike Rhodes, popular with young and unattached women in Kimberley.

'Pickling', as he was nicknamed, became Rhodes' closest friend. He was always ready to listen sympathetically to Rhodes' sometimes only half-articulate outpourings about what he felt he must achieve. Always discreet and good-tempered, Pickering supplied a welcome balance to Rhodes' own sombre character.

They shared a small wood and corrugated iron cottage opposite Kimberley cricket ground. Callers remarked that inside it was like an under-graduate's room, with empty soda water bottles on the floor, clothes just left where they fell. Often Rhodes did not even have a pillow on his bed, but used a Gladstone bag. Furnishings were bare and masculine, with horsehair mattresses and wooden chairs. A coloured man cooked for them and some-times cut their hair.

One day a visitor to Kimberley was shown into the house by a mutual friend in the absence of the occupants.

'An outside door opened from the street into the small, shabby bedroom,' he said. 'On the iron stretcher an old Gladstone bag, sagged in the middle, served as a bolster for a dingy pillow. That is the bed of a man worth £100,000. I consider it one of the sights of Kimberley.'

Pickering had been thrown from his horse into a clump of thorn bushes. The huge sharp thorns had cut him badly and slowly poisoned him. For two years he remained in indifferent health, and then his condition suddenly began to deteriorate.

Rhodes had made a will in Pickering's favour, leaving everything to him and giving him total responsibility for carrying out his own intentions regarding South Africa.

'They shared the same office, and the same dwelling house, worked together, played together, rode together, shot together.'[4]

Sauer had arranged for Rhodes to sign a contract for gold-bearing land that, in his opinion, would make him one of the world's richest men. But as soon as Rhodes heard that Pickering was so ill all interest faded in this project and he told Sauer abruptly, 'I'm off'.

Rhodes could not get a seat in a coach going to Kimberley, 300 miles

[4] Colvin, op. cit.

135

away; all were booked. He tried desperately to organize a coach to take him on his own, but none was available. Finally, he came to an arrangement with the driver of a mail cart, sitting up on top of a pile of mail bags, which were roped together, and holding on to the ropes in case he was flung off into the veld, for the entire fifteen hours the journey would take.

Sauer took the papers for Rhodes to sign as he sat on the mailbags as the cart was preparing to leave, but Rhodes was so distraught he could not bring himself even to sign his name. Instead, he promised Sauer he would wire him from Kimberley, but he never did.

As soon as Rhodes reached Kimberley he rushed to Pickering's bedside. Dr Jameson was looking after him, but it was clear that, although he survived for some time, he was already beyond all medical aid. Pickering whispered to Rhodes, 'You have been father, mother, brother and sister to me.' Rhodes held him as he died.

At the funeral Barney Barnato totally understood the grief Rhodes suffered at the loss of his closest friend, possibly his only friend. Barney wept too, while Rhodes 'alternating hysterically between laughter and tears, said in his high falsetto, "Ah, Barney, he will never sell you another parcel of diamonds".'

Shortly afterwards Sauer's brother-in-law Caldecott saw Rhodes and Pickering's brother, William, facing each other across a table in Rhodes' office. On the table lay a gold watch and chain that belonged to Neville Pickering. The two men were both in tears and kept pushing the watch and chain back and forth, each insisting that the other had a greater claim to it.

'You are his brother,' said Rhodes.

'You were his greatest friend,' William Pickering replied. 'You should have this last memento.'

Rhodes felt Pickering's death as deeply as he had felt the death of his own mother. Both had instinctively understood him when few others had even attempted to do so. With both he could unbend and share his most private thoughts. Both, in their different ways, had valued him and sympathized with his moods. And to both he had given his total trust. Now, for the second time in his life, Rhodes not only felt alone in the world, he realized he was alone.

Rhodes liked to be surrounded by men, never by women. He would blush if forced to talk to a young woman at some social function, for he was never at ease with them. He did not understand them, nor did he attempt to do so. With men he was instantly at ease, and especially with men a few years younger. With them he could appear as a young schoolmaster in relation to sixth form pupils. They called him 'the old man' and people much older than Rhodes would often refer to him as 'the old man' because Rhodes always seemed old in outlook, in attitude. He had many acquaintances, many colleagues in Kimberley and Cape Town, but, apart from Dr Jameson now, none became very close to him.

Gordon Le Sueur, one of his later secretaries, wrote: 'Rhodes was not a good judge of men on first sight. He was almost as often grievously disappointed.'

It was important to Rhodes that, like him, the young men he employed as his secretaries were bachelors. They could then devote more of their time and energies to his affairs than married men, or, worse, married men with families.

When Rhodes achieved prominence as a diamond magnate and politician, he always employed at least one male secretary, sometimes two or three. He would give them his full confidence and keep no secrets from them. He also gave them a free hand to make their own decisions.

Le Sueur described this group of young men, who were known sometimes simply as 'The Queenstown gang' because many had come from Queenstown or nearby, as 'a sort of bodyguard . . . in whom he was interested, and were chosen on account of various and varied qualifications.'

Philip Jourdan, who worked with Rhodes for the rest of Rhodes' life, first met him in 1890, after Neville Pickering's death. Jourdan was then a minor official in the Cape House of Assembly, the Parliament, when Rhodes was elected. Jourdan's office was a small room through which Rhodes would pass on his way to the Chamber, to leave his hat and coat. He usually wore a tweed suit and what Jourdan described as a 'peculiarly shaped' brown bowler hat.

Jourdan held the post of Clerk of the Papers, which sounded more important than it was. When Rhodes required any Parliamentary papers Jourdan would produce them and they might have a brief chat together. Once, Rhodes asked Jourdan whether he knew Dutch, and if he could write short-hand.

'No,' Jourdan replied.

'You must learn shorthand,' Rhodes told him firmly.

Jourdan did not take this advice. He soon left to join the Cape Civil Service, but he always remembered Rhodes warmly and, as Rhodes' political and business career advanced dramatically, with increasing admiration.

Jourdan admitted frankly: 'I felt that I could do anything for him and developed the strongest imaginable hero worship for him. I was never happier than when I was with him. That he was present in the House was a source of happiness to me.'

Jourdan had the wish to become Rhodes' secretary and, when Rhodes became Prime Minister of the Cape, he was delighted to receive a letter from another civil servant telling him that Rhodes had asked him to appoint

Jourdan as his Chief Clerk. On the day Jourdan started work Rhodes called him in.

'I suppose you thought I'd forgotten all about you,' he said. 'Do you know shorthand?'

Jourdan had to admit that he still did not.

'You're a fool,' said Rhodes shortly. 'Did I not tell you to study shorthand? How long would it take you to learn it?'

'Six months.'

'Well, you must acquire a knowledge of it as soon as possible. I want you to do my private letters.'[5]

Jourdan applied himself to learning shorthand and from then on became Rhodes' private secretary. When Jourdan fell ill with typhoid Rhodes paid his hospital bills and gave specific instructions to the hospital matron that everything possible was to be done for his comfort and he would be responsible for all expenses.

Jourdan's colleagues regarded his ability to write shorthand with undisguised respect. Harry Palk, the only one of Rhodes' several secretaries not to be born in South Africa, could also write shorthand. He had first been drawn to Rhodes' attention by his command of bad language.

Palk was then an officer aboard a Union-Castle liner. One day the small boat conveying Rhodes to the ship from the shore was a long time drawing alongside. This was watched with increasing irritation by Palk, standing at the head of the gangway.

Finally, he enquired 'with much profanity' why the ship was being held up for one man. The reply, in tones of great reverence, was that the ship was being kept waiting for Mr Rhodes.

'Palk then rapped out with a string of expletives and said he did not care a ha'porth who it was but the ship was to be kept for no one.'

Palk's brusque attitude greatly impressed Rhodes, who hired him as secretary. Because Palk had never attempted such work and had no knowledge of what would be required of him, Rhodes sent him to stay in London with W.T. Stead, the editor of *The Pall Mall Gazette*, who advised him on books he should read, and also to learn shorthand.

After Palk had been with Rhodes for some time, he married, much to Rhodes' disapproval. One day Palk told Rhodes he would have to leave temporarily because his wife was expecting a baby. 'Rhodes,' wrote Le Sueur, 'was extremely annoyed and never really forgave Palk.'

Resentment about Palk putting his wife before Rhodes' interests rankled him for years.

[5] *Cecil Rhodes, his Private Life by his Private Secretary*, Philip Jourdan, The Bodley Head, London, 1911.

'Imagine him leaving me alone at Salisbury with no one to do my letters just because his wife was going to have a baby,' Rhodes remarked to a friend. 'Why didn't he tell me before he left. He must have known, mustn't he?'

When Rhodes had first arrived in Kimberley he became friendly with three families – Dr and Mrs Grimmer, the Pickerings and the Curreys. Dr William Grimmer was the first doctor superintendent at the Carnarvon Hospital. He and his wife had eleven children, one of whom, John, more usually known as Jack, a tough, strongly built, clean-shaven young man, also joined Rhodes as his secretary.

Jack Grimmer had been working in De Beers as a clerk and asked Rhodes if he could join the column being recruited to march to Mashonaland as a prelude to opening up the route to the north.

'No,' Rhodes told him. 'They only want men with beards.'

Jack Grimmer later joined the police and then became another of Rhodes' 'young men'. Rhodes admitted that Grimmer was the only man he feared. If this was so, Grimmer was certainly not afraid of Rhodes. As someone who knew them both well declared afterwards, Rhodes seemed to be in a subservient situation, almost as though Grimmer was his keeper.

He was brusque, rough and lacking in manners. Once, when a stranger wrote politely to ask whether there was any possibility of a job with Rhodes, Grimmer scribbled a reply to him on a half sheet of paper: 'Dear Sir, In reply to your application, Mr Rhodes says No. Yours faithfully, John R. Grimmer.'

Grimmer could also be extremely rude to his employer. One day Rhodes pointed out conversationally that he weighed 15 stone, exactly the same weight as Grimmer, Le Sueur and Charles Metcalfe, his company engineer and a contemporary from Oxford. Instead of acknowledging this remark in a pleasant way, Grimmer retorted, 'Le Sueur and I are hard muscle and bone, but you and Metcalfe are all blubber.'

Rhodes, for his part, liked to needle Grimmer, to tease him, as a cat might tease a mouse, or a little boy some tame and harmless animal. Rhodes would pretend to be angry with Grimmer, but Grimmer would only smile. Once, Grimmer sat reading a newspaper and would not answer Rhodes when he spoke to him. He deliberately kept on ignoring Rhodes' repeated attempts to rouse his interest. At last Rhodes said tartly, 'I want you to write a letter for me.'

Now Grimmer acknowledged Rhodes' request.

'Let Le Sueur do it,' he said. '*I'm busy.*'

Harry Currey, another of Rhodes' secretaries, had qualified as a barrister, as Rhodes had earlier considered doing, and later became secretary to Consolidated Goldfields in Johannesburg, before he returned to the bar.

Bob Coryndon, another secretary, was born in Queenstown, but his father was a lawyer in Kimberley. After he left Rhodes, Coryndon had a successful career, becoming Governor of Uganda, then of Kenya and High Commissioner of Zanzibar. He was also a keen hunter and shot one of the few remaining white rhinoceros, which the Hon Walter Rothschild had commissioned him to do for his museum.

When Rhodes heard about this, he asked Coryndon if he would shoot another for the Cape Town museum, but did not proceed when Coryndon replied, 'Rothschild paid me £400'.

When Rhodes went to London he would often take Coryndon and Grimmer with him. They would ride each morning in the Park. A number of young women in London were greatly attracted to Rhodes, partly because of his wealth and the legendary tales of his achievements in South Africa, and possibly because he showed no interest whatever in them. One of these persistent ladies was a titled heiress.

'She used to ride with me in the park in the morning,' Rhodes recalled. 'And do you know, Coryndon thought she came to see *him*. Of course she didn't. She came to see *me*.'

In Kimberley Jourdan suffered an attack of malaria and Rhodes asked him to nominate someone else as secretary until he had recovered. Jourdan suggested a friend, Gordon Le Sueur, who was then working in a Government office, but about to move elsewhere by train. Rhodes wired to a railway station at which the train was due to stop, asking Le Sueur to report to him in Kimberley. Le Sueur did so and stayed with him for the rest of Rhodes' life.

Rhodes was not over-generous with his secretaries' salaries, although he left several £10,000 each in his will. When they travelled with him, of course, they had very few expenses to meet. In London he would pay their tailors' bills and seats in any theatres they wished to visit, and all their restaurant bills. He would also pay for as many books as they cared to put down to his account at Hatchards in Piccadilly.

On one occasion Le Sueur accompanied him to London and, like Rhodes, arrived in the capital with virtually only the clothes he wore. This was because Rhodes had the habit of giving away items of clothing as presents to Africans who had helped him in some way. To find something suitable Rhodes would simply go to the kitbag of whichever secretary was with him and take out a shirt or a jacket to give as a present.

After several such forays, the secretary could find that he had little to wear, perhaps not even a change of shirt, so in return he would take what he needed from Rhodes' stock. It was fortunate, therefore, that they all were roughly of the same size and build. On one occasion Rhodes gave so much kit away, including their blankets, that he and Le Sueur had to share a sheepskin rug when they slept rough in the veld.

On this London visit Le Sueur had to follow what he called 'the colonial custom of buying a silk hat and an overcoat "off the peg" which would cover one until clothes could be made'. As a result he ran up an unexpectedly high bill for tailoring. Rhodes paid, but grudgingly, writing on the bill, 'Seems rather a large amount for a secretary'.

Rhodes enjoyed the company of men younger than himself simply because they *were* young and, even more important, they were cheerful. He always laboured under the disability of his heart problems with a consequent shortness of breath. His secretaries were the sort of men he would like to have been – uncomplicated, healthy, extrovert. He lived by proxy through them and did not mind their occasional rudeness and their schoolboy jokes. Indeed, he appeared to revel in a level of behaviour and humour more suited to the boarding school he had never attended, or a regimental mess when boisterous young subalterns take it over in the absence of their seniors.

One day, after some argument, Rhodes told his secretaries sharply that he would like what he called 'a proper secretary', someone who would call him 'Sir'. For the rest of that day, his secretaries childishly kept putting 'Sir' after every remark. 'Do you want to do this, Sir?', 'that, Sir,', 'the other thing, Sir,' as a way of baiting him.

Rhodes claimed, 'I can read them like a book'. This is probably true. He and they were all relatively young in years but only Rhodes' secretaries were young in outlook.

He always treated them with kindness and consideration. They, and indeed everyone who worked for him, knew the value and truth of their saying, when something went wrong, 'Rhodes will see everything put right'.

But Rhodes was not always easy to work with or for; he was too fond of making cutting remarks. Le Sueur thought that he spent time in thinking out things he could say simply to hurt people or annoy them. On the other hand, when Le Sueur mentioned he wished he had qualified as a doctor instead of reading law, Rhodes immediately offered to pay all his fees at a medical school. Le Sueur, then 23, did not accept the offer; he thought he was too old.

When any of Rhodes' young men fell ill he not only paid their medical bills, he also settled their debts without question. In a sense, they were like surrogate sons to him. To them he appeared as a kind of father figure, a strange, mixed-up man with the gift to inspire others – and sometimes to let them down afterwards.

Sauer had offered Rhodes the opportunity to repeat with gold his earlier success with diamonds, and then double, treble, quadruple it. But because his best friend was so ill Rhodes had immediately abandoned this prospect of immeasurable wealth. In the end Rhodes' sacrifice was unnecessary, because Pickering lived for some time after Rhodes reached Kimberley. But money, for its own sake, was of little importance to him: real friendship was without price, priceless.

'Rhodes, like most of the men in South Africa then, knew nothing of gold mining, and still less of gold-bearing ore bodies, and in the back of his mind was the fear that the whole thing might turn out to be a frost,' Sauer wrote later.

'If he had taken up all or the greater part of the properties which I had secured under option for the matter of a few thousand pounds, he would undoubtedly have become one of the richest men that has ever lived.'[6]

Life on the gold fields in the early days was not only rough, and so far as Sauer was concerned, disappointing; it was also dangerous. Rhodes had a horror of snakes, especially of the hooded black spitting cobra. The area was thick with cobras; Rhodes and his party killed nearly a hundred in less than a year. In Johannesburg he rarely went out at night in case he encountered a snake, and he slept in his wagon, high off the ground. After dark someone would usually escort him from the mines to his wagon, carrying one or more powerful lanterns to keep any snakes at bay.

Although of great moral, political and financial courage, Rhodes was rather less sure of himself in the veld. When he and others would need to sleep in a tent and there was the danger of lions attacking after dark, he would invariably choose to sleep in the middle of the tent, as far as possible away from the door.

Once, in daylight, a cobra reared up under the nose of the mare Rhodes was riding. The animal shied, stumbled and fell, throwing him heavily. Fortunately for him, he did not fall within striking distance of the serpent, which could eject poison for more than three yards. Cobras always aimed at the eyes of any assailant. Rhodes had not seen the snake and was very angry at being thrown, although the fall could have saved his sight, and possibly his life.

He tried to persuade Beit and Robinson to amalgamate their gold companies with his, but Robinson would not agree; he was making too much money on his own. He was always a difficult and quarrelsome business partner and, after long arguments about the relative values of various sites, he and Beit decided to go their own ways so far as gold mining was concerned.

Robinson, always on the lookout for a quick profit, sold half of his share in their mine for £50,000, which seemed a good sum at the time. He was agonized when the value of what he had sold soared to £18 million and, quite irrationally, held Beit to blame.

Although Rhodes' investments in gold were nothing like so huge as those

[6] Sauer, op. cit.

of his competitors, they were still very large. He and Rudd formed The Gold Fields of South Africa Limited in 1887, with an initial capital of £125,000. Within a few years it was re-named The Consolidated Gold Fields of South Africa and the capital had increased ten times.

The annual dividend for shareholders was 50%. Rhodes' own cheque from his initially modest investment was soon between £300,000 and £400,000 a year. This company, incidentally, had a Trust Deed worded so that, as with De Beers, it could help to finance his political ambitions if the need arose.

While Rhodes was ignoring extraordinary opportunities in the gold mines, to Dr Sauer's continuing anguish and incomprehension, Barney Barnato was also not greatly enthused about gold mining. His cousin, David Harris, was, however, and Barney and Woolf agreed to pay his expenses if he would go and report on possibilities for all of them.

Harris travelled from Kimberley to Johannesburg, taking three days and nights in a coach pulled by twelve horses. The knowledge that fortunes could be made so swiftly had caused the price of farms in the area to soar from a modest £700 to £70,000. The town was so crowded that Harris could not find anywhere to stay in comfort and in the end was thankful to be offered a bagatelle table as a bed for his first night.

Harris, methodical as ever, stayed for a couple of weeks and in that time carried out more than 100 tests for gold. He was astonished at the good results, which showed the presence of gold in such huge quantities that he wanted Barney to come and see for himself as soon as he could.

The quickest way to contact Barney was by wire, but the nearest telegraph office was in Pretoria, more than 30 miles away. Seats on coaches had all been booked, and Harris had to sit with the driver of a cart through a torrential rain storm that lasted all night.

Barney cabled back that he was too busy to leave Kimberley. Instead, he sent two employees who had spent some time in the New Zealand gold fields and so were held to be experts. These two men were contemptuous of Harris' claims.

'We could find more gold on the sea shore back home than all the gold here altogether,' one claimed dismissively. The other thought that in one of the sites Harris had surveyed there might be just enough gold to salt other claims and so persuade credulous punters that they were actually solid with gold. Their pessimistic reports were similar to those of Gardner Williams about Sauer's enthusiasm.

'Dr Sauer,' Williams had said, 'if I rode over these reefs in America, I would not get off my horse to look at them. In my opinion they are not worth hell room.'

Despite such damning opinions from so-called experts, thousands of people in South Africa and elsewhere took a totally different view. They left homes, careers, families to come from as far away as North America and Australia to dig for gold, as others had trekked to Kimberley with equal optimism just a few years previously.

So many companies were being formed to raise capital for gold mining that in June, 1887, a local Stock Exchange was opened. Business was so brisk that hundreds of brokers, share touts and potential investors crowded the street outside it. Soon the street had to be closed to traffic.

On Saturdays and public holidays business still continued and, to give a place for buyers and investors to meet in the open air for after-hours deals, iron posts were driven into the ground, linked by chains. What was known as 'between the chains' eventually became one of Johannesburg's landmarks.

Barney came to Johannesburg in the following year and was not initially impressed by what he saw. His interest increased, however, when he saw how successfully Rhodes and Beit were now involved and he realized that the two men he had sent earlier had given him inaccurate reports.

Barney found so many Jews already in Johannesburg that Kruger's Government gave them a plot of land for a cemetery. President Kruger had already given four plots, known as stands, so that churches and chapels could be built for various Christian denominations, but he only gave two stands for a synagogue.

When Jewish protests were made at this apparent discrimination, he replied: 'Your people believe in only half the Bible. The others believe in the whole of it. When you change, I'll give you the other two stands!'

Later that year Barney belatedly changed his initial opinion about the possibilities of finding gold and admitted this in a speech he made at a banquet on St Andrew's Night, 30 November, in the Theatre Royal, in the newly named Market Street.

He was by now an accomplished public speaker. He had realized that public speeches were not unlike theatrical performances. He took elocution lessons from a retired schoolmaster and studied the delivery of actors and music hall artistes. He knew that it was more effective to memorize a speech, as he had memorized parts in plays, than to read from notes.

On this occasion Barney stood up, glanced at his notes and then ostentatiously tore them up and handed the pieces to a waiter. This was a piece of theatrical 'business' which brought instant applause. He then proceeded with his speech, which he had previously memorized.

'I came for a visit,' he said, 'but I shall stay for months, and I look forward to Johannesburg becoming the financial Gibraltar of South Africa.'

He did his best to make this prophecy come true. Jack Joel and Barney's brother Harry were in London, and Barney informed them of his intention to move into the Rand as a serious investor. On his instructions they arranged for larger offices in Draper's Gardens in the City, while in Johannesburg he and Solly Joel surveyed areas still available for mining.

Barney and Solly made an excellent team together. They were complementary. Barney would sense instinctively whether a proposition was sound or had too high an asking price. Solly, lacking what Stanley Jackson called Barney's 'truffle-hound nose for a bargain', would check and cross-check all figures involved and assess the likelihood of profit, loss or stalemate.

He was particularly interested in buying land and property, calculating that Johannesburg would grow enormously. New homes, offices and factories would then be needed, and he bought plots of land wherever and whenever located. But on one occasion he could not understand why his uncle bought a plot near the Market Square on which the owner had built some shoddy tin shacks. Barney explained that he was not interested in the properties, but the land on which they stood. This was clay – necessary to make bricks to build the houses on the sites Solly had acquired.

Barney was still basically the East Ender out on the spree, the little fellow at the races who had placed a lucky bet and was now enjoying himself hugely by placing more.

He was drinking heavily, as he had always done. Some people said that this habit stemmed from the time he had worked in his brother-in-law's public house, The King of Prussia, but instead of the dregs of beer he might have drunk then, now he only drank champagne. He ate little and irregularly, as he had always done. In the bars he still gambled, either with dice or playing a local game called 'tempting flies'. Each player would put a gold sovereign on the bar counter and cover it with a sugar lump. The player who owned the sovereign on which the first fly settled could claim all the other sovereigns.

As a character, smoking and drinking almost incessantly, sleeping very little, always on the move, Barney attracted hangers-on as these sugar lumps attracted flies. He was the personification of success as they perceived it. He had only to be seen 'between the chains' for there to be a surge in Stock Market prices as people tried to find what shares he was buying and buy some themselves.

But not everyone was enamoured by Barney or his attitude; he was too brash, and much too successful, for some tastes. In the Stock Exchange one day someone referred to him as a 'cheap little Yid' who should go back to the East End, where he would be more at home.

Barney heard the remark, as perhaps was intended, although he was standing some feet away. At once he crossed the floor, hit the speaker on the jaw and knocked him down. As a result, the Committee of the Stock Exchange declared that they must both resign.

'How can I resign when I *own* the bloody place?' asked Barney contemptuously. No one explained. Indeed, there was no explanation, for he held the majority shares in the company which owned the Stock Exchange site.

Later he pulled down the building to replace it with Barnato Buildings, large enough to contain a new Stock Exchange hall, 100 office suites and a covered market 350 feet long. Solly engaged architects from the Cape to design it. The design and construction were so complex that, although workmen were working day and night in eight-hour shifts, it took more than a year to complete.

Meanwhile gold shares were becoming as volatile as Barney – and as unpredictably feverish as his behaviour sometimes seemed. In a couple of days they could double, then treble their value and suddenly fell back to their original price, or below.

It seemed to matter little whether new mines being quoted on the Stock Exchange possessed either equipment or staff, or indeed much more than the prospectuses which were printed in profusion. Their shares could still leap from £1 to £25 in a single day – and then fall the following morning.

Rumours spread that virtually all the gold had been dug out, just as rumours had spread about diamonds in Kimberley. Almost overnight share prices dropped from pounds to pennies. Banks desperately tried to collect collateral given for loans and overdrafts, but the collateral was often only paper shares which were now worthless. Three banks closed. Diggers deserted the mines. Barney remained supremely optimistic.

'Money and patience will overcome all difficulties here, as they did in Kimberley,' he insisted, possibly not realizing that, while he had both in abundance, many in Johannesburg had neither; they were determined simply to survive.

When Fanny Barnato arrived to lay the foundation stone of Barnato Buildings the atmosphere was thus not one of festivity, for which Barney had hoped, but of gloom. The bubble appeared to have burst; the boom could be sliding into slump. Barney valiantly tried to raise everyone's spirits in his speech on that occasion.

'I have never made any mistake in speculation or in the investment of money,' he told his guests. 'My only regret is I did not come here two years ago and put money in bricks and mortar. You see, I am making up for lost time and doing it today in the face of depression.'

The slump in the value of gold shares coincided with a prolonged drought, so severe that food ran short. Food shops were looted. Hundreds of oxen and mules died of thirst and starvation. President Kruger called for a national day of prayer to pray for rain, but still no rain fell.

Earlier, an electrical engineer had formed a syndicate to buy several hundred acres of land on which to sink wells and build a pumping station to supply water for the town. Now he had run short of money and confidence. Banks and shareholders were demanding that he pay back money they had invested in his scheme, which he could not afford to do. He approached Barney, who gave him £30,000 out of his own funds, so that work could continue on a facility now so desperately needed.

This was more than an act of generous charity by Barney; it was also a sound investment. Without sufficient water, Barney could not keep his mines working and the value of his properties would drop.

When Barney took over the waterworks he believed that many people were using the company's water, but not paying for it. He had recently met his first Kimberley partner, Louis Cohen, and one Sunday morning he and Cohen were up early and walked round houses with gardens, making a note of hoses which had been left running all night.

After spending the whole morning walking, they called in at a bar and Barney asked for a whisky with water.

'This is very good water, isn't it?' he remarked to the barmaid. 'You don't have many complaints, do you?'

'Oh, no, the water is very good, but they don't often collect the water rate,' she replied. 'They haven't been here for over six months.'

Cohen also admitted that he had not paid water rates for ten months.

The next morning both received a summons for their arrears.

Barney and Solly later bought several building sites from the Waterworks Company for £12,500. These fetched £800,000 within three years. Later still, Solly sold the company for more than £1,000,000 to the municipality. It seemed that the Barnatos simply could not stop making money.

These deals might be thought considerable by many of their contemporaries. To the Barnatos, compared with the size and scope of their diamond, gold and other enterprises, they were not much more than petty cash.

All the time, in bad times as in good, Barney kept up his extraordinary life-style, smoking, drinking, gulping down rushed meals or parts of meals, racing from place to place with an almost insane energy. He lived as though he would never grow old, as though he was totally indestructible. And then, just as, years earlier, Rhodes had claimed that he had seen 'a ghost', barricading himself in his room in case it should return, Barney experienced sudden, unexpected and unwelcome evidence of his own mortality.

To help raise money for Johannesburg's new synagogue, he took the main role in a play, 'Ticket of Leave Man'. He was a great success and revelled in long and loud applause. Hardly had the final curtain come down than he was off to celebrate. But, leaving a hot and crowded theatre for the cold night outside, something happened that had never happened to him before: he caught a chill. Within hours the chill turned to something far more serious.

Dr Matthews, who had originally practised in Kimberley, was called in to see him. He was so concerned about Barney's chances of recovery that he asked Woolf to contact the rabbi in case the patient did not recover.

Barney's chest was congested through his almost constant smoking; years of heavy drinking had harmed his liver. But Barney had a very tough constitution and a supreme will to live, no matter how serious his illness might be.

'I *will* be all right,' he assured the doctor. 'Anyway, what a devil of a fight there'll be over the chips! But not yet, doctor, but not yet. They'll all have to wait a bit longer.'

The doctor thought that Barney must be delirious. To whom was he referring, and who would fight for the chips – the money – when he did die? Dr Matthews knew, or thought he knew, of the warm family bonds and mutual regard which united Woolf, Solly and Barney.

But afterwards Barney's words had an ominous echo. They would be remembered when much else had been forgotten.

CHAPTER 9

'LIKE GIVING A MAN THE WHOLE OF AUSTRALIA'

Now that the first land obstacle to Rhodes' march north – Bechuanaland – had been dealt with, he faced a second, much more difficult problem: how to 'square' the country of the Matabeles so that he could find a way through it.

Matabele means, literally, 'the hidden people'. This name was given to them because of their warriors' fearsome appearance when they went into battle behind huge shields of ox-hide. They were of Zulu origin, and when the Boers had left the Cape in 1837 on The Great Trek, they drove the Matabeles before them.

Their king, Moselikatze, established his headquarters south of the Zambesi River by defeating the indigenous people who occupied this rich area. The Matabeles called them Mashonas, a term of contempt, and forced them to move to an area north-west of Matabeleland, then called Mashonaland. When Moselikatze died two years of internal fighting followed, until his son, Lobengula,[1] became king at Bulawayo.[2]

Matabele men were brought up as warriors: most stood at least six feet tall and were not allowed to marry before they were 25 years old and had killed a man in battle. They ate huge quantities of meat and, before any battle, indulged in a complex sequence of war dances to heighten their own aggression and frighten their enemies.

Around their foreheads they tied strips of otter skin, wound ox-tails around their legs and wore a cape and headdress of ostrich feathers, all combining to make them appear even larger and more formidable. They did not train for battle with manoeuvres and war games; they trained by carrying out real raids on neighbouring tribes.

[1] The king's name is spelled as two words in early references, but as Lobengula in later published material.
[2] At that time Bulawayo was known as Gbulawayo, but the more familiar spelling came into use soon afterwards.

Rhodes believed that 'Someone has to get the country, and I think we should have the best chance. . . . I have always been afraid of the difficulty of dealing with the Matabele king. He is the only block to central Africa as, once we have his territory, the rest is easy. . . . Simply a village system with separate headmen, all independent of each other.'

Lobengula distrusted Germans, Boers, Portuguese and English because he believed, with cause, that they wished to take over his country. Of them all, he was least distrustful of the English, largely through the efforts of a missionary, John Smith Moffat, the son of a missionary father, who had explained to him how Queen Victoria in England ruled like Lobengula and regarded her subjects with warm benevolence. They, in turn, were loyal to her as the Matabele were to him. Lobengula trusted Moffat, whose father had been highly regarded by Lobengula's father.

The Portuguese were so eager to gain control of Matabeleland that they actually produced totally false maps showing that it was already in their possession. Rhodes also learned that a Boer horse trader, Pieter Johannes Grobler, claimed to have agreed an alliance (drawn up by President Kruger) between the Matabele and the Transvaal. This, it was said, would lead to 'perpetual peace and friendship' between them. Under its provisions, Lobengula would supply troops for the Transvaal, if called upon to do so, and agreed to accept Grobler as the Transvaal consul in his country.

Grobler did not live long enough to take up this appointment. On his way back to the Transvaal natives killed him; they believed he had sold an unsound horse to their leader because the animal died shortly afterwards.

With such strong interest already being shown in Matabeleland, Rhodes realized that he must move quickly before the initiative passed irretrievably to others. President Kruger wanted the north, and if he succeeded in securing it he would, using a mining metaphor, hold the equivalent of a solid block of claims from the Orange River up to the Zambesi. If this happened, he could control trade, which the British sought, and land, which the Dutch wanted. If Kruger achieved this aim, any furthering of Dutch and British interests would be on his terms. He would, indeed, be on a fair way to making all South Africa into the Republic he sought. These possibilities greatly concerned Rhodes because they were diametrically opposed to his own ambitions.

The best emissary Rhodes could think of to help him was Moffat, who had been born in a Ngwato village near Matabeleland. After leaving missionary work, Moffat joined the colonial service. He was then in late middle age and Lobengula regarded him as honest.

Through January and February of 1888 Moffat, on Rhodes' instructions, held long talks with Lobengula and his advisers, known as indunas. He explained that the Transvaal was deceiving them. The Boers would interpret their agreement with the King rather differently from the way Grobler had set it out, in which he had described a British threat to the country.

Moffat finally secured an agreement which said that 'peace and amity shall continue for ever between Her Britannic Majesty and her subjects and the Amandebele people'. It also pointed out, almost as an aside, that Lobengula 'will refrain from entering into any correspondence or treaty with any foreign state'. This, it was hoped, would keep him from agreeing to allow any other people to have concessions that Rhodes wanted. But the two men, Moffat and Lobengula, were discussing something which only one of them clearly understood.

The Matabeles were a nomadic people. They moved on according to the grazing of the cattle in which they counted their wealth. They had no idea of frontiers, borders or concessions. They did not own the land they grazed; it was alien for them to think of people who might do so or wish to do so. Lobengula trusted Moffat and Moffat genuinely thought he was acting in the best interests of all when he signed the document on 11 February, 1888. Lobengula placed his cross at the bottom of it and Moffat wrote: 'I certify the above a true copy, signed J.S. Moffat, Assistant Commissioner.'

While Rhodes' word was paramount in South Africa, for he was one of the richest men within its borders, in London he was far less well known. The Prime Minister, when his name was mentioned, replied, 'Rather a pro-Boer M.P. in South Africa, I fancy?'

Two men who, between them, possessed only a tiny fraction of Rhodes' wealth, but who had the asset he lacked of good social and political connections in London, were Lord Gifford 'for whom the development of colonialism was more than a source of livelihood: he devoted himself to it body and soul'[3], and George Cawston, a successful London stockbroker.

Earlier, they had formed the Bechuanaland Exploration Company and, when they learned of Moffat's agreement, they decided that they would extract a similar one in their interest from Lobengula. Both felt that this area must contain vast quantities of gold; between the Zambesi and Limpopo Rivers was the Land of Ophir from which Solomon's navies had transported gold and precious stones in huge quantities.

Gifford and Cawston recruited a former British Army officer, Edward Maund, who had visited Lobengula as an official British emissary some years earlier, and published a report estimating the mineral wealth of the country. He agreed to return for a share in the profits.

In May, 1888, Cawston asked the British Colonial Secretary for approval to this scheme. The reply was cautious; he said he would have to consult the officials in the area, but there were no officials in the area. Rhodes was the

[3] *Cecil Rhodes and his Time*, Apollon Davidson, Progress Publishers, Moscow, 1984.

nearest person of influence and he was totally unofficial. Now he knew he had to move very quickly indeed.

Maund arrived in Kimberley in July. Rhodes was still not ready, but he had infinitely better contacts in South Africa than Maund, Gifford or Cawston. Sir Hercules Robinson, the Colony's High Commissioner, was a director of De Beers and a shareholder in two other companies Rhodes controlled. Sir Sidney Shippard, who represented the government in Tswana, was an old friend, had been named as a trustee in his first will and would become a consultant in Rhodes' gold-mining company and then a director of the Chartered Company. So, while Rhodes might be a late starter, he was confident he would finish in the best position. His friends would not help Maund or make his journey easier.

Rhodes asked Charles Rudd to go north to Lobengula and persuade him to grant a concession which would give Rhodes a firm toe-hold in his country. Rudd took with him Rochfort Maguire, a lawyer, who had been an undergraduate at Merton College, next to Oriel, where Rhodes first met him. Maguire was a fellow of All Souls; his task would be to draw up a legal concession agreement. The third member of Rudd's team was Frank Thompson, who had grown up in the Cape and spoke the Tswana language, which Lobengula also understood. Thompson had organized the compounds in which African workers had to live during the months they were under contract in Kimberley.

Sir Hercules Robinson was not at first very enthusiastic about Rhodes' proposal.

'We have enough territory already,' he pointed out cautiously.

'The builders of the original fortress on Table Mountain said, "We have enough territory" and look where you are now,' Rhodes replied.

'And where will you draw the line?'

Rhodes pointed on the map to the south of Tanganyika. Robinson was still not entirely happy. He could see all manner of problems ahead, but eventually he agreed reluctantly, saying, 'I will leave you alone.'

He was discovering the truth of Barney Barnato's admission: 'The worst of Rhodes is that, when you have been with him for half an hour, you not only agree with him, but imagine you've always done so.'[4]

Robinson provided a letter for them, written as 'the White Queen's representative'. He introduced them to Lobengula as 'gentlemen of the utmost respectability'. The letter was placed inside an impressively large envelope, 12 inches by 18, and sealed with a huge red wax seal to stress its importance.

Thompson made the arrangements, telling people who wondered why he needed two mule teams, wagons and three months of provisions, that he was

---

[4] *The Great Barnato*, by Stanley Jackson, Heinemann, 1970.

8. Rhodes, with umbrella; J.B. Robinson, hand in pocket: 'proverbial for stinginess' (p.105); Sidney Shippard, seated: 'one of his earliest photographs showed them together outside his iron-roofed house' (p.49).

9. Cecil Rhodes with Jack Grimmer: 'Rhodes admitted that Grimmer was the only man he feared' (p.139).

10. Rhodes' partner, Charles Rudd (see p.52).

11. Woolf Joel: 'Fanny and Barney were impressed by Woolf's common sense and natural ability with figures' (p.98).

12. 'The president of the Boers, Paul Kruger... who never drank any alcoholic beverage and who to the end of his days believed that the earth was flat' (p.113).

13. Alfred Beit: 'His kindness and generosity were remarkable in a harsh and acquisitive world' (p.118).

14. Dr Leander Starr Jameson: 'Many women in Kimberley found Jameson charming and, on occasion, extremely useful' (p.159).

15. Dr Rutherfoord Harrris 'abandoned medicine to work for Rhodes' (p.160).

16. 'A huge well-dressed man, with moustachios,... he introduced himself as Franz von Weltheim' (p.222).

17. Groote Schuur: 'outside Cape Town stood an old building... originally built as a government granary' (p.208).

18. The grave of Cecil Rhodes: 'He wished to be buried in the Matopos' (p.232).

going on an extended hunting expedition. The three men set off on 15 August.

They had to cross the Kalahari desert where their water supplies ran short. Men and mules were parched with thirst. Mules died. Spokes broke in wagon wheels. Axles collapsed. They came to an area where the chief said that no white men had permission to pass. Rhodes, informed of this, 'squared' missionaries who persuaded the tribesmen to let them through. Although they started after Maund they reached Bulawayo on 21 September, several weeks ahead of him.

Rudd did not have an easy job persuading Lobengula to grant a concession for all mining rights in his country, which is what Rhodes wanted. Indeed, Rudd began to believe his whole mission had been in vain. He wrote in his diary, 'I fear the king will not do anything with us till he has seen Shippard.'[5]

Lobengula would not invite Sir Sidney Shippard to Bulawayo, but he came to lend his authority to Rudd's request. The reason he gave was that he was enquiring into the disappearance of Pieter Grobler. Shippard had originally wanted to bring an escort of twenty-five soldiers with him to impress Lobengula, but the King would not agree to this, so Shippard brought with him only two Majors, a Captain and a Corporal Major of the Life Guards. All had been chosen because of their magnificent stature and military bearing. In their red tunics, with highly polished breastplates and helmets and black-topped boots, they created a great impression. Shippard was also dressed to stress the importance of the occasion. He wore his medals on his frock coat, kid gloves and a white topee. This visit turned the discussion in Rudd's favour and towards the end of October Lobengula agreed to his proposals.

Of Lobengula's indunas, only one was in favour of agreement. The others were strongly against any involvement with white men. The King's witch doctor even claimed that when members of Rudd's party bathed in a river they bewitched the water for ever, but Lobengula, despite this strong hostility, allowed to give the visitors the concessions they sought.

In return he and his heirs would receive a monthly rent of £100, 500 Henri-Martini rifles, 5,000 rounds of ammunition and as much again when mining was actually starting, plus an armed steamboat on the Zambesi River. This last provision was suggested by Rhodes who thought that it would appeal to Lobengula. It did.

Thompson claimed afterwards that a saying of his – 'Who gives a man an

[5] Walter Montagu Kerr, *The Far Interior: A Narrative of Travel and Adventure from Cape of Good Hope across the Zambesi to the Lake Regions of Central Africa*, Vol. 1, Sampson Low, Marston, Searle & Rivingstone, London, 1886.

assegai if he expects to be attacked by him afterwards?'[6] – had helped to persuade Lobengula to allow them the concessions. For his part in translating between both parties, Thompson was nicknamed 'Matabele' Thompson.

Lobengula realized that he could not hold out against the white men for ever. A war between them would only have one result: his defeat. Of all the white men, the English were the least distrustful. That might not be saying much, but it was something, and he knew that if he did not agree now he would almost certainly have to do so later – and possibly then the terms might be worse.

A local missionary, Charles Helm of the London Missionary Society, acted as interpreter during the talks. He genuinely believed that he was doing the best for all parties and told the London Missionary Society that only a very powerful company should have the right to mine for gold. In his view Rhodes, Rudd and their company, De Beers, were best suited for this.

When the concession came to be signed, Helm later recalled how Rudd and his companions 'promised that they would not bring more than 10 white men to work in his [Lobengula's] country, that they would not dig anywhere near towns etc., and that they and their people would abide by the laws of his country and in fact be as his people'.[7] Helm added, naively but crucially, 'These promises were not put in the concession'.

Although the concession related entirely to minerals that could be dug out of the country and not to the country itself, many people took it to mean that the country of the Matabeles had been ceded to Britain. Newspaper articles in South Africa repeated this error and, while this news might be agreeable to their readers, it was not at all agreeable to the white people who formed part of the 10,000 inhabitants in Bulawayo.

Thompson held a low opinion of many of the whites in Bulawayo. He thought they were fugitive criminals, 'white scoundrels', who would trade in girls who the Matabele warriors had captured in tribal raids and sell them on elsewhere. Not all of these people wished to return to England or to live anywhere else among other white people. They had formed relationships with Matabeles and now they feared for their future.

This fear spread from the whites to the locals. Thompson and Maguire, who Lobengula required to stay behind while Rudd took the concession agreement back to Rhodes, now found themselves in a most unpleasant situation. Lobengula became so concerned about his own survival that he had

[6] Captain Robert Patterson, 'Notes on Matabeleland' from the Proceedings of the Royal Geographical Society, August, 1879.
[7] Walter Montagu Kerr, op. cit.

the induna who had advised him to accept the terms publicly executed with his family.

The whites in Bulawayo translated Lobengula's unease into an announcement which was sent to all the newspaper editors:

'I hear it is published in the newspapers that I have granted a concession of the mineral in my country to Charles Dunell Rudd, Rochfort Maguire and Francis Robert Thompson.

'As there is a great misunderstanding about this, all action in respect of said concession is hereby suspended pending an investigation to be made by me in my country. Signed LOBENGULA.'

If this notice were believed, Rhodes' ambitions would suffer a severe blow, nor were Lord Gifford and George Cawston disposed to give up easily. Lobengula, increasingly concerned about his own position as ruler, when it seemed possible that his whole country could slip out of his control, allowed Maund to take two indunas to London in an attempt to rouse public opinion against Rhodes.

Rhodes thought of using his influence to prevent them leaving South Africa, but in the end allowed them to go. Well-meaning members of the Aborigines Protection Society shepherded them around London. Queen Victoria asked to see them. They paid a visit to the Royal Mint, toured the London Zoo, saw a ballet performance and spoke to each other on the telephone. What amazed them here was that such a small machine could apparently learn their language so quickly. They came back to Bulawayo with strange impressions of England.

Rhodes, meanwhile, decided that the best way to advance his interests in England was to go there himself. He wanted to set up what was then called 'a Chartered Company'. Although formed privately, such a company was actually authorized by the Crown to rule the territory in which it operated, and so would be invaluable to him.

The most famous chartered company had been the East India Company, which had controlled India until the Mutiny in 1857, when the British Government took over. The Canadian West had the Hudson's Bay Company, and when the Spanish and Dutch threatened to seize Borneo, Gladstone's government in 1881 granted a charter to a group known as the British North Borneo Company with powers to rule North Borneo. In Africa there had been the Royal Niger Company and the Prime Minister, Lord Salisbury, had chartered the Imperial British East Africa Company to look after British interests in Uganda and Kenya.

Lord Gifford and George Cawston also had plans for their own chartered company. They now asked Lord Knutsford, the Colonial Secretary, whether they could receive a charter for their Bechuanaland company. Knutsford knew that they were not very strong financially –

but what if they could join forces with Rhodes, who had millions?

Cawston approached Rhodes with this proposal of amalgamation and Rhodes was delighted. He thought it possible that neither group might gain a royal charter on their own, but with his influence in South Africa and Gifford and Cawston's standing in London, the future was assured.

So, ironically, while Maund was taking the indunas to London, hoping to influence the British public in their favour, the deal had already been done. As Rhodes liked to say, 'If you cannot manage a thing one way, try another.'

He had earlier realized that his proposals might have difficulty in going through Parliament, so he had 'squared' the Irish parliamentary party, which held eighty-five seats in the House of Commons, and used these to try and gain Home Rule for Ireland. He gave the party £5,000 and promised another similar sum. Eventually, when the charter was granted to his company, the Irish parliamentary party was 'strangely silent on the matter, in some contrast to its attitude towards other chartered companies of the time'.[8]

On 30 April, 1889, Rhodes formally petitioned the Crown for a Royal Charter. The Colonial Secretary recommended the proposal, giving two unarguable reasons. First, if they did not give a Royal Charter, Rhodes might still go forward without it. Secondly, and to the political mind much more important, this Chartered Company could 'relieve Your Majesty's Government of diplomatic difficulties and heavy expenditure'.

The British Government realized that, if they did not move, other countries, notably Germany and Belgium, could seize even more of Africa, and then it might be too late for such decisions.

When Rhodes conceived the idea of a British South Africa Company, not only as a successful commercial concern but to extend British influence from the Cape to Egypt, from the Indian Ocean to the Mediterranean, 'if not in government, then in flag and by the ties of railways, telegraph and commerce,'[9] he was following the initiative of the Germans in South-West Africa.

Their colonization, ironically, owed much to the enterprise of a British subject, Aaron de Pass. He had founded a shipping company with trading posts and fisheries on the west coast, including one at Angra Pequena, from which he exported shark liver oil and dried fish; then he branched out into selling guano found on Ichabo Island. His son persuaded the Cape Government to annexe islands off the South-West African coast, which contained even more guano, and lease them to their company.

[8] Flint, op. cit.
[9] Colvin, op. cit.

Britain had no interest in declaring sovereignty over the Angra Pequena mainland, which was largely desert, where winds blew so strongly that locals said it could blow for eight days a week. Because of the huge waves, boats could only be launched from the shore on a few days every year. But Adolf Lüderitz, a Bremen tobacco merchant, realized that this remote and desolate region would be a toe-hold for Germany in Africa.

'An enterprising and energetic businessman, with imperialistic visions similar to his English counterpart, Rhodes, he rightly believed that by setting up a trading outpost and requesting German protection, colonisation had to follow.'[10]

Lüderitz reached an agreement with the local Hottentot chief. For £100 sterling and 200 rifles Lüderitz would obtain all land within five miles radiating from the harbour. Three months later a second agreement ceded the coast from the Orange River to 26 degrees latitude north of Angra Pequena and 20 miles inland. The German Chancellor, Bismarck, was then petitioned to protect this German settlement. He responded by sending a German naval vessel, *Nautilus*, which anchored off the coast for a month. In the following year two German frigates arrived and the German flag was raised at Angra Pequena.

Mr de Pass now became annoyed with Herr Lüderitz; he complained that so many guns were being fired from German warships in honour of the Kaiser that they were frightening away sea birds and damaging his guano trade. De Pass did not realize that while he shovelled seagulls' excrement for a modest living, an incalculable fortune in diamonds lay literally under his feet.

Lüderitz did not make much money out of his colonial enterprise either, but his actions had one unexpected result: they roused the sleepy British authorities from their torpor.

The Government was, however, unwilling to incur unnecessary expenditure in making any movement. Rhodes had the vision and the money, so it made sense that he should be allowed to go forward – at his own expense.

Rhodes was told that, in the description of Lord Salisbury, the Prime Minister, he would require directors of 'social and political standing'. Some he approached declined his offer of directorships, but the Duke of Fife, a son-in-law of the Prince of Wales, agreed.

According to a contemporary *Who's Who* he owned 'about 249,300 acres'. The second nobleman to accept Rhodes' offer was the Duke of Abercorn, who owned less than a tenth as much land – 26,000 acres – but he had been Lord of the Bedchamber and later Groom of the Stole to the Prince of Wales. Neither duke had any real business experience or aptitude, but both were

[10] *Diamonds in the Desert*, Olga Levenson, Tafelberg, Cape Town, 1983.

agreeable to become directors of a company with such great potential. Other directors of what became known as 'The Chartered' were Rhodes, of course, Alfred Beit, Lord Gifford, Earl Grey and George Cawston.

The opening clauses of the charter explained the company's credo.

'That the existence of a powerful British Company, controlled by those of Our subjects in whom We have confidence, and having its principal field of operation in that region of South Africa lying to the North of Bechuanaland and to the West of Portuguese East Africa, would be advantageous to the commercial and other interests of Our subjects in the United Kingdom and in Our colonies.'

The concession Lobengula had agreed with Rudd gave Rhodes and his company 'the complete and exclusive charge over all metals and minerals situated and contained in my kingdoms, principalities and dominions, together with full power to do all things that they may deem necessary to win and procure the same and to hold and collect and enjoy the profits.'

Rudd also secured the King's authority to prevent others securing rights for prospecting in his kingdom.

Having this concession with Lobengula was one thing; making sure that it could be honoured was another. In Rhodes' view, it was important for the new British South Africa Company that miners should start digging for gold, and the sooner the better. The man Rhodes entrusted to achieve this was Dr Leander Starr Jameson, with whom he shared a house in Kimberley after Pickering's death.

Jameson was a complex character, born in the same year as Rhodes. His father was first a Writer to the Signet in Edinburgh, and then edited a Scottish local newspaper. He inherited money and used this to buy two local newspapers in Suffolk. They proved so unsuccessful that he was forced to sell at a heavy loss. He died when Leander was fifteen and the family was supported by Mrs Jameson's father, a retired general.

Leander had three brothers. The eldest, Tom, became a naval doctor. When Leander was six he drank a glass of sherry and at once exclaimed, 'Now I feel as if I could go and do *everything*!' This supreme self-confidence stayed with him throughout his life.

He was seventeen when, with £100 borrowed from his brother Tom, he entered University College in London as a medical student. Later he became resident medical officer at University College Hospital. Another brother, Julius, working in South Africa, sent home a diamond, which greatly impressed Leander. Thus, when an American physician, Dr James Perrott Prince, wrote from Kimberley to the hospital asking them to nominate a potential partner, Jameson volunteered.

Like Cecil Rhodes and Barney Barnato, he had not expected to find Kimberley so primitive: dust thick as an abrasive fog, heaps of rotting rubbish that were not cleared away and 'a variety of unspeakable stenches' from the carcasses of horses and oxen. The town still consisted largely of crude shacks made from hammered-out biscuit tins and gunny bags, and shanties of corrugated iron and matchwood.

Prince planned to retire within three years and make over his practice to Jameson, but then one of his patients, a hysterical young woman, suddenly claimed that Prince had sexually assaulted her in the course of a medical examination.

Prince was old, mild and shy, and the charge was ludicrous, but her husband, described by Rhodes as 'an exceedingly excitable man', vehemently took up his wife's case and challenged Prince to a duel.

Dr Prince reluctantly went to law; Rhodes and Jameson gave evidence of his good character. The court found for Dr Prince, but he decided he was too old to endure such unpleasantness and made over his practice to Jameson, who now found himself earning the huge income of £5,000 a year.

In the neighbouring Orange Free State, President Brand was being treated for Bright's Disease by an old German missionary, who prescribed soup made from tortoises found in ditches. This did not help the President's health, but when Jameson was called in, his treatment did. So Jameson's reputation increased and Louis Cohen claimed that 'he was recognized as the best doctor who ever practised in South Africa. With the fair sex, although not particular about complexion, he was undeniably most popular, and it is conceded that he shone more as a squire of dames than a Bonaparte of battalions. . . .

'No matter what happened to be the trouble with matron, maid or widow, a visit from the dexterous Doctor would always set things right. He was the Popular Specific and enjoyed himself accordingly. . . .

'Ladies who did not want children and those who did – especially those who did – flew to Dr Jameson for advice and assistance, which he rendered with a perseverance which must have been quite pleasing to the husband who paid the coming Premier's bill with gratitude.

'I knew a chap once who had been very successful in life and whose only trouble was that his charming wife had not presented him with a tiny image of himself. He confided in me, and on my initiative consulted Dr Jameson, with the result that, hey presto! before the year was out, and on the first of April, too, he became the proud pater of bounding twins. The doctor was indeed a life-giver.'[11]

Despite the fact that so many women in Kimberley found Jameson charming and, on occasion, extremely useful, he never married. Like Rhodes, he was devoted to his mother.

[11] Louis Cohen, op. cit.

159

In Kimberley he led a very social life. He gave dances, adjudicated at boxing matches and was a great gambler. One session involved a poker game with Dr Sauer, who wagered his oxen, his wagon, his guns, his clothes, his instruments, finally even his top boots – and Jameson beat him with a straight flush.

'I rose from the table broke to the wide world,' wrote Sauer later. 'Jameson kindly returned me the top boots and my surgical instruments.'[12]

This was the man Rhodes now entrusted to develop the concessions Rudd had obtained. Jameson took with him on his journey north to see Lobengula another Kimberley physician, Dr Rutherfoord Harris. Also a bachelor, Harris had qualified in Edinburgh and then came to Kimberley. He had some money difficulties shortly after his arrival and abandoned medicine to work for Rhodes. From then on he suffered no further financial troubles.

Their contingent contained twenty wagons, all loaded with rifles and ammunition, part of the quantity agreed in the concession. They had a long and dangerous ride until they reached the granite hills of the Matopos. On guard here stood Lobengula's frontier warriors, bearing ostrich feather capes, ox-tail garters, ox-hide shields and carrying their assegais, short stabbing spears.

Jameson had brought with him a supply of pink glass beads, rolls of blue calico, brass buttons and other trinkets as evidence of their friendly intentions. He gave some of these to the guards as tribute, and passed on for a further 40 miles, when their convoy was again stopped.

The guards allowed Jameson to ride on into the King's capital, Bulawayo, in the centre of a plain covered by mimosa scrub and dried grass, and surrounded by mountains. An oval ring of huts surrounded what was known as the buck kraal, or royal enclosure.

The King sat on a packing case that had once contained cans of condensed milk and was leaning against the posts of a small stage on which, in his honour, four oxen were slaughtered every day. Dr Harris described him as 'a man of about 5 ft 11 inches in height. His weight measurement must be about 300 lbs and his chest measurement is from 55–60 inches. His walk is most imposingly majestic; he treads the ground in a manner that shows he is conscious of his absolute power.'[13]

Lobengula was very fat, naked except for a small loin cloth. He lived in this kraal surrounded by huts containing sixty wives. To bring rain, and to prevent the witchcraft of enemies, he mixed specifics by crushing roots in a

[12] Sauer, op. cit.
[13] Dr Harris' recollections of the journey were published in *The Diamond Fields Advertiser* of 28 June, 1889.

calabash. He slept in a wagon which he had taken from a passing trader, his head and arms on the box where the driver would have sat.

According to Harris, when Lobengula wished to eat, 'great masses of meat, like the pieces they give to the lions in the zoo, but as if thrown into a great big fire' were brought up by relays of servants, 'to be torn to pieces with a kind of stick' and then eaten, 'altogether very much like a wild beast'. The doctor noted that Lobengula had a pleasant smile and a curious expression on his face, 'partly good natured, partly worried and partly cruel'.

Lobengula had considerable cause to worry. He was well guarded with an army of 15,000 who lived in their own military villages, but for how long could he keep the white men on their side of the border?

The country Lobengula controlled, bounded on the south by the Limpopo river, on the east by Mozambique, on the west and north by the Zambesi, was as large as Germany and France put together. He ruled it partly by his own shrewdness and partly by terror. As many as thirty courtiers stood behind him every day, and when he spoke, they began a chorus of flattery after each sentence, calling him 'Stabber of the sun', 'Mountain of Zulus', 'Eater of men', 'The man who owns all the cattle'.

It was the custom for everyone approaching Lobengula to crawl on his hands and knees. Jameson did not observe this custom. He had been told that the head of anyone who approached the King must be lower than Lobengula's head, so because Jameson was small and slightly built he walked in without kneeling, without crawling.

Lobengula had a reputation for cruelty. Jameson diagnosed that this was at least due in part to the pain of gout, which his witch doctor blamed on spells cast by ill-disposed persons. The witch doctor wisely chose scapegoats who owned cattle. When these scapegoats were killed for causing pain to the King their cattle automatically became Lobengula's property.

Jameson now explained that gout came from 'up above' and not from the envy or hatred of others. It was visited especially on the great kings of Europe, as the result of too much brain work which meant they could take too little exercise. He injected the King with morphia, which brought immediate relief. Incidentally, Jameson, when ill with fever and unable to sleep, would also regularly inject himself with morphia, so he knew from experience its power to mask pain.

Lobengula now called his witch doctor and told him that, in future, instead of blaming individuals for gout, he would blame Providence. That year no one was sacrificed because of the King's gout.

Lobengula was so pleased with Jameson's treatment that he appointed him an induna and gave him an ostrich-feather cloak and ox-tail garters of a tribal notability.

Lobengula believed he had given permission for ten white men to dig in his country. Now it appeared that many times this number wished to be involved. Also, emissaries from other countries sought similar concessions because, as Rhodes said, 'our concession is so gigantic, it is like giving a man the whole of Australia'. Lobengula wanted Jameson to hand over to him the rifles he had brought, but he remained reluctant to allow more white men into his country to dig for gold.

His hesitation irritated Rhodes beyond further endurance. As always, he felt he was working against time, and now against more than one time-scale. From his own point of view, he needed to hurry because he believed he had not long to live. From a political standpoint, he feared other countries would leapfrog ahead and gain their own concessions, simply for commercial purposes, while he placed his need on a totally different level. He decided that it was of paramount importance for him to achieve his aim and no one would question what means he used so long as he was successful.

He approached a 23-year-old, Frank Johnson, and an American prospector, Maurice Heany, with a proposal to accelerate negotiations. Johnson had run away to sea as a boy, jumped ship at Cape Town, volunteered for a local regiment and transferred to the Bechuanaland border police. Here he had seen gold dust in vulture quills, and formed a syndicate with Heany – the Northern Gold Fields Exploration Syndicate – financed by Cape Town businessmen, who each advanced £25, to search for gold.

Rhodes now proposed that, at his expense, they should recruit 500 men, then march to Bulawayo and kidnap Lobengula and as many of his indunas as they could. If they failed to kidnap him, he could be killed.

The fee Rhodes offered for this was £150,000 each in cash and 100,000 acres of land. The cover story for their action would be that Lobengula had sent a party of his warriors against a friendly king – an act which was believed could be the first step towards an invasion of Bechuanaland.

This was agreed, and then, on the eve of their departure, Heany, who had been drinking, stupidly revealed the whole scheme to a missionary. Understandably, he was horrified and warned Sir Sidney Shippard, who then contacted Sir Henry Loch, the new Governor, who asked Rhodes whether he knew of this scheme. Rhodes denied being involved and the plan was quickly aborted.

Because no such direct and possibly finite action could now be taken against Lobengula, Rhodes decided that the miners should trek into Mashonaland, next to Matabeleland, and his road to the north could still go ahead through that country.

Rhodes sounded out Colonel Frederick Carrington, who commanded the police force in Bechuanaland, for his professional opinion as to the feasibility of this new plan. Carrington said he could carry out this assignment if he was promoted to Major General and given 2,500 men, with full equipment. This was too great an expense for Rhodes to underwrite, so, over breakfast one day in the Kimberley Club, he discussed the matter with Frank Johnson.

'Give me 250 men and I'll walk through the country,' Johnson assured him confidently.

'You will?' asked Rhodes in surprise.

'Of course I will.'

'And what will it cost?'

Johnson had only made his claim conversationally. When he saw that Rhodes was taking him seriously he realized he had no idea of its cost.

'Give me till tiffin time and I'll work it out,' he said.

On a single sheet of paper Johnson calculated that the cost would be exactly £97,400.

'Right,' said Rhodes at once. 'You go, Johnson! You command the force. You go!'

Rhodes handed him a cheque for £20,000, with two directives. First, the force should contain men from every part of South Africa, including the Boer Republics. He calculated that the whole country would then wish for the success of the expedition.

Second, in addition to being first-class shots and riders, and being officially described as 'miners', they should actually represent all sorts of trades, professions and abilities. Thus, when they reached their objective in a country 1,600 miles from Kimberley and possibly 1000 miles from any other civilized place, they could form the nucleus of a whole new nation.

As a guide for the expedition – and following his own habit to choose an expert whenever he could find one – Rhodes selected a professional big game hunter, Frederick Courtenay Selous. Years earlier, at the age of nineteen, Selous had also visited Lobengula, seeking permission to shoot big game in his country. The King was amused at this request, but told him, 'Go where you will. You are only a boy.'

Since then, as boy and man, Selous had successfully shot elephant, buffalo, lion, rhinoceros on a professional scale, selling tusks, skins and horns to museums and collectors. He readily accepted Rhodes' commission and worked out a plan to reach Mashonaland by going eastward from the Bechuanaland border and so not risk crossing into Matabeleland.

He proposed that he should first aim for a hill called Mount Hampden. Here he would meet one of Rhodes' agents who had promised to bring in 100 Matabele labourers to begin constructing the road to the north.

These labourers did not arrive, so Selous went to ask Lobengula the reason. The King now claimed that he had never given permission to Dr

Jameson for such a right of way and told Selous earnestly, 'Go back and take Rhodes by the hand and bring him here.'[14]

Rhodes could not accept this offer, but asked Jameson to return to Lobengula to resolve his problems. Lobengula admired Jameson. He actually laughed in the King's presence, which none of his people were ever allowed to do. Most important, he carried a magic needle that could ease the pain of his gout.

Lobengula's army was growing increasingly restive and, having heard that a column of white men was on the march, wished to destroy them while they could. The King's own position as ruler was by no means totally secure, nor, so it seemed to Jameson, were the lives of Europeans in Bulawayo. Jameson advised them to leave, but the King refused to give them permission to go. In any case, several missionaries refused to leave, claiming that they were 'men of peace'. Lobengula promised that, so long as the missionaries remained, 'There will be no trouble for the white men in this country'.

In the early stages of their negotiations, he had asked Jameson rhetorically, 'Can a man be happy without cows and bulls?'

Rhodes immediately responded by ordering two white bulls from England. They eventually arrived at Kimberley and were put on a huge ox-wagon for the journey to Bulawayo, under the charge of a young British transport driver with an African escort. When they reached Matabeleland they were surrounded by warriors, who chased away the escort and threatened the driver with death.

At that moment a witch doctor, who must have known the reason for this journey, approached the hostile crowd. He threw the knuckle bones on the ground and asked them quietly, 'Do you mean to kill this white man?'

'We do,' came the instant and unequivocal reply.

The witch doctor nodded as though he quite understood their wish, and then he pointed to the bulls standing under a net in the wagon.

'Can any one among you lift those two bulls?'

'No,' came the reply. 'That is impossible.'

'So you say. Yet this white man, a youngster, lifted these bulls on to the wagon,' the witch doctor replied, adding caustically that if these warriors could not do the same on their own, how could they return to their kraals and admit such failure?

'If you kill him, you will be scattered as the wind scatters the dust,' he assured them scornfully. This message was received and understood, and the bulls were allowed to proceed.

Lobengula, shaded from the sun by a white umbrella, looked them over critically when they arrived.

[14] Michell, op. cit.

'Why did you not bring me a white bull and a red bull?' he asked petulantly.

A red bull represented an enemy, a white bull a friend. This was Lobengula's way of pointing out that peace or war had still not been decided.

At dawn on 6 May, 1890, a group of 179 potential settlers, known as Pioneers, with 500 mounted police and Volunteers, possibly 1,000 men altogether, left Kenilworth, a Kimberley suburb, for the north. So little was known about their route that Lord Methuen, the Deputy Acting Adjutant-General of the Cape Command, made a joke about it as he inspected them before they left.

'Gentlemen, have you got maps?' he asked them. The officers replied that they had.

'And pencils?'

'Yes, sir.'

'Well, gentlemen,' said Lord Methuen. 'Your destination is Mount Hampden. You go to Siboutsi. I do not know whether Siboutsi is a man or a mountain. Mr Selous, I understand, is of the opinion that it is a man; but we will pass that by.

'Then you get to Mount Hampden. Mr Selous is of the opinion that Mount Hampden is placed ten miles too far to the west. You had better correct that; but perhaps, on second thoughts, better not. Because you might possibly be placing it ten miles too far to the east. Now, good-morning, gentlemen.'

Rhodes would have liked to go with the Pioneers, but he could not do so for the best of reasons. At the age of 36, he had just been appointed Prime Minister of the Cape Colony.

As one of the richest and most highly regarded men in South Africa, a life governor of De Beers, a director of this new company 'The Chartered', and as such virtually given a personal charge to forge a private empire in Africa without any controls, Cecil Rhodes was a natural choice for Prime Minister. But the actual transition to the supreme power politically came as a result of unexpected moves by others.

The existing Prime Minister, Gordon Sprigg, was defeated on a vote when Jan Hofmeyr set the votes of the Bond against him. Sprigg had to resign. Other candidates were proposed for the premiership, but the Bond would not support them. Finally, Sir Henry Loch summoned Rhodes; he was the one man all would support.

Thirty-six, for many men, is a time when they are at their peak of intellectual and professional achievement. Their health is usually good; old age and death are not yet visible on even the most distant horizon. But for Rhodes, 36 was rather different. He was already becoming short of breath. His face was puffy and swollen. He had put on weight and, from being slim, his body was thickening. He looked old long before his time and he believed he had not much time left. Thus, what he had to do he had to do as quickly as possible. There could be no standing on ceremony, or considering the wishes or feelings of others. His wishes, his needs, his aims were paramount if he were to succeed and make his dreams reality.

His political policies had already brought him the support of the Afrikaner Bond, largely made up of Dutch-speaking farmers. The new British South Africa Company, with its motto, Justice, Freedom, Commerce, offering new opportunities for successful investment in the north, now added considerably to Rhodes' influence with the English-speaking community.

Rhodes needed the support of the Cape, but the Cape needed him just as much, because from the Cape railway lines, roads, and telegraph wires would spread to the north. Settlers would also go north, and, as Rhodes grew closer to achieving his dream, the Cape could become stronger and so eventually virtually independent of any control by the British Government 7,000 miles away.

As Rhodes explained it: 'I thought of the positions occupied in De Beers, and the Chartered Company, and I concluded that one position could be worked with the other, and each to the benefit of all.'

Rhodes now showed how he could amalgamate politicians as successfully as he had amalgamated companies. He took into his cabinet Afrikaners of rigid outlook and English settlers of more liberal views, because these were the only two groups which, either singly or, worse, together, could thwart his ambitions.

On his theory that every man had his price, before British South Africa Company shares could be bought on the open market, Rhodes distributed 125,000 shares among politicians whose support he needed.

Politicians he could not persuade to his own views he quietly moved sideways out of his way to positions where they could not oppose him, one to become a judge, another an administrator. He needed a Government powerful enough to be able to carry out his plans without being sniped at by Opposition speakers.

To maintain the support of the Dutch-speaking Afrikaners he commissioned an enquiry into the teaching of Dutch in schools and, out of his own resources, financed a company to print Dutch language newspapers.

So the column set off on their 1,600 mile march. The Pioneers were paid seven shillings and sixpence (37½p) a day and when they reached their destination each was assured he would receive 3,000 acres of land. Many of them might not intend to live on this land permanently, but in 3,000 acres of land, in what they were told was the world's richest gold-bearing country, they would surely find some gold. Rhodes promised each one fifteen claims. In addition, according to Sam Kemp, who wrote his account of the march,

Rhodes told them very simply: 'Stay with me . . . and I'll send you home a millionaire.'[15]

This was a challenge that many men without careers or hope were very glad to accept. The only qualification asked of them was that they had to be physically fit.

Their assembly point was Mafeking, where they were given horses, rifles and khaki shorts, woollen socks and thick cloth puttees to wind round their legs against snakes, especially the deadly black mamba.

The prospect of future riches spurred them on, despite many cruel setbacks. They were struck down with black water fever, for which they had no specifics; the supplies of rum and quinine they carried were useless. Many fell ill with dysentery and assorted fevers from ticks that bit them, from tsetse fly, from mosquitoes. When they camped, lions would attack their horses and elephants trample their tents. Each night, to minimize such risks, they outspanned, drawing up their ox-wagons in a circle, with searchlights borrowed from the naval base in Simonstown and machine guns at the ready. So many died on the journey that burial parties dug graves nearly every night.

Lobengula was concerned at reports he received of this approaching army. He sent a message, translated by a European in Bulawayo, to Jameson: 'Has the King killed any white man, that an impi (army) is collecting on its border, or have the white men lost anything they are looking for?'

Jameson replied, 'These men are a working party, protected by some soldiers, and are going to Mashonaland along a route already arranged with the King.'

Lobengula now denied that he had ever agreed to this. He felt increasingly alarmed that permission for a few prospectors had so rapidly resulted in a thousand men, half of them armed, now apparently marching to the border of his country. How had he been bamboozled into this appalling situation? Could he possibly extricate himself before it was too late?

The answers to both these questions were the same: he had been ensnared by Rhodes' cunning. There was now no escape for Lobengula; indeed there never had been. He had trustingly agreed to one proposition which quite inexplicably – almost unbelievably, because he had relied on Jameson – had somehow become another.

So the Pioneer column moved slowly onwards, with Selous leading a squad of local labourers to hack a road through rough country. They marched by the observations of an astronomer from the Cape observatory who guided them by sun and stars. They also had a former ship's captain with them; he brought along a sextant and compass to help keep them on course.

[15] Sam Kemp, op. cit.

By September they had reached their destination and they set up three forts. The most southerly they called Fort Victoria, after the Queen. The second was Fort Charter, after the Chartered Company. The most northerly was Fort Salisbury, named after the British Prime Minister.

When the Pioneers were dismissed from their last formal parade they instantly ceased to be a military force and became civilians, pledged to build 'a civilised state in the wilderness – to cut forests, make roads, lay out farms, mine for gold, and build towns'.

They lived here for more than two years without any trouble from the Mashonas or the Matabeles just across the border. It seemed that the Pioneers and the neighbouring Matabeles could live in peace indefinitely. Rhodes claimed: 'We are on the most friendly terms with Lobengula. He receives a globular sum of £100 a month in sovereigns, and he looks forward with great satisfaction to the day of the month when he will receive them. I have not the least fear of any trouble in the future from Lobengula.'

This was, unfortunately, wishful thinking. The Matabeles had always looked with contempt on the Mashonas and considered them their slaves. They still did, and would send armed groups across the border to collect cattle from them as tribute. Any resistance was met by death, except for young men and girls who might be useful to them.

Then, in April, 1893, 500 yards of telegraph wire linking Kimberley with Salisbury was cut from the line. A Mashona chief admitted the offence; the wire was very useful for other purposes besides transmitting messages.

Jameson, who had stayed in charge of the settlers, fined him in cattle, and at once Lobengula claimed that all Mashona cattle were his by right.

Seventy Matabele warriors came over the border armed with rifles – ironically, part of the consignment that Rhodes had supplied to him earlier under the agreement – to back up the King's claim. This raiding party was sent back and the Matabeles responded with a huge force of 3,500 warriors. They killed 400 Mashonas and set their kraals ablaze, but Lobengula still honoured his pledge not to kill any white men. His warriors killed their servants instead, and then stole the cattle.

Fort Victoria, 188 miles south of Salisbury, and closer to the border of Portuguese Mozambique, was guarded by a fort, with a tower at each corner, surrounded by barbed wire and with two Maxim and Gatling machine guns. All work stopped in the town when the Matabeles marched on the settlement. Survival was suddenly top priority among all the white settlers.

The *Mashonaland Times* described how the 'Rev Sylvester . . . preaching from an ammunition case on Sunday,' had assured his congregation that 'the Sons of Ham would all be cleared out'. And the report of a meeting held in the Market Square in Victoria on the previous day declared that, 'Dr Jameson must settle the Matabele question at once, now and for ever.'

Jameson agreed to meet Lobengula's representatives to discuss the situation. To receive them he sat on a wooden chair outside the fort, facing the indunas who arrived with two or three hundred men as guards. The talks ended indecisively. The Matabele withdrew and then squatted with their shields and assegais nearby. Jameson sent out an army captain with thirty-eight mounted men to persuade them to move. His orders were to shoot them if they refused.

The Matabele had left by the time they arrived, but, it was said, only to round up cattle 'at the point of their spears'. The captain's men fired. The Matabele fled.

Meanwhile, Dr Sauer had arrived in Fort Victoria. Jameson told him that a number of Dutchmen were in Victoria and asked how many men Sauer thought it would need 'to fight the Matabele nation'.

'One thousand men,' Sauer reported.

'I'll do it,' said Jameson.

He telegraphed to Rhodes that he therefore proposed to deal with them. Rhodes replied briefly: 'Read Luke xiv. 31.' Jameson looked up his Bible and found this text: 'Or what king, going to make war against another king, sitteth not down first, and consulteth whether he be able with ten thousand to meet him that cometh against him with twenty thousand.'

Jameson cabled to Rhodes that he had read the verse and that 'it was all right'.

Unease increased among the citizens of Fort Victoria. They told Jameson that they believed they must either fight or leave. Their native labourers had either deserted them already or were in the process of leaving. When the rains came the Matabele could return and massacre everyone who remained.

When Rhodes cabled that he had no money to sustain a campaign such as Jameson proposed, Jameson cabled back: 'By this time tomorrow night you have got to tell me you have got the money.'

Rhodes found it by selling 50,000 of his shares in the Chartered Company.

Jameson now hastily worked out a plan. All available men would ride out from Salisbury, Victoria and a third town, Tuli. They would each take rations for three or four days and 100 rounds of ammunition. The officer in Salisbury, who was trying to raise 250 mounted men, now reported he had everything – except 250 horses for these riders.

Almost every white man in Mashonaland volunteered, not for money, for there was none, but because each was promised 6,000 acres of land, sixty gold mine claims and a share of all cattle, plus their existing mining claims in Mashonaland, which would remain valid for six months after the end of a war that now seemed imminent.

Jameson cabled to the Cape Town office of the Chartered Company: 'Three years of negotiations have only induced them (the Matabele) to encroach more. Work is absolutely stopped. . . . People and government have lost large numbers of cattle and I am sure work will not be recommenced or even transport carried along the roads until some definite action on our part is taken.'

Then he learned that Matabele warriors had re-crossed the border and telegraphed a message for Lobengula, demanding compensation for the damage they had done. Lobengula replied 'in a humble and conciliatory fashion'. But when the Matabeles who had marched on Fort Victoria returned to Bulawayo, they lied to Lobengula to excuse their own defeat at the hands of such an inferior force. They said they had been asked to disarm for their talks and then had been attacked and shot when they were disarmed.

Lobengula replied bitterly to Jameson: 'Had I known at the time when I dispatched my impi (forces) . . . what I know now, I would have ordered them to capture and loot all they could lay their hands on belonging to the whites to compensate myself for the people and their property which were withheld from me.'

Lobengula did not want war, but now he could not guarantee peace; his army was in a ferment of discontent. Distance, lack of communications and the feeling of isolation, of being in the centre of a gigantic and largely unknown land, were also undermining the morale of the settlers. Throughout that summer both sides waited uneasily for some sign or portent of what would happen.

By early September the Salisbury volunteers had still not received their horses. Jameson wrote a note to his brother: 'The usual thing. All heroic when only talking to be done, then demands for everything under the sun to ensure safety. . . . I always did hate the military gentlemen.'

On 5 October a patrol of the Bechuanaland border police said that they had been fired on by thirty Matabele. The High Commissioner telegraphed to Jameson: 'Whatever your plans are with regard to the advance of the columns . . . they had better now be carried out.'

On the following day Jameson cabled back ambiguously: 'I am now acting upon Your Excellency's instructions to carry out my plans.' So the whole force set off.

In the meantime Lobengula had sent emissaries south to try to keep the peace, even at this late hour. One was his own half-brother, with two indunas and an Englishman as interpreter. They reached one column of the advancing troops and the interpreter went to see Selous.

While they had a few drinks they received word that the two indunas were trying to escape. The column commander thought they were 'just two natives' who had simply followed the interpreter from Bulawayo and had put them under arrest. One snatched a bayonet from a trooper, stabbed two guards and tried to escape. The other joined him – and both were killed.

Lobengula's half-brother was arrested and by what was later called in an official enquiry 'a series of extraordinary mischances, for which neither the officers nor the men of the police were to blame'; the message that Lobengula still wished for peace was never delivered.

When the Cape parliament rose in early September Rhodes went by ship to Beira, and then travelled overland to Salisbury. Jameson sent Sauer to meet him. Sauer could not understand why Rhodes seemed to wish to go forward as slowly as he could. When Sauer told him that they could reach Salisbury that night, Rhodes replied that where they were would be 'a very nice place to camp'. Then a messenger rode out towards them from Salisbury. Rhodes' face changed as he read his message.

'Jameson has started,' he said. 'Let's get into Salisbury.'

He did not wish to move until he knew it was too late for the British Government, or anyone else, to change their mind.

As armament the column had one Nordenfelt gun, a Gardener gun, two Maxims 'on galloping carriages', and one seven-pounder gun. The Victoria column brought three galloping Maxims,[16] a one-pounder Hotchkiss, a seven-pounder gun, plus riders and marching men with 'a native contingent of 400 friendly Mashonas'. Their searchlight proved very useful in an unexpected way. The Matabele called it 'the white man's eye' and it caused great consternation among them.

At four in the morning on 25 October the Matabeles attempted a surprise attack. As dawn lit up the sky, they advanced down a slope 'in a most casual way, without hurrying or attempting to take cover'. When they reached the bottom, they sat down and began to fire. Sporadic fighting went on for nearly a week. Finally the Matabele attacked in a group.

'I believe that no civilised troops could have withstood the terrific fire they did for at most half as long,' reported one British officer with the column. They lost nearly 1,000 men, literally mown down by the machine guns. The columns suffered one fatal casualty and three died afterwards of their wounds.

'In such fashion the fate of the Matabele War was decided,' wrote Ian Colvin in his life of Dr Jameson.

Lobengula was not a strategist and his troops had never been taught how to use their rifles to the best effect. They believed that the higher they raised their sights the harder their bullets would hit. Instead, most soared harmlessly over the heads of Jameson's column.

They also believed that the shells which landed in their midst were full of

---

[16] These were Maxim machine guns mounted in very light two-wheeled carts, each pulled by one horse. Part of the seat in the cart was removed to allow space for the Maxim.

tiny white men who, as soon as the shell burst, ran out to kill everyone in sight. So whenever a shell landed among them the Matabele fired wildly in every direction to destroy these phantom midgets – and wasted much of their ammunition.

With such huge losses the Matabele will to fight evaporated. When Jameson entered Bulawayo two Englishmen came out to meet him. They reported that the royal kraal had been completely burned down. Lobengula had fled, but before he left he had charged his most senior chief upon his life to keep all the white men safe.

Jameson immediately sent out patrols to find Lobengula; he believed that there could not be any lasting peace without his agreement, although what this would be worth after such a catastrophic defeat was debatable. A week later Jameson received a message saying that Lobengula would come to see him, but he did not do so. More patrols went out to try to find him, but they were unsuccessful. It was later reported that Lobengula had died, either, as some said, of smallpox, or, as others claimed, of a broken heart.

Rhodes, and Jameson as his subordinate, had acted on the basis that the end would justify any means they used to achieve it. Lobengula, on the other hand, had acted honourably throughout all the negotiations; he had always kept his word.

In his last months of power Lobengula would often have long conversations with Charles Helm, the missionary who had acted as interpreter in the first negotiations with Charles Rudd.

'Did you ever see a chameleon catch a fly?' Helm recalled Lobengula had once asked him reflectively, when he finally realized he had been duped by men he had trusted.

'The chameleon gets behind the fly and remains motionless for some time. Then he advances very slowly and gently, first putting out one leg and then another. At last, when well within reach, he darts out his tongue and the fly disappears. England is the chameleon and I am that fly.'

In fact, Lobengula was only half right. The chameleon was not England, but Cecil Rhodes.

CHAPTER 10

'PEOPLE COME HERE TO MAKE MONEY, NOT GET INVOLVED IN POLITICS'

Rhodes was now in control of a million square miles of Africa and all it contained or could produce, above ground and underground, a private empire which his company, in effect, owned.

He and his directors, who invariably agreed with his opinions and proposals, could appoint judges and administrators and give land, except for two areas marked 'native reserves', to whoever they wished.

Like Caesar, Rhodes came, he saw, and it seemed that he had conquered. The whole area was called Zambesia. The new country was first called Rhodesia in 1895. Two years later it was proclaimed as the official name of Rhodes' own country.

When Rhodes learned of this, he asked, not entirely rhetorically, 'Has anyone else had a country called after their name? Now I don't care a damn what they do with me.'

What 'they' did was to appoint him a Privy Councillor. Such was his popularity and fame that, when Rhodes came to London, strangers, recognizing him from photographs and cartoons in the illustrated newspapers, would spontaneously raise their hats to him or shake his hand warmly. Rhodes could not pass a bus without the driver shouting a cheerful greeting to him; cabbies touched their hats and waved their whips in salute as he walked past.

The British South Africa Company – 'Chartered' – had more than 9,000 shareholders, many of whom lived on the Continent of Europe. A number of its shareholders would buy only one or two shares, not because they wanted the investment, but simply because ownership made them eligible to attend annual meetings where they could see Rhodes and listen to him. Such was his reputation that these meetings were held in the largest room in London available, in the Cannon Street Hotel. 'Chartered' meetings held here were so crowded that hundreds of shareholders could not even get inside the building.

Rhodes had achieved so much politically and financially, and yet somehow his success had an empty, solitary flavour – the taste of loneliness. What he lacked was someone close to him, like his mother or Neville Pickering, who would not only listen to his plans, but, much more important, could say if they did not approve of them.

Instead, as Rhodes grew richer and more influential, his increasing health problems made him more and more irritable. Like many rich and lonely men he was largely surrounded by sycophants who agreed with whatever he said or proposed, as Lobengula's indunas had praised their master fulsomely whenever he spoke.

In the ancient world emperors knew the value of having at least one unbiased critic close at hand. At the height of their fame, when they rode in their chariots, leading a triumphant parade with their defeated enemies marching dejectedly before them, the shouts and cheers of the crowd would blot out every other sound except one – the most important. They employed a slave to stand at their side in their chariot, to whisper in their ear that all power is temporal and most of it ephemeral; nothing lasts for ever.

Rhodes lacked any criticisms just when he needed this healthy reaction most. He was attracted to doctors – Jameson, Rutherfoord Harris and Sauer were three of several more, but of these three only Sauer had anything like independence of thought or speech. The others were virtually echo-chambers of Rhodes' own views. This was a state of affairs that did not improve as he grew older and had more need of at least one other unbiased opinion to balance his own.

He was thick now in his body and his face was often flushed and bloated, which caused rumours that he was drinking heavily. This was not so. He was abstemious and would only have a whisky and soda or a beer or a light hock at lunch and before dinner. At dinner he might drink a whisky and soda or a glass or two of champagne.

Barney Barnato, like Rhodes, was also instantly recognized whenever he walked through London. This was not often, since he preferred to travel in his magnificent coach. But with his distinctive pince-nez, his moustache with carefully waxed ends, his silk cravat, a fresh flower in his buttonhole, cigarette in his hand, his face cheerful and his manner ebullient, Barney Barnato could never be mistaken for anyone else. People might be awed by Rhodes and respect his achievements, but they genuinely liked and admired Barney. He was still one of them, only richer, very much richer.

He was in London when he learned that Rhodes had been appointed Prime Minister of Cape Colony; he immediately ordered a portrait of Rhodes and a huge graph that showed the enormous rise in De Beers' profits. He hung these in the waiting room of his City office. Visitors who did not know Barney could then see instantly the sort of man he was without having to be told: friend of a premier and life governor of the world's largest and most profitable diamond company.

In February, 1894, Gladstone, by then 85 years old, was replaced as Prime Minister by Lord Rosebery. He had British interests in South Africa very much in mind, indeed had married a cousin of Nathanial Rothschild, who had been involved, first with the diamonds business and then with the gold-fields. Lord Kimberley, after whom Colesberg Kopje had been re-named, was now Foreign Secretary in Rosebery's new government.

Barney Barnato approved of these changes. Previously, although he had spoken of Johannesburg's prospects in the most enthusiastic terms, he had been listened to with reserve. Now the wheel had turned; it seemed that everyone wanted to invest.

Two weeks after Rhodes had received the Royal Charter for the British South Africa Company Barney registered the Johannesburg Consolidated Investment Company Limited. This was a grouping of Barney's other commercial undertakings on the Rand, and the issue of shares was handled by banks in London and Paris, who reserved half the shares for themselves.

This meant that shares offered to the public were relatively few and this rarity increased the demand. When they appeared on the open market their price soared. If investors could not buy shares in Barney's companies they bought shares in other companies on the Rand; these South African shares were known as 'Kaffirs'.

Barney appointed his cousin, David Harris, to be his proxy at De Beers' board meetings when he could not attend. Harris, like Barney, did not appreciate Rhodes' habit of calling such meetings at very short notice, whenever he needed more money for his own political projects. Neither of them could understand Rhodes' total lack of concern about money. He appeared to keep no proper books. Diamonds worth thousands of pounds would turn up wrapped in twists of paper in the pockets of discarded jackets. Money to Rhodes was only useful because it could buy power, and power was essential if he was ever to fulfil his dream.

Barney grew concerned when payments from De Beers to the British South Africa Company rose to more than £500,000. Money, to him, was what they were in business to make, not to give away. The greater the profits, the more businesses they could buy, the more assets they could control. He could not comprehend why Rhodes wished to spend so much money on what, to him, seemed an idle project. But permission to do this was spelled out in the company's trust deed and he had to accept it, although privately he agreed with Lord Rothschild, who said, 'We are not a philanthropic association. Our business is to get diamonds.'

Barney's business was also to guard against declining returns from gold in Johannesburg. Here he and Solly spread their interests widely. They bought into a printing company; they took over a wine and spirit concern; they involved themselves with firms making building materials and others owning wagons to transport food. They were born deal-makers; no one else could approach them for their abilities to strike a profit apparently as constantly as a tinder strikes a flame.

In London, however, Barney often felt bored. Fanny, his wife, also seemed out of her depth there. She was by nature a quiet, gentle person and had loyally adjusted her way of living to that of her husband. She fell in with what he proposed, but this did not mean she always liked what he proposed or even agreed with it. She followed where he led, but this did not stop her from becoming impatient sometimes, as, for example, when he would take two boxes for the opera at Covent Garden. In one they would entertain his friends, and then in the interval Barney would invite them to move to the second box where they could all have a better view of his wife, with her tiara.

This was not the life that she might have chosen, yet she knew how proud Barney was of her. He was genuinely in love with her and she with him.

'People thought my husband ugly,' she said once, 'but to me he always seemed a very handsome man with a smile that lit up the darkest room.'

Even so, she could never appreciate the long sessions Barney needed to hold with his friends late into the night, or his rushed meals, hasty meetings with brokers, bankers, punters, tipsters, the regular dashes from their hotel suite to the East End to visit people he remembered from childhood.

Cobbs Court, where Barney had been born, and The King of Prussia where he had worked, were both pulled down when Middlesex Street was widened. His parents and his sister and her husband had therefore at last come up west, where he bought houses for them. He also gave his father a carriage and pair, but the old man felt embarrassed by the magnificent equipage and did not want to go back to see his old friends in this carriage. Instead, he and his wife would take a bus twice a week to the East End.

Barney had no such inhibitions about his possessions, but he always remembered what it was like to be poor, and on his visits he would hand out pound notes to whoever he thought needed them. He was always willing to help an orphan girl who lacked a dowry or an old man with nowhere to sleep. But, like Rhodes, he could not bear loafers or scroungers. Once someone, who Barney remembered from boyhood had never worked, asked him for a shilling.

'I'll give you a bob for your wreath,' Barney retorted. 'No, they're not allowed in our religion. Better yet, I'll leave you a shilling in my will.'

As soon as he arrived in the East End a cheering crowd would surround him. He would play to this audience, open his collar, loosen his cravat and dance on the pavement, often juggling with bagels. Perhaps he was happiest of all here, with people who remembered him as he remembered them, a past he could now recall with a warm pink glow of nostalgia.

Only afterwards, back in his hotel room, a bottle of iced champagne at his elbow, he would realize that this was still their world; he was the one who had got away. He had enough money now to buy everything that was for sale, except, as with Rhodes, the one elusive and priceless piece in the mosaic of a successful life – happiness. Barney's frenetic routine of drinking, smoking and dashing about in London increased rather than diminished as he grew older. He was always glad to return to South Africa with its sunshine and vast open spaces. London seemed cramped and small compared with the land he now thought of as home.

Barney's almost pathological fear that he was being patronized would show itself in unusual ways. Dining in a smart restaurant where he was not known, for example, an over-obsequious wine waiter, taking him for someone unused to such sumptuous surroundings, brought a bottle of wine and introduced it as a special vintage, 'A very good Johannesburg '77.'

'Rubbish!' shouted Barney. 'Johannesburg wasn't even built then!'

Again, he was late joining a party for dinner at a Pall Mall club because he had been all day in the City. Rather than go home and change he went into an outfitters and bought a new white collar and cravat which he put on in the shop.

A stranger at the party, knowing Barney had made his fortune in diamonds, was obsessed by the stone in Barney's tie-pin and praised it very highly, thinking it to be very valuable. Barney nodded nonchalantly as though he agreed with this man's assessment of its worth.

'It's yours,' he said at last. 'If you'll pay for champagne for all of us at dinner.'

The man agreed instantly, thinking that for a few pounds he had acquired a stone worth thousands. At the end of the evening Barney removed the pin and handed it over to the man.

'Good luck,' he said. 'I paid ninepence for it when I bought this collar and cravat.'

Wherever Barney might be, in Kimberley, Johannesburg or in London, he preferred to conduct important meetings in his own room or his own office rather than in anyone else's. He would explain that this saved time. Instead of spending an hour going to another office, they could come to him. And if the meeting grew boring, or against him, he could always end it by saying he had someone else due to arrive within minutes.

In reality Barney still lacked confidence. This confidence, and the confidence of investors, was not helped by a visit Lord Randolph Churchill made to South Africa. He was writing a series of articles for the London *Daily Graphic* at £100 a time, hoping to make money, which he needed, and also restore his rapidly deteriorating health.

Churchill was dismissive of South Africa, which he called 'this God-forsaken country', a description which did nothing to increase the enthusiasm of potential investors. More importantly, however, he wrote enthusiastically about the Johannesburg goldfields.

'Not only is it certain that there is gold ore practically in sight sufficient to occupy the energies of a mining plant far larger than that which now exists for one or two generations, but the many wants of a mining population where wealth is easily and largely gained, and where luxury and free expenditure become a habit, offer to every variety of commercial enterprise promising prospects,' he declared.

Of the Boers, however, he wrote: 'One cannot but lament that so splendid a territory should have ceased to be British. . . . The goldfields, when connected by railways with the coast, will be crowded in a few years' time with thousands of Englishmen, who will impatiently jerk from their shoulders the government of the Boers. These will be out-numbered, absorbed, or scattered.

'Already, this process is perceptibly going on. All the capital invested in the Transvaal is foreign and under foreign direction. Such is also the case with all industry other than pastoral. . . .

'The days of the Transvaal Boers as an independent and distinct nationality in South Africa are numbered; they will pass away unhonoured, unlamented, scarcely even remembered either by the native or by the European settler.

'Having had given to them great possessions and great opportunities, they will be written of only for their cruelty towards and tyranny over the native races, their fanaticism, their ignorance and their selfishness. They will be handed down to posterity by tradition as having conferred no single benefit upon any single human being, not even upon themselves, and upon the pages of African history they will leave the shadow, but only a shadow, of a dark reputation and an evil name.'[1]

Barney was as absent-minded now he was rich as he had been when he was poor. Like Rhodes, he would often appear to be so lost in thought he became almost oblivious to his surroundings. For example, he would put a cigarette in his mouth and then go up to a stranger in the street and hold it out to him for a light, and be astonished when the stranger asked him angrily what he was up to.

Rhodes was also reluctant to strike a match on his own. He would wait until a companion had lit a cigarette and then light his from it.

At one race meeting Barney found he had forgetfully left his spectacles at home. His eyes were so weak that without them he could only see the jockeys

[1] Lord Randolph Churchill, op. cit.

vaguely as coloured blurs. He turned to a stranger and asked him excitedly, 'For God's sake, man, tell me what my colours are!'

Barney was superstitious about unusual things. If he set out on a journey he was always most reluctant to turn back, no matter what he had left behind. And whenever he saw a blind man he would not pass by without giving him a coin.

One day he heard of a former colleague down on his luck.

'You must help him,' he told Louis Cohen, who agreed that he would like to do so.

'Then give him £100,' said Barney.

'I can't afford it,' Cohen replied.

'Can you afford £10?'

'Yes.'

'Then you give him £10, and I'll give him £400,' said Barney, and did so.

Cohen and Barney fell out for a reason that neither ever revealed. Barney prospered while Cohen did not. They ran into each other years later in Johannesburg. Barney generously worked out a plan that would give Cohen an immediate £150 commission on a deal. When it was seen that Cohen had such a wealthy and influential friend, Cohen's own credit rose instantly.

When Barney arrived in London in the spring of 1894 the stock exchange was handling Rand shares worth around £20,000,000. By the end of that year this had risen to more than £55,000,000. Because of Rhodes' activities in Rhodesia, investing in South Africa was not only good business, it was also patriotic. Stockbrokers in the City received telegrams from Russia, Vienna, Constantinople, all with the simple and unequivocal instruction: 'Buy Kaffirs'.

Barney launched the Barnato Bank, Mining and Estate Corporation and, before the bank had even begun to conduct any business, its shares were three and a half times their nominal value.

Barney became the hero of the City. People would buy anything with which his name was associated.

'If I had proposed to make a tunnel from the Bank of England to Johannesburg, they would have snatched at the shares,' he said later. 'They would have snatched at the shares without waiting to hear a single detail of the scheme.'

He owned racing stables and was building a palatial house in Park Lane, although he had never lived in a house he owned before. Indeed, he had a residual resistance to the idea; somehow it seemed symbolic of settling down and growing old. When his house was being built he stood under the scaffolding and said prophetically, 'There it is, but I shall never live in it.'

Outwardly he remained as ebullient as ever. During a supper party at the Savoy a woman sitting next to him asked him whether it was true that he had once actually been a clown.

'Of course,' Barney answered instantly. 'And I can still walk on my hands.'

To prove it, he slipped off his coat and, dodging between the waiters, cheered loudly by the diners, he walked around the grill room on his hands.

And then, as quickly as gold shares had risen, they fell – on the Day of Atonement, Yom Kippur, the most important feast in the Jewish calendar, at the end of September, 1895.

Because Jews were observing this feast stock markets were quiet. In Paris, when a huge amount of Kaffir shares unexpectedly went on the market, because there were so few buyers, their value dropped. Within an hour some had lost as much as a third of their value. No one knew why.

Barney, who had been the man of the hour, was suddenly the man everyone blamed. He refused to sell his own shares and stuck to his view that the rise of the shares had been justified. Indeed, his stoic and coura-geous viewpoint, this steadfastness among so many running panic-stricken for cover, helped to stop a total collapse of the shares.

The Lord Mayor, Sir Joseph Renals, gave a banquet for Barney in the Mansion House, with the object of showing that the City maintained faith in its most famous son. Only two women were present, the Lady Mayoress and Fanny Barnato.

Barney was optimistic that gold production in South Africa, already larger than the gold production in the United States, was still only a fraction of what it would be in a few years' time. Such a fact was, however, of little comfort to investors who had lost money. Matters were not helped when Lionel Phillips, formerly a clerk in Kimberley, and by then President of the Johannesburg Chamber of Mines, made a speech in which he mentioned the strange relationship between the British in Johannesburg, who actually were producing the wealth, and the Boers, who were taxing it heavily.

'It is a mistake to imagine,' said Phillips ominously, 'that this much-maligned community, which consists anyhow of a majority of men born of free men, will consent indefinitely to remain subordinate to the minority in this country.'

Gold mining shares dropped again, some by 50 per cent. Shares in the Barnato Bank fell from £4 to £1 10s. Again, no one could understand exactly why such a dramatic fall had occurred, least of all Barney.

A French banker attempted to explain to his junior and worried staff that such a fall could happen when people got carried away by enthusiasm. To illustrate this, he lit a match and held it up to them.

'Imagine this match is a share,' he said. 'In lighting it, I have started a rise.'

He handed it to one of his colleagues.

'Now I sell it to you. You sell it on, and it goes from one to another.'

Finally, the last man burned his fingers.

'There,' said the banker. '*That* is the fall.'

Rhodes, meanwhile, was concentrating on politics. To consolidate his influence with the Boers, Rhodes 'squared' Jan Hofmeyr and the Afrikaner Bond, basically a party of farmers, by turning his attention to agricultural matters that concerned them. He agreed to restrict the dipping of sheep to prevent an infection that was harming the export of wool from the Cape.

The Boer farmers in general were backward and resistant to change, and especially hostile to plans to make them disinfect their flocks and goats as was done in other countries who relied on wool exports. They believed that, if the sheep were ill, then this was the will of God and it was not for men to question the ways of the Almighty.

Another motion in the House that aroused great controversy concerned compounds in Kimberley that housed native workers when they worked in the mines. Rhodes built these compounds, using African convicts, to cut down on the activities of I.D.B. merchants, to keep African labourers beyond the reach of the corrupting influence of cheap liquor and to maintain some measure of control over them.

A local doctor and member of parliament, Josiah Wright Matthews, reported favourably on one of these compounds in Barney Barnato's company. It was, he said 'a large yard, some 150 yards square, enclosed partly by buildings and the remainder by sheets of iron ten feet high. Within this inclosure were sleeping rooms for 500 Kaffirs, magnificent kitchen and pantry, large baths, large guardroom, dispensary and mess rooms.'[2]

Local traders were strongly against the compound system, not from any concern that the Africans might feel restricted, but for commercial reasons. The mining companies had their own shops within these compounds and so Kimberley shopkeepers saw their profits fall.

Rhodes had used American mining experts successfully in De Beers; now, as Prime Minister of the Cape, he brought in Americans from California to create a deciduous fruit industry. He grew oranges. He imported American vine roots, which were resistant to phylloxera, caused by insects which attack their leaves and roots, and which were decimating South African vines. When his railway line to the north was being extended, he made certain that new markets were found and new sites for farms were available alongside it.

In return, the Bond became more friendly to him over his plans for reorganizing De Beers in Kimberley, where a large number of miners had been sacked to cope with a sudden fall in the demand for diamonds. For a time Kimberley was altogether less prosperous than it had been and Rhodes became so unpopular that he needed police protection.

The Bond, and Rhodes, were concerned about future voting patterns. In 1853, the year Rhodes was born, Cape Colony had given the vote to every

[2] James Bryce, *Impressions of South Africa*, New York, 1898.

man, black, white or coloured, whose property was worth £25 a year. In the words of the Colonial Office, this was 'in order that all the Queen's subjects at the Cape, without distinction of class or colour, should be united by the bond of loyalty and common interest.'

By the time Rhodes was Prime Minister, however, there were twice as many Africans in the Cape as whites. Many of these Africans could not vote because they lacked the essential property qualification, but, clearly, their increasing numbers could not be ignored indefinitely.

The liberals would not accept any racial qualifications to be made with regard to voting. Rhodes came to a compromise by trebling the property franchise to £75, which added 4506 white voters but disenfranchised 3348 coloured voters. As a sop to the liberals, Rhodes introduced a secret ballot, although personally he was not in favour of this.

In 1894 Rhodes called a General Election, which he won, and as a result controlled two-thirds of the Parliamentary seats. The new Parliament now discussed what became known as the Glen Grey Act. Glen Grey was a district north of Queenstown, home to about 40,000 Africans. The land here was fertile, and Dutch-speaking farmers would have welcomed the opportunity of acquiring it, but it had become seriously over-grazed and overcrowded.

Rhodes proposed that Africans living there, and elsewhere, would have to accept that they could not all look forward to an unchanging pastoral life in which they could live by owning a couple of cows. They would have to change their outlook, and their jobs, and accept work elsewhere, as farm labourers in Britain had been obliged to do after the Industrial Revolution.

This change, for the Africans, meant working in towns for white people or for firms which whites controlled. In Glen Grey they would still be allowed a small amount of land each and could have their own local councils to raise taxes for local needs, such as maintaining roads and building bridges.

'As a gentle stimulus to these people to make them go on working', Rhodes advocated a tax of ten shillings a year which would be imposed, but not enforced, on Africans who did not own land and had not worked outside Glen Grey during the previous year.

In the House these proposals were strongly criticized on the grounds that they meant virtual slavery.

'I was much more of a slave than any of those natives . . . for nine mortal years of my life,' Rhodes replied. 'And it was compulsory slavery too. . . . Six years at school, I had to work five hours during the day and prepare work for the next day for three hours in the evening, while at college I was compounded in the evenings and not allowed out after nine o'clock.'

Someone shouted, 'And you never went out, I suppose?'

Rhodes had a paternal attitude towards Africans.

'I say the natives are children. They are just emerging from barbarism.'[3] He could not contemplate them simply becoming 'loafers', men who 'never did a stroke of work' but who sponged on relatives who were working, and so became prey to the sellers of cheap liquor.

When the Glen Grey Act came into force, it was copied elsewhere in South Africa. At the time this had seemed a pragmatic and reasonable solution to a growing problem. Years later it would be seen as the beginnings of apartheid.

Rhodes was Prime Minister from 1890 until 1896 and during these years he stood higher than any potential opponent. The only antagonist of any possible significance was Paul Kruger, the President of the Transvaal.

Rhodes and Kruger were not only diametrically opposed in outlook and policies, but in their own make-up. Kruger, when a young man, was out shooting when his gun burst and shattered a thumb. No medical aid was available, so he simply sharpened his knife on his leather trousers, put the end of his thumb in his mouth, and fixing his eyes twenty yards in front, slashed at it until he had cut it off.

Rhodes hated pain and the sight of his own blood made him feel sick. He also dreaded a long illness and a painful death. Once, talking with Le Sueur and Rutherfoord Harris, he told them, half joking: 'You and Harris will probably die of cancer in the throat and linger in agony, but I shall go off suddenly without any pain.'

He thumped his heart. 'This will kill me, but I shan't suffer.' But in the end he did.

Kruger believed implicitly in the Bible and could not be shaken from his conviction that the earth was flat. He regarded Rhodes virtually as an emissary of the devil, a worshipper of Mammon, which was the Aramaic word for riches. Rhodes' huge discoveries of diamonds and gold had meant that thousands of avaricious and godless foreigners had arrived in the Transvaal, hoping to emulate his success, and now they outnumbered indigenous Boers.

Rhodes was, in his own way, an idealist. He believed that the beneficent results that would come to Britain and South Africa if he achieved his aim were worth any sacrifice on his part or on anyone else's. He was not, in his own opinion, an enemy of the Boers. Indeed, his deliberate political policy was to conciliate them and so secure their support. He believed that he had gone a long way to uniting Afrikaners and English for their common good in South Africa and he was prepared to work at this wholeheartedly.

Rhodes hoped that eventually the Boer Republics of the Orange Free State and the Transvaal would combine with Cape Colony and Natal to form a Federated South Africa.

[3] George Honour: 'What Cecil John Rhodes thought about "the native question"', from *The New Rhodesia*, Vol 18, 1951.

Kruger had different ideas. He remained the steadfast champion of his own country's total independence. He remembered clearly how, as a boy, in the Great Trek, the Boers had marched north. But now Rhodes wanted the north for his own purposes. So here two powerful men were set on a collision course and the focus of their disagreement became Johannesburg, the city of gold.

When Rhodes first went to Johannesburg it was a shanty town of corrugated iron huts and tents, like Kimberley in its early days, but much more volatile. In the following eight years Johannesburg sprang, in Ian Colvin's words, 'like Aladdin's palace out of the empty desert. . . .

'Upon the main stem of the mining industry all manner of subsidiary activities contrived to exist – English accountants and bank clerks, German chemists and import agents, the British shopkeeper, Australian prospectors and mine-managers, and a cosmopolitan crowd of stockbrokers and land agents, liquor-sellers, illicit gold-buyers, pimps, and fried-fish shopkeepers, and the votaries of all nationalities of a hundred and one other trades and occupations, reputable and disreputable.'[4]

These often oddly assorted people lived and worked in a city hundreds of miles from the sea and several thousand feet above it. They felt justifiably proud of Johannesburg's new eight-storey buildings, fronted by marble, its electric light and trams, its music halls and shops. When times were good and the price of gold was high, there were no grumbles among these new arrivals, known to the Boers as Uitlanders, or foreigners. But when investment wavered or complications regarding the extraction of gold increased, so did their complaints.

Their main grievance, or at least the one most publicized, because probably most remained unconcerned, was that, although they paid taxes, they did not have a vote in the Transvaal. A similar grievance had caused the American War of Independence.

There had been rumbling discord between the Transvaal and the Cape for years. When the Cape charged heavy tolls on goods that crossed their border into the Transvaal Kruger retaliated by putting an equally heavy duty on Cape brandy. The Transvaal would have liked a Customs union and the Cape railway to be extended from Kimberley to Pretoria, the capital of the Transvaal. Against Rhodes' advice, and before he became Prime Minister, the Cape Government did not agree. As Rhodes said drily, 'The mists of Table Mountain covered all'.

When gold was discovered in Johannesburg the sudden huge increase in revenue from taxes meant that Kruger could begin his own railway from Delagoa Bay, on the east coast, to Pretoria, and so be independent of Natal and the Cape for importing and exporting goods.

[4] Colvin, op. cit.

When Rhodes became Prime Minister the Cape Government advanced money to construct a railway from the Vaal River to Johannesburg and fixed traffic rates until Kruger's railway from Delagoa Bay to Pretoria would be finished. Then, as soon as the 52 miles of track from the Vaal to Johannesburg was in use, the Boers trebled their charges for transporting goods.

Merchants in the Cape boycotted this railway and sent their goods by ox-wagon to Johannesburg. As many as 120 wagons a day would cross the Vaal river by fords, known as drifts. Kruger announced that he would put 'a barbed wire fence' along its banks to prevent this traffic. Cape merchants could then either pay the new high rates for moving their goods by rail or send them by sea round to Delagoa Bay.

The situation grew so serious that the British Colonial Secretary, Joseph Chamberlain, offered to support the Cape Government, whatever the outcome. He wanted an assurance, however, that if British troops should become involved, 'the Cape Parliament will bear half the gross expense, and that the local government will furnish a fair contingent of the fighting force as far as its resources in men may suffice, besides giving the full and free use of its railway stock for military purposes.'[5]

Kruger backed down and opened the drifts to the ox-wagons.

Before gold was discovered in Johannesburg the Transvaal was virtually bankrupt. Now, thanks to taxes on the gold mining companies and the Uitlanders who worked in them, it was on the way to becoming rich.

Almost completely surrounded by British colonies, the Boers began to receive supplies of up-to-date weapons, with instructors, from Germany, and Kruger cleverly played Germany against Britain. His philosophy was expressed at a dinner given in honour of the Kaiser: 'Our small Republic is still crawling about beneath the great powers and we can feel that when one is about to step on our feet the other tries to prevent this.'

Kruger knew that if the vote was given to the British in Johannesburg, who outnumbered the Boers, he might be on the way to losing his own power, and this was unthinkable. By 1895 Kruger was 70, almost twice as old as Rhodes, but Rhodes was convinced that he himself had not much longer to live. Time, like a tide, was running against him. He could not afford to wait until tomorrow to achieve what might be possible today.

In July of the previous year the new British Governor of Cape Colony, Sir Henry Loch, paid an official visit to Johannesburg and it was arranged that he would ride in a carriage with President Kruger. As they took their places, a crowd of British Uitlanders suddenly rushed from the sides of the road, unharnessed the horses, threw an enormous Union Jack over the carriage, and, to Kruger's amazement, pulled it forward, cheering.

[5] Telegram from the British Government, 1 November, 1895.

This apparently spontaneous demonstration against Kruger made Loch ask the British President of Mines, Lionel Phillips, what would happen in the event of any uprising against the Boers in Johannesburg. Could the Uitlanders hold out until British reinforcements arrived?

Too much importance was being given to what had simply been an act of exuberance, and which, although discourteous in the extreme, was not of serious intent. Barney Barnato probably summed up the feeling of most Uitlanders when he remarked, 'People come here to make money, not get involved in politics.' The Boers' policies and their dour outlook, like their taxes, could be extremely irritating, but they were not unbearable.

For an opinion about the feelings of the Uitlanders, Rhodes relied heavily on the advice of the American mining engineer, John Hays Hammond. He had poached Hammond from Barney Barnato for a salary of $75,000 a year, a third more than Barney had been paying him, plus the right to engage in speculative mining ventures of his own.

Hammond was an excellent engineer, but his grasp of local politics was less sure, which Rhodes did not realize. He appears to have believed that, since Hammond was correct where engineering was concerned, his judgment in political matters would be just as good, not, as events showed, a very wise assumption. Also, as an American, Hammond may not have been fully aware of the British characteristic to grumble, often when there is little to grumble about.

Hammond told Rhodes that in his opinion the Uitlanders were ready to rise against the restrictive measures of Kruger's government. He predicted a very serious situation in Johannesburg which needed to be resolved speedily.

They did not even have a municipal council. Agreed, they could become Boers by naturalization if they wished, and would then be allowed to vote, but that would mean they had to stay in Johannesburg for fourteen years, which most had no wish to do.

In Johannesburg an association called the Transvaal National Union, which began as a debating society, had become more political. It attempted to secure rights for the Uitlanders by presenting petitions to the Transvaal government. Once they succeeded in getting 40,000 signatures, but still nothing changed.

Rhodes knew that British feeling against the Boers – their bureaucracy, corruption, and their general stranglehold on enterprise – was very strong, but he overestimated their wish to be involved in violent change. He hoped that a huge demonstration against Kruger could cause the fall of this government and the election of one more amenable to the interests of the Uitlanders.

Curiously, J.B. Robinson, Rhodes' old adversary, was very much on the side of Kruger. But if the government had fallen, Robinson could possibly end up in charge. Rhodes was strongly against this possibility.

'I was not going to risk my position to change President Kruger for President J.B. Robinson,' he said afterwards.

In Johannesburg what was called the Reform Committee was formed to co-ordinate an uprising, with Rhodes' brother, Colonel Frank Rhodes, in overall charge. If the Uitlanders in Johannesburg actually rose against Kruger's government, they could hand over power to this committee. The signal that the Uitlanders were ready to act would be an attack by them on the Pretoria arsenal, believed to be very lightly guarded.

Jameson, who would just happen to be waiting on the border with 1,500 armed volunteers from Rhodesia, would march into the town. The British Governor in Cape Town could then act in a mediating role to restore order and calm. Such was the plan for a hypothetical situation, but events did not work according to it.

Some time before this Rhodes and Sauer were in Rhodesia and, shortly after lunch, while sitting in the shade of a licuni tree, Sauer saw a great bustard feeding about 900 yards away. He told Rhodes he was going to shoot it at that range. Rhodes laughed at his confidence.

'You won't get anywhere near him,' he said. Sauer aimed, fired and had a very near miss. At this Rhodes reacted in a strange way, suddenly becoming very silent and moody.

'Six months later,' wrote Sauer. 'I came to the conclusion that . . . Rhodes and Jameson had already agreed to invade the Transvaal before the year was out, (of this there is now no doubt).

'The reason why Rhodes was so upset at my accurate shooting was that he said to himself, "If the town-bred Dutchman can shoot as well as that, the veld Dutchmen, all born hunters, will shoot even better".'[6] Later Rhodes admitted that Sauer had drawn the right conclusion.

Jameson, however, still had a very low opinion of the Boers' fighting qualities. He and Sauer discussed this in detail and Sauer listed some of their remarkable victories since they arrived in South Africa.

Jameson was convinced that, since those days, they had, in his words, 'gone off'. He claimed he could drive them all out of the Transvaal and into the sea with only 500 troopers, simply armed with sjamboks – hippopotamus-hide whips.

A few days before Jameson's column started to march Sauer's brother-in-law, an army major, told Sauer that he knew 'for certain' that Jameson was going to invade the Transvaal with 800 mounted men and horse artillery. He knew this because he was a member of the officers' mess where he had heard them openly discussing the prospect.

Rhodes had made his own preparations for a march on Johannesburg.

[6] Sauer, op. cit.

Some time earlier he sent Dr Rutherfoord Harris to England with instructions to persuade the Colonial Office to cede part of Bechuanaland, which included the small town of Pitsani, to the Chartered Company. This was ostensibly requested so that the railway line could pass through it but actually was required because Bechuanaland was much closer to Johannesburg than Matabeleland, where most of the Chartered Company's police were stationed. When the Colonial Office agreed, after much discussion and some reluctance, the men who would form Jameson's force could therefore start from a base about five miles from the Transvaal border.

For several weeks before Jameson and his men set off consignments of huge oil drums had been arriving regularly in Johannesburg from Kimberley. The tap at the base of each drum was connected to a small tube of oil inside the drum. If the tap were turned on briefly, oil would flow out, which would reassure any inquisitive Boer officials who might wonder why so much oil was arriving. This ingenious arrangement had been devised by the American engineer, Gardner Williams, of De Beers. The main part of each drum contained rifles, whose total weight had been carefully calculated against the weight of a genuine drum of oil.

The plan was that Jameson's column would enter Johannesburg simultaneously with a so-called spontaneous uprising in the city. It could then be made to appear that they had answered a desperate call for help and had only moved to avert a tragedy. As the date for this approached, however, difficulties multiplied and enthusiasm within Johannesburg waned dramatically.

The original date for the co-ordination of revolt within Johannesburg and the 'relief' from outside was found to coincide with Johannesburg races. Instead of postponing the races, the Uitlanders postponed the uprising.

Jameson did not realize how much his officers had talked in the mess about these plans and was understandably concerned about the risk of discovery before his 176-mile march began. The suspicion was growing that the Transvaal was somehow aware that some demonstration would take place. For this reason the conspirators used mining terms in simple code messages to each other: an 'immediate flotation' meant immediate action.

A cable from Frank Rhodes in Johannesburg to his brother in Cape Town warned that it was 'absolutely necessary' to delay flotation. Rutherfoord Harris, back in South Africa, cabled to Jameson: 'You must not move until you hear from us again.'

Jameson remained as impetuous as he had been at Fort Victoria, when he ordered that, if the Matabele did not move away, they should be shot. He now telegraphed that if he did not hear further 'we will make our own flotation, with help of letter, which I will publish'. John Hays Hammond replied urgently: 'Experts decidedly adverse. I absolutely condemn further developments.'

On that Saturday afternoon Jameson cabled to Rhodes that he intended to leave on Sunday 'unless I hear definitely to the contrary'. This cable reached Cape Town at 5.45 in the afternoon. It had not been addressed to Rhodes at his home, however, but to the Chartered Company's office, which was closed on Saturday afternoon.

The assistant secretary of the Company went into the office on Sunday morning and opened the cable at ten o'clock. He decoded it and took it at once to Rutherfoord Harris at his home. Harris rushed with it to Groote Schuur, Rhodes' official house as Prime Minister. It was by then impossible for Rhodes to reply, because on Sunday mornings the telegraph office in Mafeking opened for only one hour, from nine to ten.

On the morning of Sunday, 29 December, Jameson, as the Administrator of Rhodesia, read a Reuter message from Johannesburg which was published in newspapers throughout South Africa.

'The position is becoming acute, and persistent rumours afloat of arming miners and warlike preparations. Women and children are leaving the Rand. . . . The market is lifeless. No business and everything politics.'

He decided not to delay any longer. Later that day he called together officers and men of the Chartered Company's police force in Pitsani near the Transvaal border. He explained that he had received an important letter from the British population of Johannesburg, asking for their assistance. He then read it out to them.

The letter explained that the British were providing the Afrikaners with their main source of revenue from their taxes, yet they were denied the right to vote because President Kruger's government considered them to be only temporary residents. Forty thousand Uitlanders had signed a petition seeking full civil rights, but that had been turned down.

'The [Transvaal] government riles the national sense of Englishmen at every turn,' read Jameson. 'What will be the condition of things here in the event of conflict? Thousands of unarmed men, women and children of our race will be at the mercy of well-armed Boers while property of enormous value will be in great peril. . . . The circumstances are so extreme that we cannot believe that you and the men under you will not fail to come to the rescue of people who will be so situated.'

Five men had signed this letter in the name of the Reform Committee. The first was Cecil Rhodes' brother, Colonel Frank Rhodes. The next was John Hays Hammond. Lionel Phillips, President of the Transvaal Chamber of Mines, also signed, as did George Farrar, who represented a French mining syndicate, and Charles Leonard, who chaired the Transvaal National Union.

When Jameson asked for volunteers (who, he pointed out, would all be financially reimbursed) every man stepped forward. That evening they set out towards the Transvaal frontier, roughly five miles away.

At the same time 400 officers and men from the Mashonaland Mounted Police also crossed the border. They brought 150 African servants, 640 horses, 158 mules, eight Maxim machine guns and three cannons. They marched all that night and by morning had only 141 miles left before they would reach Johannesburg. In the meantime they joined forces with 122 officers and men of the Bechuanaland Border Police. So a total of 522 – instead of the 1,500 originally considered necessary – were on the march to the city of gold.

What none of these volunteers knew, because Jameson had not told them, was that the Reform Committee had also sent him a second letter. In this they ordered him that on no account was he to make public the contents of their first letter until he received their permission to do so. Incidentally, their first letter was deliberately undated, so that Jameson could fill in whatever date he wished.

Kimberley, Salisbury, Pretoria, Johannesburg and Cape Town were many days' ride apart, but all were linked by telegraph lines. Jameson ordered two troopers to cut the line to Pretoria, which he believed rather naively would ensure that news of the column would remain unknown until they reached Johannesburg. Troopers detailed for this task had been drinking before the march started, and to them one telegraph line looked much like another. They cut the wrong one.

This had the catastrophic result of cutting the vital cable link with Cape Town and Cecil Rhodes, but leaving open the line to Pretoria – an exact reversal of what Jameson planned. Jameson, therefore, never received Rhodes' message: 'On no account whatever must you leave. I most strongly object to such a course.' And within days the Boers in Pretoria knew that a large armed British detachment was on the march to Johannesburg. They began to make their own plans to defeat it.

Kruger had meanwhile also received regular reports of the column's progress along its route, and also from his own people in Johannesburg. He was strongly urged to attack it before they could reach Johannesburg. He replied, in a kind of parable, that before anyone could kill a tortoise it must first put out its head. Now Jameson's head was out.

As the column marched they saw groups of Boer riders, sometimes as many as 200, who began to follow them at some distance. This was unwelcome attention, but not as worrying as it would have been had they known that their progress was being monitored in Pretoria, day by day, hour by hour.

The column's commissariat failed. Some troops found a deserted shop and searched it unsuccessfully for any food. All they could find was a cask of bad sherry, which they drank. The horses had little grass to eat: all fodder had to be reserved for the animals pulling the guns.

At Krugersdorp, twenty miles from Johannesburg, the column reached a wide track with wire fences on either side. Now they had 100 Boers following them, with twice as many visible on either side, all just out of rifle range. But Jameson, still believing that their progress was only arousing local interest, and assuming (because he thought the telegraph line to Pretoria had been cut) that Kruger knew nothing about this march – or, much more important, the reason for it – led them on towards their goal.

They reached a ridge and paused. Here they should have met members of the Reform Committee in Johannesburg, who were to stage their uprising. But no one had come to meet them. Something obviously had gone wrong. But – what? And why?

Inside Johannesburg the leaders of the Reform Committee had earlier arranged for two men to lead a squad of 100 volunteers who planned to seize the military arsenal in Pretoria. What arms and explosives they could not carry out, they would blow up. This would severely hamper any military action that the Boers might plan in retaliation.

The two leaders chosen decided that they would enjoy a meal in the Rand Club before they left on this hazardous and vital mission. At this last supper they ate and drank so well, however, that next morning they were both found asleep under a billiards table. There was thus no raid on the Pretoria arsenal.

Although Gardner had smuggled drums of rifles into the town, not all had been removed from their drums. The Committee did not possess any large-calibre weapons. To make up for this, they propped a length of steel water pipe on a cart and covered it with a tarpaulin. From the shape, shrouded as it was, they hoped that Boers in Johannesburg would believe it must be a huge gun.

In Johannesburg members of the Reform Committee asked Major Heany, who was to help organize their uprising, how could they convince Jameson he was not to come.

Heany replied, 'He will come in, as sure as fate.' But he cabled to Rhodes, 'Stop Jameson until I come.' Phillips sent virtually the same message to Beit: 'It is absolutely necessary to delay flotation. If foreign subsidiaries insist on flotation, anticipate complete failure.'

For Rhodes in Cape Town the raid on Johannesburg was not so much military as political. If the Reformers would act as they promised, then the whole thing could be excused as an answer to their appeals for help. Once more the end would justify the means. But he knew that the resolution of the Uitlanders was feeble. Ian Colvin described it as being 'like screwing up a nut with a broken thread. The Reformers simply went round and round but never reached the sticking point.'[7]

The Reformers had in fact asked Francis Younghusband, the Johannesburg correspondent of *The Times*, to go to Cape Town to impress on Rhodes that Jameson's proposed advance must be delayed. Rhodes and Younghusband walked in the garden of Groote Schuur discussing something that should have been agreed months earlier.

'Is there no *man* up there?' asked Rhodes angrily, when he heard how the Uitlanders had lost enthusiasm for revolt. Then, remembering Younghusband's record as an explorer in Tibet and as one of Britain's most successful and intrepid secret agents, Rhodes suddenly asked him, 'Won't *you* lead them?'

Younghusband felt flattered, but explained that he was not well known in Johannesburg.

'Then,' said Rhodes decisively, 'we must stop Jameson.'

To Rhodes, in the opinion of Ian Colvin, 'it was a hideous, slow-dawning contingency that Jameson might move alone. The suggestion that Rhodes ever agreed to such an isolated move could only be by malice or ignorance. The whole idea threw him into a state of nervous apprehension.'

On Saturday, 28 December, Charles Leonard, a lawyer and chairman of the National Union and Reform Committee in Johannesburg, and F.H. Hamilton, the editor of the Johannesburg *Star*, who had come to Cape Town specially to appraise the situation, warned Rhodes that any military intervention would only antagonize the Dutch, whose co-operation Rhodes needed. It would also cost the sympathy of ordinary citizens and cause immediate distrust of anything that Rhodes or the Chartered might say or do. Rhodes agreed.

'I have already sent Jameson a message not to move,' he told them. 'I shall send him another today.' But this message, if it was ever sent, could not reach him.

Meanwhile, several miles outside Johannesburg on the veld, the Boers were waiting on the far side of the ridge where Jameson had halted. The column attacked the Boers and was driven back. It then tried to change direction, go south and reach Johannesburg another way, but this route was also impassable. They were trapped, surrounded on every side.

The Boers, all bearded, wore dust-coloured shirts and trousers, and felt hats with wide, floppy brims, with bandoliers of cartridges across their chests. To the weary men who faced them they were almost indistinguishable from the dusty veld. As one British officer said bitterly, 'We were shooting at puffs of smoke'.

[7] Colvin, op. cit. p. 115

Finally the column could march no further. They had covered 169 miles in eighty-six hours and had been fighting a running and unnerving battle for the last seventeen. They were dispirited and hungry. They had eaten their last meal at eight o'clock the previous morning, seventeen miles on the other side of Krugersdorp.

Worst of all, they now realized that Johannesburg had failed them. There would be no uprising inside it, no reinforcements to ride out and greet them. They were defeated.

Someone, no one appeared to know who, ran up the white flag of surrender at 9.15 on the morning of Thursday, 2 January, 1896. Actually, the column did not have a white flag to raise. This was not the sort of equipment any army carries, but a woman in a nearby farm took pity on them and handed her white apron to one of the men. This he flew from a wagon shaft.

For Jameson it was a moment of supreme humiliation. His Raid had ended before it had properly begun. They had lost sixteen killed and nineteen wounded, plus another twenty-five or more who had fallen out on the march.

'Jameson was quite without military talent,' wrote Dr Sauer afterwards. 'With his ingrained recklessness he was probably as bad a soldier as could be imagined.'

The Boer commander was at first reluctant to accept his surrender. His information was that 20,000 armed Uitlanders were expected from Johannesburg at any moment and he was wary of a trap. When he realized that no reinforcements were arriving, he rode over to Jameson and his officers who waited wretchedly in a rectangular cattle kraal walled with loose stones. The raid was over – and with it all hope for any quick reconciliation and federation of the Boers and the British in South Africa under Rhodes.

If the raid had been a success, Rhodes planned to see the Governor and explain how he had responded to appeals for help from the Reformers, but now Rhodes knew he could do nothing; it was pointless going to see him.

On Monday the Governor's Secretary called twice at Rhodes' office to give him the Governor's instructions: 'Call back Dr Jameson immediately'. But Rhodes did not leave his house all morning, so he never received the message. By then, of course, the time for sending and receiving instructions was long past.

Rhodes sat alone, brooding. Hamilton called to see him and found him almost in despair; Jameson had gone against his orders, he said, and he was ruined. Then he recovered from his gloom to tell Hamilton shrewdly that they had at least twenty-four hours before the public would know anything about this fiasco. Hamilton agreed to see editors of Cape Town newspapers and persuade them to prepare the public for what had happened.

Rhodes asked Rutherfoord Harris to cable to *The Times* in London the letter that Jameson had read to his troops. And then, ironically, he found he had to entertain to lunch Lord Hawke's English cricket eleven who were touring South Africa.

That afternoon, freed from any need to appear cheerful in front of his guests, he went up alone to Table Mountain and stood looking down at the sea, wondering what would happen to him. He had not exaggerated his position to Hamilton. He might still be a very rich man, but politically he was ruined.

That evening he asked the Attorney General, William P. Schreiner, to come and see him. Schreiner described Rhodes as 'a man I had never seen before. His appearance was utterly dejected and different.'

Before Schreiner could speak, Rhodes said, 'Yes, yes, it is true. Old Jameson has upset my apple cart.'

He repeated the sentence, 'Old Jameson has upset my apple cart. He has ridden in.'

Schreiner had seen Rhodes the previous day and now asked him why he had said nothing about Jameson then.

'I thought I had stopped him, and I did not want to say anything about it,' Rhodes explained. 'Poor old Jameson. Twenty years of being friends, and now he goes in and ruins me. . . . I cannot go and destroy him.'

On Tuesday morning the main topic of conversation in Cape Town was the raid. Rhodes called on the Governor to offer his resignation.

'From that moment, with some few exceptions, Dutch and English in South Africa fell back into opposite and hostile camps. The raid was like a bugle call dividing them.'[8]

Rhodes did not sleep for five nights. He locked his bedroom door, and Tony, his personal servant, could hear him pacing up and down. By five o'clock each morning Rhodes would be out, riding along the mountainside. When his secretary brought him cascades of telegrams that had arrived he appeared uncharacteristically indecisive.

He would pick up one telegram and glance at it, then a second or a third, as though unable to understand their messages and incapable of framing answers. Meanwhile, all the friends he had made in the good years were either preparing to stand by him – or to abandon him.

Jan Hofmeyr, with whom Rhodes had for years worked amicably, sent a telegram to President Kruger: 'I hope your burghers will acquit themselves like heroes against Jameson's filibusters.'

'Now that I am down,' Rhodes said, 'I shall see who are my real friends.' Later, he added, 'It is worthwhile being down to see who are your real friends.'

[8] Colvin, op. cit. p. 126

Jameson and his colleagues in the rectangular stone cattle kraal outside Doornkop appeared to have no friends, although their captors did not treat them harshly. Indeed, relations seemed so cordial that on the way to Pretoria, where they were taken under strong guard, both sides drew teams and held a shooting match at targets. Ironically, the column's marksmen won. Then, in Pretoria, they were imprisoned in the capital's jail.

In Johannesburg, meanwhile, the Reform Committee had made a futile show of distributing arms and having trenches dug. Little groups of men with rifles rode importantly here and there. Many Uitlanders believed that Jameson and his columns were expected at any hour. When news began to come in that they had been captured and all this warlike activity was only play-acting many besieged the headquarters of the Reform Committee, shouting angrily: 'Judas! Judas!'

At first opinion in Britain was strongly against Rhodes and Jameson. Then, from a totally unexpected source, came news that instantly made them heroes in the eyes of the British.

The Kaiser was so incensed at the thought that the Boers, who had been armed largely by German companies and trained by German instructors, could be in any danger of attack that he resolved to send a detachment of German Marines to the Transvaal to protect German residents and to make the strongest representation of his displeasure to the British Government. His ministers dissuaded him; Germany did not possess a navy capable of carrying out such an action.

The Kaiser then proposed declaring a Protectorate over the Transvaal if need be. Again his ministers calmed him, and finally he grudgingly agreed that all he would do was to send a telegram to Kruger.

'I express to you my sincere congratulations that you and your people, without appealing to the help of friendly powers, have succeeded, by your own energetic action against the armed bands which invaded your country as disturbers of the peace, in restoring peace and in maintaining the independence of the country against attacks from without.'

When this telegram of congratulations appeared in British newspapers the British public rallied instantly to Rhodes and Jameson. There is something about what can be plausibly portrayed as a gallant defeat that rallies British public opinion almost as strongly as a victory.

Anti-German feeling in Britain exploded – as did anti-British feeling in Germany. Many used this outburst of (carefully orchestrated) popular feeling as an excuse to promote the construction of a more powerful Germany navy.

CHAPTER 11

'IT IS OCCASIONS LIKE THIS THAT MAKE LIFE WORTH LIVING.'

Barney Barnato was in London at the time of the raid and his cousin, David Harris, was standing in for him in Cape Town. When Harris went to see Rhodes to remind him that the De Beers' general meeting was due within a few days he found Rhodes unshaven and distraught. Harris showed him the accounts and Rhodes thumbed through them mechanically as though they had little meaning for him. He told Harris that he could not make any public appearance for the moment and asked Harris to take his place at the meeting.

Meanwhile London newspapers were reporting from Johannesburg on conditions in the town. Crowds of refugees had arrived from outlying farms and homesteads to avoid being caught in any battle between Jameson's column and the Boers. Prices had risen so steeply that many people simply could not afford to buy food. Barney at once approved a cheque for £5,000 which would be given by Barnato Brothers 'for the alleviation of distress in the community'.

Lionel Phillips travelled to Pretoria with three colleagues to see the Boer Chief Justice in an attempt to defuse the situation. The Chief Justice appeared co-operative and promised that the Kruger Government would lower railway charges, abolish duties on various goods and make other gestures of goodwill.

He then made the point that the Reform Committee members in Johannesburg were – technically, at least – rebels, and he asked Phillips to prove to him that they genuinely believed they represented the Uitlanders.

Phillips was gratified by what he took to be a sincere attempt to deal with the matter and naively presented the Chief Justice with a list of all those involved, including Solly Joel, who, like Dr Sauer, had joined the Committee very belatedly. Solly Joel and Dr Sauer were then both arrested at the Rand Club and, with John Hays Hammond and George Farrar – and Lionel Phillips – were put in jail. By nightfall sixty-four Reform Committee members were behind bars.

As an immediate reaction shares in Barney's companies dropped sharply. The Johannesburg Stock Exchange was closed for two days and hundreds of investors in Britain bombarded Barney with letters demanding the return of their investments, a hysterical request obviously impossible to implement.

One man, who had illegally used his employer's funds to buy shares for himself in the hope that he could sell them at a profit and so conceal his theft, feared that his dishonesty would now be discovered. He shot himself, leaving a note: 'Barnato's Bank is the cause of everything.'

Barney called a special meeting of shareholders in the grand room of the Cannon Street Hotel to try to explain the situation in a rational way. He realized that this would be a harrowing occasion for them, and for him, and a serious test of his own abilities. He therefore dressed with particular care, like an actor who knows he faces a very hostile audience and must give an impeccable performance. He wore a flower in his buttonhole, a crimson waistcoat, pince-nez on his nose, and had his moustache carefully waxed. Unusually, he asked his wife Fanny to be present, which showed that, despite his outward appearance of confidence, Barnato was inwardly greatly concerned about the outcome, as he had much cause to be.

So many shareholders arrived to hear him speak that, as when Rhodes would address a meeting, hundreds could not even get into the building. Of those who could, some cheered Barney and others jeered him angrily and shouted abuse.

Barney stood up on the dais, a small and lonely figure. He gave no outward sign of his real feelings, but was determined to control the meeting. He held a silver tankard in one hand and sipped from it as he spoke. He regarded this meeting as a supreme test of his abilities and handled the shareholders as adroitly as he had handled other unappreciative audiences years earlier when he was appearing as The Great Barnato.

He explained that he had been in South Africa for twenty-two years and so was not likely to destroy all his work in as many weeks. He spoke quietly and rationally. He drew the attention of the shareholders to the huge dividends they had received in earlier years, sometimes 36 per cent, or even 60 per cent on their original investment. Gradually the heckling stopped as Barney explained candidly that setbacks beyond anyone's control could upset even him, with his astonishing record of making money for investors as well as for himself.

From time to time he paused dramatically, raised the tankard and drank from it. Shareholders imagined that he was drinking a pint of beer and admired him for doing so at such a moment. He was a card all right, was Barney. Fancy having a pint when he was addressing such a momentous meeting – and so early in the morning! In fact the tankard did not contain beer but champagne, which helped to give Barney much more confidence than he could ever have found in a jug of ale.

He ended his speech, following his own maxim of always ending with a good curtain: 'I tell you that the name of the Barnato Bank will not die out while the name of Barnato Brothers lives!'

Afterwards some shareholders might think on reflection that this statement was meaningless, but at the time Barney's ringingly confident words cheered them – and they cheered him. He left to a round of genuinely approving applause, prudently before he faced questions for which he might not have ready answers.

Privately Barney felt that Jameson and Rhodes had acted with almost unbelievable folly. He had personally lost a great deal of money as shares went down, but his loyalty to his colleagues was very strong. Never did he publicly criticize either Jameson or Rhodes.

Meanwhile the Transvaal Government agreed that Jameson and others involved as leaders could be brought to England to stand trial. They appeared initially at Bow Street police court. Then six out of the original fifteen were committed for trial at the High Court. Other members of the Reform Committee remained in Pretoria jail.

It was announced that they would be tried under Roman Dutch law, which maintained the death sentence for treason. The accused were informed, however, that, if they pleaded guilty, they could expect lenient sentences. If they pleaded not guilty the prosecution could press for the maximum sentence.

Barney travelled to South Africa and visited them in jail. Solly Joel's wife was a regular visitor, smuggling in some luxuries to them. She put packets of cigars on her head under her huge hat and once even concealed two ducks in her bustle.

Instead of employing a local judge to try the prisoners, Kruger engaged Judge Gregoroski, the State Attorney from the Orange Free State. At first this seemed to augur well for a totally fair trial, which would be unbiased by the considerable anti-British feeling that the raid had aroused among Boers in Johannesburg and Pretoria.

Before the trial the usually lugubrious President took a number of drives around Pretoria in a new open State coach. He wore a Republican sash and waved to cheering crowds who threw flowers at his escort. At first these outings also seemed to augur well for the trial. As a showman, Barney believed that these rather theatrical appearances were Kruger's attempt to show himself to British and Boers alike as a kindly, almost avuncular figure. His nickname was Oom Paul – Uncle Paul – and these drives could reinforce this comfortable Pickwickian image.

Then someone told Barney that the judge had been asking whether anyone in Pretoria could provide him with a black cap, which he would need to wear should he have to pronounce the death sentence. Immediately Barney realized that his friends and colleagues could be in very serious trouble. He was right.

Death was the sentence that Judge Gregoroski passed on John Hays Hammond, on Frank Rhodes, Lionel Phillips and George Farrar. Other members of the Reform Committee, including Solly Joel, were sentenced to two years' imprisonment, with a £2,000 fine each, and banishment from the Republic for three years.

Barney was in court when the sentences were announced and at once he rushed up to the judge, shouting abuse at sentences of death being passed on his friends. Had anyone else behaved as Barney did then, they would have been escorted from the courthouse at the least, and probably charged with contempt. But Barney's position as one of the wealthiest men in the Transvaal, and its largest employer, was too well known to allow any such reaction. A single word from him, so many Boers believed, could fire the uprising that Rhodes and Jameson had so signally failed to ignite.

Later that day, in the Rand Club, Barney saw Judge Gregoroski and a further shouting match began.

'You are no gentleman,' replied the judge coldly.

'And you are no judge, Mr Gregoroski!' Barney retorted furiously.

Rhodes retreated into himself when he realized that the raid had been a total and terrible failure, what he called a 'fyasco'. He locked himself in his bedroom at night, walked alone on Table Mountain by day. Barney had neither time nor stomach for such negative responses. He was instinctively a man for action. Recriminations and lamentations for what might have been, and what some said so easily could have been, were never for him. From boyhood he had followed his father's sound advice on the importance of getting his blow in first. Now he realized that he held the only possible key to freedom for the prisoners, but he must act quickly. To delay could be fatal for those under sentence of death.

Barney had for long realized the importance of keeping on good personal terms with President Kruger. While Rhodes classed Kruger as a potential enemy, Barney had early on decided that it would be wiser, and far more profitable, to cultivate the President's friendship. Barney would visit Kruger regularly, not to seek some immediate favour, but simply to talk, man to man, about mutual interests and concerns.

This policy had paid initial dividends. When Barney's waterworks company ran into unexpected difficulties, for example, Kruger's personal influence speedily resolved them. As a result, Barney bought shares in the concession which Kruger had given to his son-in-law to extract water from the Vaal River. Both men therefore owed each other a favour.

Barney knew that Kruger wanted to construct a railway line to Delagoa Bay, a project which Rhodes was totally unwilling to subsidize. He called this project 'Kruger's little hobby'. Barney suggested that the railway line from the Cape should go on to Pretoria, with a branch line to Johannesburg. If Kruger agreed with this, then the Cape could help him with his line to Delagoa Bay.

Barney appeared to be on such good terms with the President that individuals and companies in Johannesburg would often seek his advice when they needed a quick decision over some matter that the labyrinthine and notoriously sluggish bureaucracy of Kruger's government was delaying without any apparent reason.

Kruger appreciated Barney's visits. Other Britishers who came to see him would often talk down to him, or so he thought, and usually wanted something from him. Kruger resented this as much as Barney resented any real or imagined condescension. But Barney, as head of enormous financial concerns, could speak on equal terms to the man who was head of a country. Kruger liked their relationship and once told a delegation from Johannesburg exactly why.

'When Mr Barnato wants anything, he always comes to see me himself and we talk it over. But the others always send someone else, unless they want to talk about what they call their rights, and then they all come together.'

The two men would sit on the stoep (verandah) of Kruger's house drinking black coffee. Barney would smoke cigarettes and Kruger a pipe, with a spittoon handy on the floor.

So now Barney went to see Kruger, the only man in the country who could save his friends. For this crucial interview and to emphasize its importance, Barney dressed theatrically, as though going to a funeral. He wore black, with a thick band of black crepe around his hat. The excuse he gave to the President for his visit was that he wished to apologize personally for the offensive remarks he had made to Judge Gregoroski.

Kruger knew that Barney had not been involved in the raid or its planning and was not a member of the Reform Committee, but he still received him coldly. The atmosphere between them became even cooler when Barney declared bluntly that he considered that Boer lawyers had tricked the accused into pleading guilty. Kruger replied that both the trial and the sentences had been entirely fair. Barney sensed that further discussion on these lines would be fruitless, so he came immediately to the very grave decision he had taken if the death sentences were not commuted.

'Mr President,' he said bluntly. 'I have 20,000 whites on my pay-roll and 100,000 blacks. If I close down, I will put more white men out of work than you have burghers in your entire State.

'My concerns also spend £50,000 every week, which will be lost to you. Already, thanks to this political crisis, my mines have lost £20,000,000 in production. Do you want to ruin your country for good and all?'[1]

'The law must be respected,' replied Kruger. 'I will report your views to my Executive Committee.'

To show Barney that their discussion was at an end, he pointed towards the door. Barney went out, and immediately had notices printed and personally posted them up on the gates of his companies. They were brief and unequivocal.

'Notice is hereby given that all our landed properties in this State will be sold by public auction on Monday, 18 May, 1896.'

Kruger could understand and cope with political or military threats, but for the Transvaal's entire economy to be attacked in this way, with potentially disastrous results that would become evident almost immediately, was an attack against which he could not marshal any defence.

Two days later he commuted the death sentences. The British and American Governments had also urged him to show clemency, but Barney's threat was the most potent persuasion. Shortly afterwards Kruger announced that the other members of the Reform Committee would be released after paying their individual fines of £2,000.

The four men who had been sentenced to death were now released on payment of £25,000 each. Cecil Rhodes and Alfred Beit paid their fines.

Rhodes admitted later that, all told, the raid had cost him £800,000. More importantly, it also cost him his Premiership of the Cape. He now left for Kimberley, where the whole town appeared to turn out to meet his train. Rhodes was deeply touched by this spontaneous demonstration of loyalty and affection.

'I am proud to see that at this crisis I can count on so many trustworthy friends on the diamond fields,' he told the crowd. 'There is an idea abroad that my public career is quite at an end. On the contrary, I think it is just beginning, and I have a firm belief that I shall live to do useful work for this country.'

He left for England on the same day as Jameson, but aboard a different ship. In London the Chartered Company's solicitor was already working on Jameson's defence and wished to use a number of telegrams that had passed between the Company's offices in Cape Town and London before the raid. Some of these were thought to have revealed that the Prime Minister and the Colonial Secretary had known of plans for the raid, which could be crucial to Jameson's case.

---

[1] Quoted in *Barney Barnato*, Richard Lewinsohn, E.P. Dutton & Co. Inc., New York, 1938.

If they were made public, however, they could have unprecedented political repercussions in Britain. In such a situation Rhodes guessed that, in retaliation, the British Government might well revoke the charter that allowed his company to administer Rhodesia. He had no intention whatever of allowing this to happen.

Soon after he arrived in London he had an appointment to see the Prime Minister. Earlier that day he instructed the Chartered lawyer to visit the Colonial Office, where he would reveal casually that he held certain telegrams which *could* be used at Jameson's trial. The inference was clear. When Rhodes met the Prime Minister shortly afterwards, the question of ending the charter was not mentioned. Rhodes had squared the opposition. He now returned to South Africa – to face another crisis.

In his absence the Matabeles had taken advantage of the fact that their police force had been denuded to supply men for Jameson's column. Their witch doctors realized that this provided an exceptional opportunity for the warriors to rise up against the whites who had taken over their country.

Exaggerated accounts of the Jameson defeat had reached them. Rinderpest, also known as cattle plague, was decimating their herds. These two catastrophes combined to convince them that the power of the white man was waning. Now was the time to rise up and drive out these interlopers for ever, for such a chance might never come again.

The Matabeles had already killed twenty-three Europeans, and what was especially alarming about this was that the killers were native policemen who the Company had recruited, helped by other men from neighbouring villages, including Lobengula's brother.

The revolt spread rapidly. By mid-April the rebels were in control of the country, except for the towns of Bulawayo, Salisbury and Victoria. Matabele warriors now marched on Bulawayo, the capital of their old King, Lobengula, and encamped around the town on three sides, leaving clear a fourth, to the south. They appeared to think that, since this road was deliberately left open, the settlers would use it to escape. When they realized that this was not going to happen, and that the British were staying on in the town, some proposed that they attack immediately.

British troops had meanwhile arrived from the Cape with armed volunteers and Chartered Company police, but the Matabeles had learned from the example of the Boers outside Johannesburg how to stand up to adversaries trained in text-book tactics of attack and defence. They simply dispersed to the Matopo hills, which are about seventy miles long and thirty miles broad. Here the Matabeles hid in caves, behind boulders, among rock outcrops. A British patrol might drive them from one hide-out, but as soon as the patrol had gone, within an hour they would be back in position again.

War on this scale could take years, and neither Rhodes nor the Chartered had years available to them. Yet if Rhodes and the Chartered did not quell this rebellion, the British Government was unlikely to shoulder the burden. Rhodesia could be abandoned and, in the words of Rhodes' secretary, Philip Jourdan, 'revert to barbarism again'.

As Rhodes considered how best he might achieve this, he received a telegram from the Prime Minister in London. It requested him and Alfred Beit to resign as Chartered Company directors. Rhodes cabled back characteristically: 'Let resignations wait – we fight Matabele tomorrow.'

Since Rhodes would not resign, he was dismissed as a director. Then he suffered a further setback.

The Shonas of Mashonaland, who Rhodes had always regarded as his allies, because he had broken the Matabeles' hold over them, now joined the rebellion. He had to stop this spreading revolt urgently or shares in Chartered would fall disastrously and the whole company could collapse. Worst of all, he feared that then the name Rhodesia might be changed.

'They can't take that away,' said Rhodes desperately, trying to convince himself. 'They can't change the name. Did you ever hear of a country's name being changed?'

Rhodes had no intention of allowing this and travelled to Bulawayo to resolve what seemed to many to be an intractable problem. He stayed with Earl Grey, who had followed Jameson and was administering Rhodesia from Government House, built on the site of Lobengula's burned-out kraal. Early one morning Rhodes went to see his host. During the night he had been pondering his present unhappy situation, and then characteristically had decided he still possessed advantages on which he could congratulate himself.

'Have you never realized,' Rhodes asked the surprised Earl, 'that you might have been a Chinaman, or a Hottentot, or that most degraded of men, a Mashona? But you are not. You are an Englishman, and have consequently drawn the *greatest* prize in the lottery of life. I always think of that when I am bothered, and it carries me through all my troubles – I am an Englishman.'

On a personal level, Rhodes was ill with malaria, contracted some weeks earlier. He could not be rid of the lingering fever and the physical weakness that accompanied it. Also, he was now acting on his own. Jameson, his ally for so long, was awaiting trial and Rhodes knew that he personally was also due to face a Committee of Enquiry in Cape Town, and then a more important Parliamentary Enquiry in London into the background of the raid.

Time was even more pressing than it had ever been before, and he realized that a direct attack on the Matabeles would be useless. The only way out of these increasing political and military difficulties was to meet their leaders face to face, come to terms with them and, hopefully, square them.

Out of power, out of office, Rhodes' personality and charisma still made him the only man in all Africa who had any hope of ending this conflict. He therefore sent out agents to the indunas to arrange a meeting. Their reply was uncompromising: 'If the whites are tired of fighting they can come and surrender to us here.'[2]

Rhodes then discovered that one of the wives of Lobengula's father was still alive. She knew the leaders of the rebellion personally and was persuaded to use her authority to help Rhodes make contact with them. Finally, after several false starts, they agreed to meet him, but only on the strict condition he was not accompanied by more than three other men. They feared a trick. But, from Rhodes' point of view, was their apparent willingness to talk only a trick to kill *him*, or maybe to capture him and hold him to ransom?

These were the risks Rhodes knew he had to take. The rebellion was costing the Chartered Company about £4,000 a week. They simply could not afford to spend such a sum indefinitely without any guarantee or even prospect of ultimate success.

Rhodes therefore agreed to their conditions and, as evidence of his good faith, moved two miles away from where the nearest British forces were encamped. If the Matabele attacked him and his small party, it would be impossible to attempt a rescue. He would be out on his own.

He had a tent wagonette in which he slept. His interpreter, Johann Colenbrander, a frontiersman from Natal, slept in another tent. Philip Jourdan, Rhodes' secretary, slept in the open air, which he preferred. One day, some time after they had taken up their position, they were surprised to see a British rider approach with an escort of twenty armed men also on horseback. One carried a huge Union Jack.

Rhodes, who was sitting on a biscuit box, watched with surprise the arrival of these uninvited visitors. The leader turned out to be a British official from Bulawayo. He had felt offended because Rhodes had not confided in him exactly how he hoped to resolve the fighting. Now he wanted to find out for himself what was happening.

Rhodes possessed only one chair. This the official now sat in and asked when the chiefs were due to arrive. Rhodes ignored his question and pointed to the flag.

'What is this?' he asked.

'The Union Jack.'

'I am well aware of that, but what is it doing here?'

'It is my symbol of authority,' replied the official. 'Do you expect the Kaffirs to come? I thought you had arranged for them to meet *me*.'

'They will come and see me,' Rhodes corrected him. 'But when they have

[2] Terence O. Ranger, *Revolt in Southern Rhodesia 1896–87*, Heinemann, London, 1967.

seen you arrive with an armed escort, they will assume that there is someone to be arrested and shot. You will think me a funny fellow. I *am* a funny fellow. But you must remember, I am a Privy Councillor.'

So Rhodes bid the official and his escort farewell. He then had to wait for six weeks before Babiaan, one of the indunas who years earlier had gone to London with Maund, came to see him.

Babiaan looked old and withered and nervous. He still feared that this meeting could be a trap in some way, but Rhodes explained that it was a genuine attempt to end the conflict quickly, with no loss of face and, most important, no further loss of life.

Rhodes entertained Babiaan so well that he remarked that this life was better than the one he had grown accustomed to, living rough in the hills. Rhodes' valet, Antony de la Cruz, known as Tony, part Chinese, part Goanese, was an excellent cook. There was plenty of game to be shot and Babiaan and Rhodes enjoyed the chops Rhodes preferred when out in the veld.

According to one of his secretaries, Rhodes was 'a valiant trencherman – one might almost call him a gross feeder'. He liked to have the joint in front of him on the table and then would cut off 'great hunks of meat'. At dinner in the civilized surroundings of Groote Schuur, he would go to a side table, carve himself meat and carry it over to his plate on the fork.

Whenever Rhodes travelled by ship between South Africa and England chickens were taken aboard to supply him with fresh eggs, and a cow for milk. He was also very partial to potted meats and sometimes reserved a whole cabin to be packed with delicacies from Fortnum and Mason. Here the food was less sophisticated but much enjoyed by Babiaan, who stayed with Rhodes for two weeks and then returned to explain to his fellow indunas that it would be perfectly safe for them to come and talk with Rhodes as well. So they arrived, one by one, to stay for several days.

During these weeks of negotiation Rhodes received the news from Bulawayo that Jameson and the other leaders had been sentenced; Jameson received the harshest sentence – 15 months imprisonment, without hard labour. Rhodes sat silent for a moment when he heard this news and then remarked drily that the sentences were 'a tribute to the unctuous rectitude of my countrymen who have jumped the whole world!'

Sometimes, when no indunas were with Rhodes, British visitors would ride out to his camp. One was Father Barthelemy, who was in charge of the Jesuit mission in Bulawayo and had been extremely helpful to men in the Pioneer column.

The conversation turned on religion and the priest was surprised when Rhodes described in accurate detail the seventeen years of probation Barthelemy had undergone before he could be called 'Father'.

'How is it, you know so much about us and our course of training?' Barthelemy asked him.

'I study all these questions,' Rhodes replied. 'I am not at all sure that if I were not as I am I should have not been a Jesuit.'

'You say, if you were not what you are. What *are* you?'

'Ah, there you have asked me a very difficult question,' Rhodes admitted. 'Let us think it out. I suppose you would call me an agnostic – *agnosco*, I don't know.

'I believe in a future state, but what it is I don't know and what is more, *you* don't know. I have never found anyone who could tell *me* what it is, and you have never found anyone to tell *you*, but I believe that if one does one's best in this world, according to one's lights, and does no harm intentionally to anyone, I shall get as good a place in that future state as you will who make a profession of your religion.

'In fact, if I was to go before the Almighty tomorrow, and He was to tell me that He thought I had acted very badly at times and had wronged some people wittingly, say Kruger, for instance, well – I should be prepared to have it out with Him.'

'Upon my soul, Mr Rhodes,' was the priest's reply. 'I believe you would.'[3]

Rhodes could see value in every belief in a God, no matter the name by which this God might be known.

'A man who says there is no God is a fool,' he would say. And on another occasion, after listening to colleagues having a heated religious argument, 'Let a man be a Buddhist, let him be a Mohammedan, let him be a Christian or what you will; let him call himself what he likes, but if he does not believe in a Supreme Being, he is no man – he is no better than a dog.'

The talks with the indunas lingered on, usually lasting late into the night. Rhodes never lost patience and, indeed, seemed to acquire extraordinary physical strength and stamina during these prolonged sessions.

Every morning he and his colleagues would ride from five o'clock, often until noon. Jourdan admitted that by then he sometimes felt almost too tired to dismount, but Rhodes showed no apparent signs of fatigue. He ate breakfast and then he would frequently talk to the chiefs staying with him, through the heat of day, until four in the afternoon. Horses were then saddled up again and he would ride until dusk. After dinner Rhodes would chat for several more hours with whoever was staying with him.

Sometimes, after an unusually long ride on an exceptionally hot morning, Rhodes would leave the breakfast table and literally throw himself down on the earth in the shade of the nearest tree. He would sleep there for half an hour and then get up refreshed.

[3] Michell, op. cit, p.177

When Rhodes was staying in Groote Schuur he usually rode twice a day and played bridge until late most evenings. As a result he would often rise later next morning; gradually his rides became shorter and then tailed off altogether. It was noticed that his heart condition became more troublesome when he stopped riding. His habit of playing cards until the early hours and smoking heavily most of the time did nothing to help his health. His face appeared swollen and bluish and his temper did not improve.

It had been agreed that all the negotiators would be unarmed, but one day more than 400 armed Matabeles came down from the hills and faced Rhodes. He and Colenbrander, with Mrs Colenbrander and her sister, who had come out to see them, were on horseback.

'Keep on your horses!' shouted Colenbrander warningly, but Rhodes ignored this advice. He dismounted and walked towards the nearest leader.

'How can I trust you?' he asked him. 'You asked us to carry no guns and stated that you would not. Until you lay down your weapons, I will not discuss a single point.'

Some of the warriors began to mutter among themselves. Rhodes turned to several of the older indunas.

'Why do you permit this?' he asked them. 'These young men are out of hand. You cannot control them.'

The chiefs admitted that this was so, explaining feebly, as old men tend to do when excusing their diminishing authority, 'The young men of today are no longer to be controlled as they were when Lobengula was alive. They are too much for us.'

'Do not allow your authority to be set aside in this fashion,' Rhodes told them bluntly. 'I will stand by you. Order your men to put down their guns at once, or we shall go back and the war will begin again.'

For a few moments no one moved; then, one by one, the warriors placed their rifles on the ground.

Within ten minutes all arms had been laid down. Rhodes then asked them to tell him their grievances, and promised that they would all be examined thoroughly, and redress made.

'Now for the future,' said Rhodes when they had explained the injustices that had caused them such distress. 'Is it peace or is it war?'

One by one the chiefs placed their own spears on the ground, a sign that the war had ended.

Rhodes walked back to his wagonette, amid shouts from the Matabeles of 'Inkosi!' ['Master! Chief!']. He turned to his colleagues and said with quiet satisfaction: 'It is occasions like that make life worth living.'

Africans admired him; some would say they almost worshipped him. They called him 'The Separator of Fighting Bulls' because by his own example he had been instrumental in ending a war that could have destroyed the infant

Rhodesia. Yet Rhodes at that time was acting solely on his own initiative. He had no political authority, no military command, no Chartered Company to give him authority. He was simply Cecil Rhodes. This success in ending a war virtually on his own was hailed as the greatest achievement of his career.

From the ruins of everything for which he had worked for so long, Rhodes' reputation – in Africa, at least – now stood higher than it had ever previously been. But whether he was being acclaimed or criticized, Rhodes never changed his own views – or lost sight of his ultimate aim. He was a man of little ostentation. Like an iceberg, nine-tenths of his feelings were almost always below the surface, out of sight. And of all the sayings of Marcus Aurelius, which he read time and again, one probably influenced his life most strongly: 'It is in thy power, whenever thou wilt, to retire into thyself; and nowhere is there any place whereto a man may retire quieter and more free from politics than his own soul. Constantly, then, you must retreat and renew thyself therein.'

All who knew Rhodes and worked with him recalled his early morning rides, when often he would not speak, but simply sat on his horse, brooding, retiring into his own thoughts. Others recalled how he loved to walk alone on Table Mountain in good times or in bad. As the psalmist in the Bible put it, 'I will lift up mine eyes unto the hills, from whence cometh my help.'

Rhodes liked old things; the past was a country he was always pleased to rediscover. Outside Cape Town at Rondebosch stood an old building which the Dutch governor, in the days of the Dutch East India Company, had originally built as a government granary, known as Groote Schuur, the great granary. Later, it had been adapted as a house.

Rhodes bought it and engaged a young British architect, Herbert Baker, to restore it completely, to look as it had appeared when originally built. This house became a central point in his life. It reflected his own taste and outlook.

Baker's brief was that Rhodes wanted it 'to be big and simple, barbaric if you like . . . I like teak and whitewash.'

Rhodes had a rare instinct for personal craftsmanship and an equally strong dislike for items made by machines. Baker had to replace all imported ironwork such as hinges, and even screws in the doors, and then engage local craftsmen to remake them in bronze and brass. The rooms were simply furnished with solid teak beams, and panelled walls. Teak was not indigenous to South Africa but the original builders used it because they could not find local wood of the strength they wanted. So in recreating the house, Rhodes ordered teak. The ceilings were plastered and whitewashed.

Rhodes found old furniture – chairs, benches made by Boer hunters, pinned together, and inlaid with dates or initials in animal bone or ivory. His bedroom faced Table Mountain. In Groote Schuur he entertained all visiting dignitaries from Lord Randolph Churchill to Rudyard Kipling, who came out every summer to stay in a house on his estate.

Groote Schuur was surrounded by 1,500 acres, mostly undergrowth when he bought it, but a park within a very short time. 'I have bought all this,' Rhodes would say. 'But I don't possess it.' His estate was open to the public to walk through and enjoy. He installed a huge menagerie of wild animals, not in cages but on the open land. It was his pleasure that others, less rich or fortunate than himself, should enjoy what they might have no other chance of seeing.

One of the most interesting rooms in Groote Schuur was Rhodes' library. From boyhood he had been fascinated by writings of the Roman emperors, Gibbon's 'Decline and Fall of the Roman Empire' and of course the sayings of Marcus Aurelius, were always in his mind. On his first journey north from Cape Town to Kimberley, he had carried (and lost) Plutarch's 'Lives of the Greeks and Romans'. So now his library contained a huge selection of such works.

He commissioned Hatchards in London to provide translations of the original sources that Gibbon had used when writing 'Decline and Fall'. His instructions were that they should all be 'absolutely unabridged'. They were now typewritten and bound in red morocco. They stretched to several hundred volumes and Rhodes spent between £8,000 and £10,000, until he was convinced he had copies of all the sources in his possession.

The books also went into full details of the perversions of later emperors and empresses, and were illustrated by drawings taken from medallions and coins which, in Le Sueur's view, were 'of a decidedly erotic nature'. So erotic were they, indeed, that when he catalogued the volumes he felt that a number of them should be locked away.

After Rhodes died, he went through these books, and found that 'despite all precautions, the illustrations were cut out and removed . . . I have a shrewd idea as to the culprit.' He did not say who this might be, but such a mass of printed and illustrated erotica was strange to find in the library of a man 'who was said to blush at the slightest mention of sex'.[4]

The library also had a cabinet which contained phallic carvings from the Zimbabwe ruins where apparently a form of phallus worship was once the religion. That Rhodes was surrounded by young men who, although loosely described as secretaries, had little secretarial experience, aptitude or qualifications, and the fact that no women servants whatever worked in Groote Schuur, added to rumours that Rhodes, while outwardly puritan,

[1] *Cecil Rhodes and the Princess*, Brian Roberts, Hamish Hamilton, 1969.

inwardly might not have been quite so puritanical. The fact was that Rhodes preferred the company of men with whom he could be at ease, rather than women.

The house that Barney Barnato was building in Park Lane, London, was very different. It was constructed of Portland stone, had five storeys and was more a sign of his own prodigious success than a symbol of his good taste.

It had two billiard rooms and, unusually, a complex central heating system with radiators in every room. The interior was in the Renaissance style. The children's rooms had their own kitchen, bathroom, nursery, schoolroom, all on one floor. From the top rooms he could see the Crystal Palace to the south, and the hills of Highgate to the north. The cost soon soared from the original £40,000 estimate for building and £30,000 for decorations – despite his strange premonition that he would never live in it himself.

Other diamond magnates, such as Joseph B. Robinson, filled their London mansions with paintings, as an investment as much as for any artistic interest. Barney only bought one painting in his life. This was a pastoral scene by Sydney Cooper entitled 'Group of sheep'. He would say he only bought this because he thought that one of the sheep looked like him.

Despite this, dealers and others tried to interest him in paintings. Once, at the theatre, he noticed a young woman who kept looking at him and smiling in a most friendly fashion. In the interval, she introduced herself, and said she had a collection of valuable paintings which, for personal reasons, she would have to sell. Perhaps Mr Barnato would be interested?

'You really must find time to come and see my Watteau,' she said.

Barney gave her a long look.

'Do you mean that?' he asked.

'Of course.'

'Fine,' he said. 'When's your old man out? Or perhaps we'd better meet somewhere else?'

Only then was it explained to him that Watteau was an artist.

Barney seemed to need to draw attention to his money, because his wealth was a carapace against insults and sneers he had endured from childhood.

Louis Cohen could not understand how Barney was still so worried about money and about his many businesses. He did not appreciate how Barney, like many another who had come from great poverty to great riches, could scarcely believe that the transformation was true, that it had indeed happened to him.

Cohen had heard that Barney was then worth £20,000,000, the equivalent today of several billion. Was this true?

'Yes,' agreed Barney. It was. 'But,' he added, 'I still need another five million to feel *quite* comfortable.'

Like Barney, Rhodes could be spontaneously generous. Once, he invited a deputation of Boer sheep farmers to lunch. They had opposed his bill to make it compulsory for farmers to wash scab-infected sheep with disinfectant. According to the Boers' religious beliefs, this was going against the will of God. If sheep were ill, then that was the wish of the Almighty. When Rhodes' butler suggested to Rhodes that since very few of these guests would have tasted good wine – indeed, any wine at all – he proposed putting out an indifferent vintage for them. Rhodes disagreed.

'No,' he said at once. 'Give them of my best.'

When the men left, one of them picked up a small stone from the gravel path as a memento of their meeting. Rhodes at once took a silver snuff-box from a collection he had, and gave it to the man as a farewell present.

He hated any dirt or untidiness in his house, or ash left by smokers. A number of old brass cuspidors or spittoons were placed on the floor. If guests scattered ash carelessly, Rhodes would pick it up and put it in the spittoon himself. And when he was travelling, he would always look for a camping site which previous travellers had not littered with paper and rubbish.

Cecil Rhodes, like Barney Barnato, preferred simple food, and he was very casual about his clothes. His servant, Tony, bought pairs of the pepper-and-salt trousers he wore, literally by the dozen. He often appeared so shabby, that once he was refused admission to a fete which he had been asked to open.

On any journey or visit he would invariably pick one particular coat or suit and wear it day after day until the cloth was worn through. On one occasion, he finally had to admit that his suit needed cleaning and mending. It was sent to a tailor who returned it with a note to Rhodes' secretary:

Dear Sir,
Herewith the Right Honourable C.J. Rhodes' coat, uncleaned and unmended. We regret that all we can do with the garment is to make a new coat to match the buttons.'

When Rhodes was visiting London, he was commanded to go to Windsor Castle to meet the Queen. He had no court dress; and no idea what clothes he should wear or when. A tailor was approached. He promised to make suitable suits if his staff worked all night. They did, and shortly before the train taking Rhodes to Windsor was due to pull out of Paddington station, a messenger ran along the platform with a suitcase of clothes. The first time Rhodes put them on was when he was dressing for dinner with the Queen.

Barney Barnato, on the other hand, was a natural actor and liked the limelight. When he had stood as a candidate for the Cape parliament, he knew he might face considerable hostility, because some diggers had previously asked him to stand as their representative, and he had declined. Politics did not really interest him – yet now he knew that they would say he was 'hand in hand with Rhodes', and standing not as their representative – but as the ambassador of De Beers.

Instead of driving round his constituency in a Cape cart, Barney sat in a coach drawn by four matching grey horses, which he had been at great pains to find from various farms.

He hired a young man who beat the big drum at local fairs, dressed him in a scarlet frock coat with gold buttons, a velvet cap and top boots, and gave him a trumpet which he had specially sent up for the occasion from Cape Town. The young man blew this trumpet loudly as they went through the streets. On the coach, behind Barney, stood two tall footmen in green livery with gold lace; his postillions wore scarlet jockey caps.

The coach had Barney's monogram painted on each door, and on either side rode six riders also in livery. He wore a silver greatcoat with scarlet lapels, a grey top hat, the biggest carnation he could find in his buttonhole. No one could mistake him. He was the candidate – and he won the seat.

Barney was no longer the little clown who had once been offered five shillings to make people laugh. Now he wanted to impress them, and he did, though some people shouted at him, 'Tomorrow you'll have six horses to draw your coach, while we have to shut up shop'.

This was a reference to the fact that De Beers controlled (and sold) most of the goods imported into the area. They did this, they said, to protect their workers from the high prices local traders were charging. Local traders looked at it differently. They thought they could be crushed unless this could be stopped.

Barney knew their fears, and when people talked to him about such a gloomy prospect, he took them into the nearest bar and bought them a drink, explaining that his father had also been a poor shopkeeper. He was not going to let them suffer.

For Rhodes, Groote Schuur was an expression of his own character; he loved it – but only as an inanimate possession. What affection he had for people he reserved for only a few: his mother, for Neville Pickering, and, latterly, for Dr Jameson.

On his way to take ship for England after the end of the Matabele rebellion, Earl Grey met Rhodes, and said he had bad news for him. Rhodes feared that this concerned Jameson, who he knew was in poor health, and in jail. Had he died?

Grey explained quickly that his news was not about Jameson, but about Groote Schuur. It had been destroyed by fire – with all its contents. Rhodes accepted the news philosophically.

'Is that all? I thought you were going to say that Jameson was dead.'

Then he added: 'Providence has not been kind to me this year. What with Jameson's raid, rebellion, famine, rinderpest, I feel like Job – all but the boils.'

He left for England in the following January 'to face the music', the Parliamentary Enquiry into his involvement in the raid. Travelling through South Africa, Rhodes was impressed by the obvious sincerity of the crowds of people who lined the streets to cheer him.

'It is very moving to see one's fellow beings feel so kindly to one,' he said. 'Such appreciation as this usually comes after a man is dead.'

In South Africa he was still a hero, even to those who condemned the raid; they remembered his past services to the colony. In London, however, he was not so sure of his reception.

At first, the findings of the enquiry went strongly against him. He attended the enquiry twice a week for the three weeks it lasted. He would listen impassively, eating sandwiches and drinking stout in the corridor when the meetings adjourned for lunch.

When Rhodes spoke, he agreed his responsibility for the raid, but went into great detail explaining conditions in South Africa at that time. He also listed his own achievements on behalf of the British Empire, which he maintained far outweighed what he considered were political charges against him.

Throughout the proceedings he appeared reserved, as though the deliberations of the members conducting the enquiry did not really concern him. He might have been an observer, not the person whose conduct was under scrutiny.

When Rhodes was asked specific questions, he refused to answer, giving as his reason the possibility that they might implicate others. When questioned about letters written during the raid, he replied shortly, 'I never write letters.'

In the end, Rhodes was reprimanded, but he retained the title of Privy Councillor. One reason for this result was the strong belief that he knew who in the British Government had known about the raid before it began – and that he possessed cables that would prove this.

He repeatedly refused to reveal details of any relevant telegrams that had passed between the Company's offices in Cape Town and London, explaining he did not have the cables in his possession. This was absolutely true. As he spoke, they were in the briefcase of his counsel sitting by his side.

None of the political parties appeared eager to dig too deeply into who might have known what and when – and why. The Conservatives wished to protect Joseph Chamberlain, the Colonial Secretary. The Liberals lacked enthusiasm for enquiring whether Lord Rosebery or Sir Henry Loch, the Governor of the Cape, had prior knowledge.

The single member of the Irish party, remembering the £10,000 Rhodes had paid to his party, saw no reason for giving further publicity to this. In essence, the enquiry was a charade.

But just in case Sir Hercules Robinson became too loquacious, Chamberlain made it impossible for him to come to London before his successor, Sir Alfred Milner, left England for the Cape. Robinson's secretary, Graham Bower, and a Colonial official, who died before he could appear, eventually took the blame for knowing about the raid but not passing on this knowledge to Sir Hercules or Joseph Chamberlain.

So Rhodes, virtually vindicated, left for South Africa, travelling by way of Europe. Being reprimanded meant little to him. And soon, he would regain his position on the board of the Chartered. He had always been confident that he would 'square' all allegations.

'I arrived in London and saw the busmen and cabbies and other working men touch their hats to me in a friendly way,' he said later. 'I knew I was all right and that the man in the street had forgiven me.'

In Berlin, Rhodes had an audience with the Kaiser. He sought his permission to run telegraph lines across German territory in Africa as part of his intention to link the South with the North. This was given. The Kaiser then asked Rhodes what he personally thought about the congratulatory telegram he had sent to President Kruger at the time of Jameson's raid on Johannesburg.

'I will tell you, your Majesty, in a very few words,' Rhodes replied. 'It was the greatest mistake you ever made in your life, but you did me the best turn one man ever did another.

'You see, I was a naughty boy, and you tried to whip me. Now, my people were quite ready to whip me for being a naughty boy, but directly *you* did it, they said, "No, if this is anybody's business, it is *ours*."

'The result was that your Majesty got yourself very much disliked by the English people, and I never got whipped at all!'[5]

In the middle of their conversation, Rhodes glanced at the clock and suddenly stood up. Court etiquette demanded that he should wait until the Kaiser asked him to leave, but Rhodes simply said: 'Well, goodbye. I have to go now, as I have got some people coming to dinner.'

Back in South Africa, Rhodes and Milner, another bachelor, got on extremely well. Rhodes had aroused strong Imperialist support in Britain, first by his success, then by the failure of the Jameson raid. Admiration, laced with sympathy, has always been a potent combination for influencing the British public.

The Transvaal, with German backing, meanwhile orchestrated a strong anti-British campaign among the Boers. Joseph Chamberlain explained in

[5] Michell, op. cit.

the House of Commons that requests by British subjects in the Transvaal for voting rights had all been refused. The Government appealed to the country 'to support us, if the necessity should arise, in any measures we may think it necessary to take to secure justice to the British subjects in the Transvaal.'[6]

Rhodes did not believe there would be a war between the Boers and the British. Such a conflict could signal the end of everything for which he had worked. He cabled to Beit in London: 'Remember that Kruger, if the Home Government are firm, will in the end give way. All they need to do is to continue preparations as openly as possible. Nothing will make Kruger fire a shot.'

Milner declared ominously that 'The right of Great Britain to intervene to secure fair treatment of Uitlanders is fully equal to her supreme interest in securing it . . .'

Milner and Kruger met at Bloemfontein to try and resolve their differences. Kruger still refused to give the vote to British settlers, and Milner would not discuss any other matters until the President changed his mind. The British then asked for votes to be given to adult Uitlanders after five years' residence in the Transvaal. Kruger replied that he would give them the right to vote (if they had certain other qualifications) after seven years.

So both sides dug themselves in doggedly. Chamberlain told the cabinet in London: 'The position of Great Britain in South Africa, and with it the estimate formed of our power and influence in our colonies and throughout the world, is at stake.'

Jan Christiaan Smuts, the Transvaal's Attorney General, noted: 'War between the Republics and England is certain.'

Twelve thousand British troops were already in South Africa. Ten thousand more were due to arrive in October. The two Boer republics, the Transvaal and the Orange Free State, could probably count on twice as many local volunteers.

Kruger declared that the British should settle all their differences with him by arbitration, withdraw troops already in the Cape, and not land a further detachment, otherwise there would be war. Milner's reply was that the British government considered such conditions 'impossible to discuss'.

Both sides were playing for time. The Boers were waiting for the spring grass to appear on the veld, so that they could have enough to feed their horses in any campaign. The British were waiting until reinforcements arrived.

[6] Parliamentary Debates, 4th series, Vol. 75, 1899.

CHAPTER 12

'MURDER!'

Gold shares were dropping quickly and nowhere was this slide larger than in shares in Barnato companies, which only months previously had reached record heights. Solly was now chairman of the Johannesburg Stock Exchange and took a more reasoned approach to this savage fall in the family enterprises. But to Barney a loss of pennies seemed a crisis, and of pounds the onset of ruin.

Louis Cohen could not understand why Barney still kept on working so hard, and worrying so much.

'If you make five million more, what good will it do you?' he asked him.

'No good,' Barney agreed, and then pointed to a photograph of his two baby sons. 'When I am dead, I would like those two boys, as grown up men, to point to my portrait and say, "Well, he was a clever little chap, that father of ours".'

Clever Barney certainly was, and always had been, but now he appeared to be increasingly consumed by melancholy. Barnato Bank seemed in terminal decline and was taken over by another family company, Johannesburg Consolidated Investments. Many shareholders and others loudly criticized this move. Solly Joel, concerned about his uncle's unusual gloom, proposed to him that one day they should build a huge hotel and a theatre to seat an audience of 1,000. This alluring prospect briefly rallied Barney.

One day he happened to meet Leo Weinthal, who edited the *Pretoria Press* and had acted as interpreter when he met President Kruger. Weinthal told him he was having two large marble lions carved as ornaments for his house. Barney knew that Kruger had hunted lions as a young man, and indeed killed his first at the age of 14. He told Weinthal that he would like to give two lion statues to the President to show that recent events had not undermined his feelings of friendship towards him. Weinthal agreed and it was arranged that Barney would present them to Kruger on the President's 71st birthday in October. Having something definite to look forward to cheered Barney, if only briefly.

He sailed for England late in July. Here his returning confidence received a setback when he found that work on the huge house he was building in Park Lane was behind schedule. The builders promised, however, that all would be finished before Queen Victoria's Diamond Jubilee in the following June.

Barney spent that summer largely passing time. He went to the theatre, to the races, and drove around London in his splendid carriage, but somehow the sparkle had gone out of his life. He seemed no longer the ebullient, irrepressible Barney. News of Barnato Bank's being absorbed – after a public meeting, called so quickly that shareholders in Britain and the Continent had no chance to vote – had turned an always volatile public opinion sharply against him. He began to receive threatening letters, at first only a few, then by the dozen.

Henry Labouchere, the editor of *Truth*, who had frequently attacked Rhodes as 'this Empire jerry-builder who has always been a mere vulgar promoter masquerading as a patriot, and the figure-head of a gang of astute Hebrew financiers with whom he divided profits', now turned his journalistic attentions towards Barney. Driving past his half-finished mansion one day, a friend asked Labouchere what he thought huge stone figures being hauled up to its roof were supposed to represent.

'Barnato creditors petrified while awaiting settlement,' replied Labouchere at once.

Barnato went on from London to Paris, but here Press comment was so hostile that he felt glad to return to London. His mental trauma at this sudden evidence of hatred showed in his face and, indeed, in his whole attitude. Sometimes he forgot to shave, or did not bother, but he never forgot to drink.

He became obsessed with the thought that he was losing all his money, although this was absurd. He began to dread that he might go back to his starting point with a barrow in the East End; full circle, rags to riches to rags.

He would visit his parents' graves in Willesden Cemetery and recall days and incidents of his youth. Once, at the height of his fortune, walking down Bond Street he had seen a magnificent overcoat, priced at £150, in the window of a tailor's shop. He bought it for his father but then, realizing that the old man would never appreciate how much the coat had actually cost, told him he had only paid £30 for it, which was still a very large sum to pay for an overcoat.

Barney's father did not wear the coat, but a few days later, handed Barney back £30. 'That coat you gave me – I sold it for £75. You may know a lot about diamonds, Barney, but you can't teach me anything about clothes.'

So Barney gave his father a second expensive overcoat, with strict instructions to wear it, not sell it.

Such memories, like his immense and genuine popularity, were all in the past and he began to feel that was where he also belonged. He could not understand how things seemed to be going so terribly wrong for him.

Fanny Barnato became so concerned about her husband's state of mind and the hostility which now he appeared to attract, despite his lavish donations to charities in London and South Africa, as well as to individuals, that she gave him a malacca cane to carry when he went out, in case he should ever be physically attacked. When Solly Joel came to London, he took a far more rational view of the future, and indeed was thinking of buying a huge yacht, an extravagance that Barney could not begin to comprehend, although in the past he might have applauded such a purchase as obvious evidence of deserved prosperity.

When Solly returned to South Africa, Barney travelled to Southampton to see him off. He was reluctant to see Solly go and appeared to have been drinking, for he was oddly dressed in a pair of striped trousers from a morning suit and a tweed sports jacket under a fur-lined overcoat. He looked altogether so woebegone and wretched, totally out of sorts, that Solly suggested he accompanied him as far as Madeira, where the ship made a brief stop. The sea voyage would do him good, he said. Barney agreed instantly and was aboard ship within minutes.

In Madeira a number of business telegrams from Johannesburg awaited Solly, and, still wearing his unusual clothes, Barney decided he would go on with him to Cape Town; the prospect of working cheered him considerably.

From Cape Town Barney travelled to Johannesburg where he found that he had really very little to do. The days of the entrepreneur who could make instant snap decisions to buy, sell, consolidate or close down, now seemed, like his memories, to be part of the past.

Only a few months earlier he could frighten President Kruger with the threat that he would close down all the mines, but now Kruger, preparing for an election by introducing more measures against foreigners and those he classed as 'undesirable immigrants', appeared to have soared out of Barney's power to influence. Indeed, Kruger was at that time discussing what was termed a treaty of 'friendship and mutual defence' with the Orange Free State, which clearly envisaged Britain as a potential mutual enemy.

Stanley Jackson, Barney's sympathetic biographer, described Barney's mood graphically: 'For days at a time he would climb into his bottle and pull the cork after him.'[1]

He was becoming irrational. One moment he thought he faced imminent ruin; the next he agreed to spend £80,000 on rosewood panelling for his

[1] Jackson, op. cit.

Park Lane house, and planned to add a minstrels' gallery. He complained of nightmares. The Stock Exchange was burning. Faces of long-dead diggers he once knew stared at him accusingly from rising waters in flooded diamond mines.

Subsequent events pointed to a specific reason for his sudden and uncharacteristic unease, but at the time Barney's doctor, faced with a very rich patient whose complaint he could not readily diagnose, fell back on that old medical specific in such cases: a long sea voyage.

The Prime Minister of the Cape, Sir Gordon Sprigg, and the Chief Justice, Sir Henry de Villiers, were sailing in June aboard the Union Line *Scot*, as South Africa's representatives at Queen Victoria's Diamond Jubilee that month. Barney willingly agreed to go in the same ship; ostensibly he could represent the South African mining industry.

Barney now travelled like a king, which indeed he was in all but name. Whereas he had first sailed steerage to South Africa, below sea level, down with the rudder chains, now he and his wife and their three young children occupied the best state rooms aboard the best ship of the line.

His elder son, Jack, celebrated his third birthday on board. Barney, very much a family man, showed the crew the present he had brought for him, a little bicycle. Barney seemed in good spirits, but unusually interested in the speed of the ship and when they could expect to reach Madeira where mail and newspapers from England would be waiting. Each morning he would go into the saloon and rip another page from a large calendar that hung on the wall. It was almost as though he had an appointment to keep – but when and where and with whom?

After lunch at the captain's table on Monday, June 14, exactly one year to the day since he had rescued Solly Joel and other members of the Reform Committee from jail in Pretoria, Barney invited the Prime Minister and Chief Justice to join him in the smoking room for brandies.

Shortly before three o'clock the party broke up. Barney had been unusually abstemious on the voyage, but at lunch had treated all the guests at the table to champagne. Now he suggested to Solly that they should take a walk round the deck.

The ship was making 17 knots through heavy, rough seas and the deck rolled and heaved. Solly was not at all enthusiastic; he would much rather lie down in his cabin. Many passengers favoured a siesta after lunch in such sailing conditions.

Barney would not hear of this. He took his nephew's arm and persuaded Solly that he should walk with him. So they set off, walking round and round the deck. Finally, Solly said that he must sit down and chose a deck chair facing the rail.

'What is the exact time?' Barney asked him.

'By my watch it is 13 minutes past three,' Solly replied. He closed his watch and put it back in his pocket.

Farther along the deck, the *Scot*'s fourth officer, William Tarrant Clifford, was dozing in a deck chair. Suddenly, he heard a cry, '*Murder!*'

Clifford jumped up in time to see Barney leaning far out over the rail, with Solly holding on to a trouser leg.

'What is it?' asked Clifford, still half asleep.

'For God's sake, save him!' cried Solly as Barney overbalanced and fell over the side.

At once Clifford ripped off his coat and vaulted across the rail into the sea. Bells clanged. Cries went up: 'Man overboard!' People threw life-belts. The *Scot* slowed and began to turn in a great white flurry of foam. Passengers could see Clifford swimming steadily through huge waves, but was still possibly 50 yards from Barney, who was floating face downwards in the water.

A boat was lowered with a doctor aboard and passengers crowded the deck rails to see Barney and Clifford being picked up when they were barely ten yards apart. The onlookers thought that the rescue had been successful and cheered loudly. The Cape's Prime Minister and Chief Justice were so impressed at Clifford's bravery in diving into the sea that they held an instant whip-round among everyone on deck. They collected £100 at once and gave it to him as he came aboard. But despite the best efforts of Clifford and the ship's doctor to revive Barney, all attempts failed. When the ship called at Madeira, Barney's body was opened – no one can say on whose authority – but no autopsy was carried out.[2]

An inquest was held in Southampton when the *Scot* docked several days later. At this Clifford gave evidence that 'Mr Barnato had a good idea of swimming, as he kept up so well'. Solly Joel said that when Barney had asked him, '"What is the exact time?" As I looked down to my watch, I saw a flash and he was over.'

For reasons never revealed, the coroner did not consider it necessary to follow up this statement. If he had done so, the cause of this flash might have been discovered. Could it have been sunlight suddenly reflected from a window glass, as the ship dipped in the heavy sea – or from something else that Barney considered inescapably menacing? And, if so, what? A revolver, a knife?

And who had shouted 'Murder!'? Surely, in the circumstances Solly Joel described, trying to pull his uncle back from the rail, Barney would be shouting for help, not calling 'Murder!' So had Solly or someone else shouted? Or had Barney Barnato been uttering a last desperate appeal for assistance?

[2] Interview with Mrs Diana Barnato Walker, MBE, his grand-daughter.

Having heard the evidence, the coroner returned a verdict of 'death by drowning while temporarily insane'. This was kinder than deciding that Barney had committed suicide, but was it a true verdict? Barnato's widow Fanny would never accept that her husband had taken his own life.

'It was never talked about. She talked about earlier things, coming up to Kimberley from the south with her parents and her sister in their ox-cart, but not about that.'[3]

Afterwards Clifford received a Lloyd's silver medal, one cheque collected by public subscription, a second cheque from Woolf Joel on behalf of the Barnato's company, and an annuity organized by Barney's widow. He became friendly with Solly Joel and would go shooting with him on his estate. He rose to become a captain in the merchant navy. His son Eric, not two years old when Barney died, joined the Royal Navy, reached the rank of Vice-Admiral and was knighted.

So Barney Barnato, The Great Barnato, died at the age of 44. In tribute Johannesburg Stock Exchange closed for the day, as did South Africa's gold and diamond mines. And the South African Assembly, where Barney had been a member for nine years, adjourned in his memory. So his life ended, but controversy about the manner of his passing was about to begin.

After Barnato's death several questions were regularly asked. First, did he fall – or was he pushed? And if the latter, by whom – and why?

If Barney had jumped overboard deliberately, what had, apparently suddenly, forced him to do so? And in any event, why should he suddenly commit suicide?

'He had everything to live for – a beautiful wife, three lovely children, lots and lots of money,' wrote his grand-daughter.[4] 'He was coming home to receive all sorts of accolades that a poor-boy-made-good would be delighted to be given. He had got there by his own hard work and canniness. Why should he jump overboard? Not he . . . He had a lot more mileage in him.'

Under Barney's will his share in the family companies passed to the surviving partners. Solly Joel took over control of Barnato operations in South Africa. In the following February, seven months after Barney's death, he received a long letter from a stranger who signed himself, simply, Kismet, the Arabic word for Fate.

Kismet explained that his letter was 'the last resource of a desperate man whom ruin stares in the face, before seeking the only escape possible from utter misery by a bullet. . . . I must have £12,000 at once or face ruin and

[3] Interview with Mrs Walker.
[4] *Spreading My Wings*, Diana Barnato Walker, Patrick Stephens Ltd., Sparkford, near Yeovil, 1994.

disgrace, which I utterly decline to do. But if my race is run so shall yours be!

'The best police could do is to see your death avenged – never prevent it – and that trouble I shall save them as we die together. . . .

'I know I can find you when the time has come, and you will never know who I am till the moment that I strike. . . . I am plain with you, so that your death shall not be murder, but your own doing, really, though I will willingly admit all blame for removing you to a better world, this or the other side of the river Styx, where Barnato may be glad to see you again.'[5]

Kismet instructed Solly to place an advertisement in the *Johannesburg Star* and he would then give him instructions for delivering the money he demanded. Further letters threatened that, if Solly did not pay up, the writer would kill Solly and Woolf Joel as well as himself.

Like many rich men, Solly had received threatening letters from cranks, but this one he decided to take seriously and, considerably alarmed, he asked his brother Woolf for his opinion.

Woolf considered the matter important, because not only were their lives at risk, but Kismet could also pose a threat to their good name in business. He told Solly that he would deal with the matter and answered Kismet's advertisement. He agreed to meet him, with Harold Strange, the manager of the Consolidated Investment Company, which Barney had founded and which the Barnato family controlled.

Kismet proved to be a huge, well-dressed man, with moustachios. Speaking with a cultivated German accent, he introduced himself as Franz von Veltheim, involved with a group who had devised a simple but apparently foolproof plan to overthrow the Boer government, so that more liberal leaders could be elected and thus avert a possible war with Britain.

In helping him financially, he said that the Joels could also make a huge profit themselves by selling their own shares and then buying them back when the government fell and prices dropped.

Von Veltheim explained that earlier the previous year he had met Barney Barnato in London and discussed the plan with him. He claimed that Barney had then given him £500 towards it, and later, when he was in Eastbourne, an intermediary had sent him a further £500 on Barney's behalf. Barney, so von Veltheim went on, had offered £50,000 to him if the venture succeeded, plus £1,000 a month for expenses. Barney had also told him that, if the plan could be achieved within a £1,000,000 budget, it would be cheap at the price.

Woolf was unimpressed by this rambling talk of large sums of money, but although von Veltheim's story did not tally in any way with his original letter

[5] *Ace of Diamonds*, Stanhope Joel, as told to Lloyd Mayer, Frederick Muller, 1968.

he did not consider him to be particularly dangerous. He instructed Strange to meet him again and to offer him £200, which von Veltheim said he needed to help one of the group who was in financial difficulties.

At this meeting, von Veltheim said that he must meet Woolf Joel urgently in his office next morning; he was apparently leaving for Cape Town at noon that day to sail to England. With hindsight, it would have been prudent for Woolf Barnato to involve the police, or at least to have some other witnesses at this meeting, even if they kept out of sight.

But, as Woolf's nephew, Solly's son Stanhope, wrote later, 'For some reason that is forever veiled in mystery, Woolf did not do so. What hold had the adventurer over the powerful head of Barnato Brothers? What had Woolf Joel to fear from this evil man? The answer was never to come from his lips, and Solly, if indeed he knew, never revealed the secret.'[6]

Von Veltheim meanwhile reduced his original demand to £2,500, and Woolf apparently decided that von Veltheim was a man of little account; at their meeting he repeated his offer of £200, virtually to go away. Unsurprisingly, von Veltheim did not think highly of this proposal.

Before the meeting Strange had put a revolver in his jacket pocket in case von Veltheim should become threatening, and Woolf had a pistol in a desk drawer.

'Mr Strange tells me you are not going to give me any money,' said von Veltheim angrily. 'Well, if that is your final decision, you know too much, and neither of you will leave this room alive!'

Strange reached out to move a cigar box on top of Woolf's desk – a clumsy attempt to divert the German's attention while he drew his own revolver.

'Don't move!' von Veltheim told him sharply, now aiming a revolver at Woolf.

He swung round to fire at Strange, who ducked and fired back. Both men missed. Then von Veltheim fired three times at Woolf, who fell across his desk, dead. At the sound of the shots other members of the staff rushed in belatedly and seized von Veltheim.

He was charged with murder. His trial lasted for nine days. The jury of Boers, who remembered Solly Joel's membership of the Reform Committee and Barney Barnato's threat to Kruger to close all his mines, were not disposed to listen sympathetically to the prosecution's evidence. To them von Veltheim, as a German, represented the nation which had espoused their cause; he was a hero, not a criminal. As a result he walked out of the court a free man. The judge could not comprehend this extraordinary verdict. Nor could von Veltheim's lawyer, who refused to shake hands with his client or congratulate him on his totally bizarre acquittal.

[6] Joel, op. cit.

Solly Joel was now in command of the Barnato family's financial affairs. His brother Jack (formerly Isaac) did not return to South Africa and Woolf was dead. Years later Barney Barnato's grand-daughter Diana was discussing the family's early days with her cousin, Stanhope Joel.

'I said something like, "When Barney Barnato committed suicide . . ." and Stanhope looked up sharply and said, "Or Solly pushed him!" That was the son saying that about his father, who was then dead. So, in Stanhope's eyes, Barney had certainly been pushed.'[7]

'"He gave him the heave-ho overboard," Stan went on. . . . "If you flounder about and drown, the body usually submerges as the lungs fill up with water. If you go in unconscious, then your lungs are still full of air, so you float."'[8]

Since Barney floated, then, if this theory is correct, he would have been unconscious when he went into the sea. Had Solly and he come to blows and Solly knocked him out? This is possible, but Barney was very quick with his fists, and what could cause an uncle and his nephew, apparently on very good terms with each other, to have such a violent argument that it ended in blows?

After this long lapse of time it is probably impossible to discover whether Barney killed himself or whether he was killed. But it is not impossible that von Veltheim, who travelled regularly between South Africa and England under different names, seeking different sources of money from the rich, was also aboard the ship.

The prospect of meeting an immensely wealthy man who thought that achieving an aim for within £1,000,000 would be 'cheap at the price' could have fired his determination to extract some of Barney's money for himself. Von Veltheim was a confidence man who had lived on his wits – and other people's money – since, under his real name, Karl Kurtze, he deserted from the German navy.

He took with him not only an officer's gold watch but also the officer's aristocratic name, von Veltheim. Subsequently he served in various British ships, then married a wealthy Australian, spent her money, moved to the United States and bigamously 'married' a rich American.

His good looks and apparently aristocratic background proved greatly attractive to other women of means. Once, his life as a blackmailer and confidence trickster became so complex that he found it expedient to 'die'. A woman friend helpfully claimed that a body found in the River Thames was his, but by then von Veltheim was actually on his way to Cape Town.

He could have been aboard the *Scot* as a passenger or one of the crew, and

---

[7] Diana Barnato Walker, in an interview with the author.
[8] Walker, op. cit.

if, indeed, he had seen Barney in England, as he claimed, Barney *could* have arranged to meet with him at 3.13 on the afternoon of 14 June.

There is no evidence to support this possibility. But if von Veltheim *was* aboard, for whatever purpose, did he stay in the background, and then only reveal his presence with such unexpected effect that Barney jumped overboard simply to avoid him? Could the sudden glint that Solly Joel saw be sunlight shining on von Veltheim's revolver? If so, that could explain Solly Joel's remark at the inquest, 'I saw a flash and he was over'.

The matter might have ended inconclusively, lost in a mass of contradictory theories and possibilities, were it not for another strange sequence of events. As Diana Barnato Walker wrote: 'When I was told the story by my cousin Stanhope, Solly's son, I heard for the first time all about how hard Solly tried to get his hand on the company and all the loot.

'He was something of a brigand and Stan even suggested that Solly probably paid for von Veltheim's defence. He would have been quite happy to do so, because the tragedy had got Woolf out of his way. In order to realize his ambitions, Solly had needed to oust his brother from the South African end of the company.'[9]

According to Diana, Solly's ambition was always to gain total control of the family's enormous enterprises.

'It was said that he masterminded the organizing of a phony indictment of illicit diamond buying on his brother Jack. . . . My Uncle Jack didn't wait for the case to come up, but hopped it back to England out of the jurisdiction of the courts, where he continued to run the English side of the business well out of Solly's hair.'[10]

Years ago in her mother's jewel box Diana found a letter from her godmother, Jack's widow, Dorothy, who later married Lord Plunket. The letter had originally been addressed to Barney Barnato's daughter Leah.

'The letter said, in essence, well, if Grandpa Falk wants to find about this it is no loss to us. Maybe he will find something, and if he wants 20 per cent of what he finds, we should allow him this, otherwise we wouldn't get anything at all.'[11]

'Grandpa Falk' was Herbert Valentine Falk, an extremely successful Wall Street broker and the father of Diana's American mother. He had heard rumours of an argument between Barney and Solly shortly before Barney died, and he said he would be willing to retire from his company to try and find the truth – for this fee if he were successful. His investigation took him two years to complete in South Africa and elsewhere.

[9] Walker, op. cit.
[10] Ibid.
[11] Diana Barnato Walker in an interview with the author.

'Despite every conceivable difficulty being put in his way, (he) got permission to see the company's books. When he got to the very page he really needed, he found it had been torn out. . . . He then had to start again, but doggedly went on and on.'[12]

Eventually, after a court case which gave him access to the books, which Mr Falk discovered that Solly Joel had indeed swindled Barney out of nearly £1,000,000. 'This wasn't much to those boys even then, but it was enough to have a row about, when Barney had made it all from nothing, with Solly helped along on his back.' Under the terms of Barney's will, after provision for his immediate family, the sole survivor of the company 'took the kitty – and that was eventually Solly. So he did all right, didn't he?'[13]

If Barney Barnato suspected, or worse, knew that his nephew, Solly, who owed so much to his kindness and help, was actually swindling him, this could have helped to cause his frenetic and untypical behaviour before he left for England on his last voyage.

There was a court case, which was settled 'amicably after lunch on the second day of the hearing'. Solly Joel paid £960,000 to the Barnatos, and his costs; Mr Falk received his 20 per cent.

Then someone remembered the large amount of interest that would have accrued on nearly £1,000,000 over so many years. More court action followed. Solly Joel had to pay up for a second time.

Throughout his long life he appeared a strange paradox of extravagance and parsimony; possessive love for his immediate family and hostility towards any who thought to marry into it. He named his magnificent yacht *Doris* after his favourite daughter. When Doris told him she wanted to marry, Solly was devastated and grew a beard as a symbol of his mourning. They were briefly reconciled when she divorced her husband, shortly before she gave birth to a son. Then the boy died and recriminations resumed between father and daughter.

Solly Joel changed the name of his yacht to *Eileen*, after his other daughter, and ordered that all linen, gold and silver services, and crystal goblets, which bore the yacht's name *Doris*, must be thrown into the sea. To make sure that his action received adequate publicity, he gave full details to the newspapers. When people would ask him about Doris, Solly Joel would reply briefly, 'I have no daughter, Doris. For me, she does not exist.'

When Solly Joel died, Doris sent a bouquet of carnations and forget-me-nots to his funeral, with a card: 'I loved you, Daddy. Doris.'

Solly's eldest son, Woolf, after Eton and Cambridge, flew with the Royal Flying Corps in the First World War and was then given a sinecure in his

---

[12] Walker, op. cit.
[13] Ibid,.

father's London office. He found this tedious and preferred a life of gaiety and enjoyment. In attempting to finance this, he ran up huge debts gambling, and to moneylenders. Solly made him bankrupt – he had assets of £235 and liabilities of £42,345 – and Woolf left England for Egypt to try and make a new life fruit-farming.

One night, on the outward voyage, he fell down a long staircase and was found dead next morning. Because of his lifestyle it was thought that he might have been drunk, but the autopsy performed by the ship's surgeon revealed that he had not drunk sufficient to make him even faintly intoxicated.

Surprisingly, the young man had what was described as 'a nasty wound at the base of the skull which could have been caused by an assault with a lethal weapon'. However, no one had seen anything. The tragic incident was written off as 'death by misadventure'.[14]

Solly Joel became one of the world's richest men, with an estate at Maiden Erlegh near Reading, where more than seventy horses were stabled, and a stud at Newmarket. He won the wartime Derby in 1915, and the St Leger, and in 1921 headed the list of winning owners. Every investment with which he became involved was successful. He owned huge blocks of shares in theatres, hotels, a catering chain and cotton mills, plus his vast interests in gold and diamonds. But in spite of prodigious expenditure, including lavish gifts to charity, a basic mean streak remained in his character.

For example, he pursued a bookie who owed him £10 and castigated his children's French governess because she had the habit of posting letters in sealed envelopes, which required a 1½ penny stamp, instead of the ½ penny stamp needed for unsealed envelopes. Once, a guest at Maiden Erlegh dived into Solly's Italian marble swimming pool, described by his son as 'one of the most magnificent in the world', and injured his nose. He hoped that Solly might express some sympathy, but instead he simply looked at the water, now streaked with blood, and asked coldly, 'Do you know how much it costs me to fill that bath?'

Towards the end of his life Solly Joel was invited to give a lecture on 'Happiness and Wealth'. Someone asked him whether he personally was happy.

'Am I happy?' Solly repeated in genuine amazement. 'Consider what I have suffered. . . . My beloved uncle's suicide, the murder of my brother by a man who persecuted me for years when I went in peril of my life. . . . The ingratitude of a daughter I loved and for whom I made every sacrifice. . . . The tragedy of my eldest son. . . . Happy? I am a dying man.'

[14] Joel, op. cit.

As with the legendary King Midas, everything Solly Joel touched turned to gold. But perhaps, like Midas, he paid too dearly for the gift.

Two years after Barney's death, in the early part of 1899, Rhodes was in London making his will, which he changed a number of times. In the final version he outlined qualifications for the scholarships he intended to award every year to young men from different parts of the world to study at Oxford. He was determined that they would not be 'mere bookworms', because he believed that no one, however intellectual, could succeed in life unless they also possessed physical strength and strong character.

Rhodes had abandoned his early and totally impossible scheme to bring nearly all the world under some kind of British control, with the hope that this would minimize the risk of any war. Instead, he wanted to provide future world leaders with an Oxford education which, he believed, would broaden and consolidate their views and give them a unique chance to develop their individual abilities. He chose Oxford partly because it had been his own university, also because he strongly believed that the system of individual residential colleges there was especially helpful to personal development.

'Rhodes hoped that those who gained these benefits from Oxford and his Scholarships would go on to improve the lot of mankind and work towards maintaining peace between nations.'[15]

Initially he provided in his will for fifty-seven Scholarships to be given every year. Of these twenty were 'Colonial' Scholarships, thirty-two more for young men from the United States and five from Germany. He believed that such cooperation between future German and English-speaking leaders would help to prevent war between the two countries. He had been impressed by the Kaiser when he met him, and the Kaiser had been equally impressed by Rhodes.

The allocation has varied over the years. In 1996, for instance, there were thirty-two American Rhodes Scholars, eleven Canadian, nine from Australia and Southern Africa, four from Germany and India, three from New Zealand, two from Zimbabwe (formerly Rhodesia), the Caribbean and Kenya, one each from Zambia, Uganda, Singapore, Pakistan, Malaysia, Jamaica and Bermuda, making a total of eighty-six. Usually, more than 200 Rhodes Scholars are in Oxford at any one time.

In June, 1899, Rhodes received the honorary degree of Doctor of Civil Law at Oxford. He had originally been offered this in 1892, but since he had been unable to come to Oxford at that time, he was informed he could receive it whenever convenient to him. A friend then suggested that he

[15] From a paper prepared by the Association of Rhodes Scholars in Australia.

should accept the degree in 1899 at the Encaenia, the annual celebration which remembers founders and benefactors.

This particular Encaenia was to be on an unusually splendid scale. The Duke and Duchess of York, afterwards King George V and Queen Mary, were to be present. Lord Kitchener, who had commanded the troops at the victorious Battle of Omdurman in the previous year, was also to be honoured, as was the Earl of Elgin, the Viceroy of India, and several other men of distinction. Rhodes' critics protested strongly that after the Jameson Raid he should not be given this degree.

There was only one way in which it could be thwarted at such a late stage, by using a veto given to the Proctors, who hold the right to interpose in University business. Two Proctors now decided that they would exercise their veto at the one opportunity left to them, at the actual ceremony in the Sheldonian Theatre. They were not on their own; a number of Oxford residents signed a letter to *The Times* agreeing with their views.

'There was such bitter opposition to him. . . . All, of course, with a vein of truth, but so exaggerated and so indifferent to his great services,' Rhodes' friend from undergraduate days, the Rev. Arthur Gray Butler, wrote to his sister shortly afterwards.

'Then came the news that the Proctors' veto was being used to bar his degree – an old rusty weapon, quite obsolete. It would have been monstrous, but it was only got over by the Duke and Duchess of York refusing to go to the Theatre and Kitchener declining a degree if that was done. And when it was in suspense and Rhodes himself was in doubt, his friends pressed him to resist – and his telegram "Rhodes will face the music" set that right.'

That evening there was a Gaudy in Oriel, a special dinner held from time to time for former members of colleges. This was the last time Rhodes was to visit his old college. He sat between Butler and the Lord Chancellor, Lord Halsbury, and was asked to speak.

'He spoke admirably, pointing out the difference between an old and settled country and that of a country in formation. He spoke also of what he had done or striven to do, not denying his mistakes but pleading very great difficulties and provocations. It was a striking and historical scene. His humility was quite as marked as his consciousness of great achievement.'[16]

In earlier visits to Oxford Rhodes revealed his personal views about committees, and his concerns that the white population of South Africa might be swamped by the sheer numbers of black Africans.

During one of these visits, he had a conversation with Sir James Bryce, who had been Chancellor of the Duchy of Lancaster in Lord Rosebery's cabinet.

[16] *Cecil Rhodes and his College*, G.N. Clark, O.U.P., 1953.

Bryce asked Rhodes, 'How many ministers have you in your cabinet?'

'Three. Two others beside myself.'

'A nice manageable number,' said Bryce.

'Hm,' said Rhodes. 'Two too many, I think.'

At about the same time Rhodes and Jameson spent a weekend at the Provost's Lodgings at Oriel. Pelham Warner, the famous cricketer, was one of the undergraduates asked to meet him at breakfast, and sat next to him.

Rhodes asked him, 'What are you going to do when you go down?'

'I am going to the Bar and I am "eating dinners" at the Inner Temple,' Pelham Warner explained.

'Do you ever meet any coloured men there?'

'Yes. A few.'

'Do you ever sit near them?'

'Yes. We're often placed in messes of four.'

'Do you talk to them?'

'Yes.'

'Do you like them?'

'Yes, I do.'

'Well, I don't. I suppose it is the instinct of self-preservation. In South Africa we have perhaps a million or two whites and many millions more of black people.'[17]

Now Butler explained to Rhodes that his old college was having a difficult time, owing to the general agricultural depression.

'How much money would be needed to put the college right, to restore it to its full dignity and efficiency?' Rhodes asked him. The answer was that it would be a large sum.

'Would a hundred thousand be sufficient?' Rhodes asked. 'I'm going to make my will in London during the next few days. Write and tell me exactly what you want. I cannot tell whether I may not lose my money, but' – here he gave a nod – 'I don't think I shall.'

The next day the Provost, at Butler's suggestion, drew up a list of what was required. Rhodes signed his will ten days after his discussion. When he died he left his old college £100,000 free of all duty, and added, 'As the college authorities live secluded from the world, and so are like children as to commercial matters, I would advise them to consult my trustees as to the investment of these various funds for they would receive great help and assistance.'

Later Sir George Clark, Provost of Oriel in the 1940s, noted how 'the anxieties of the dons and their comparatively unenterprising attitude to the future stands in sharp contrast with the part relating to the altogether

---

[17] *Long Innings*, Sir Pelham Warner, quoted by G.N. Clark, op. cit.

new and revolutionary idea of the Rhodes Scholarships, which was Rhodes' own.'[18]

Rhodes also wrote in this final will – of seven – that he wished to be buried in the Matopos, and he left Groote Schuur, with a sum for its maintenance, as a residence for the future Prime Minister of a federated South Africa. Properties he owned in Rhodesia he left in trust to settlers there, and his properties in England to his family.

Rhodes was staying in a suite at the Burlington Hotel in Cork Street while he drafted this will. He and his solicitor worked in the sitting room, which also served as Philip Jourdan's office. One day Rhodes asked the lawyer in a jocular way, 'What shall we do about this young rascal?', pointing to Jourdan.

'I'm going to leave you £5,000,' he said. 'Will that be sufficient for you?'

Jourdan was embarrassed at this; he had not asked, nor indeed, expected, anything. Then Rhodes said, 'No, I will leave him £7,000. He's done very good work for me.'

As the lawyer started to write in this clause, Rhodes changed his mind again.

'No, make it £10,000, he deserves it.'

Rhodes disliked going out to dinner and rarely went to the theatre. In London he would receive as many as half a dozen invitations each day for lunch or dinner, or to spend the weekend in some country house. He always preferred to be the host, not the guest.

In his hotel he was looked after by the same waiter, named Arthur, a shrewd judge of character, who appeared to know instinctively who to admit to Rhodes' presence and who to turn away. This ability proved very useful to Rhodes, who was pestered by so many people for money or favours, or both, that he would invariably ask people he met for the first time, 'What do you want from me?'

When Rhodes left London, after a stay of five months, he wished to give Arthur a present. Jourdan suggested £25. Rhodes agreed, but as Jourdan made to write out the cheque he changed his mind.

'No, make it £50.' Then, 'No, do not let us be mean, make it £75.'

When Jourdan gave the cheque for this amount to Arthur – more than a year's wages – Arthur simply looked at it, touched his head with his finger and said, 'Thank you, sir.' Jourdan thought that he might have sounded more appreciative.

Rhodes bought two thousand thoroughbred stallions and two pure-bred Arab stallions to take back to South Africa to help improve the breed of horses. He planned to return by way of Egypt, where he intended to buy a

[18] G.N. Clark, op. cit.

231

number of young trees to be sent out to Rhodesia, but just before he left London he received a letter from a Russian Princess, Catherine Radziwill. She explained that she had inherited £150,000 and asked for his advice about investing it.

Rochfort Maguire, a friend of Rhodes from Oxford days, happened to be with him when Philip Jourdan opened her letter. Rhodes said he had never heard of Princess Radziwill, but Maguire reminded him that he had actually sat next to her at a dinner party three years earlier. Rhodes then agreed that he did now remember her.

'She was quite interesting, a vivacious talker,' he said.

Rhodes did not like to advise anybody about investing their money. If his advice was sound he would not receive any credit, but if it turned out badly he would get all the blame. In this case, however, Rhodes made an exception and suggested that the Princess should buy Mashonaland Railway Debentures.

He delayed his departure for Cape Town five times because he kept re-writing his will. Finally, in July, 1899, he set off aboard the *Scot*, the ship from which Barney Barnato had fallen to his death two years previously.

In the dining saloon Rhodes selected a small table to which he could invite any passenger who might care to join him for dinner. Just before the ship sailed the agent of the Union Line informed Jourdan privately that Princess Radziwill had booked on all the five ships on which Rhodes had requested passage, because she appeared very anxious to travel to South Africa with him. Jourdan reported this to Rhodes, who was surprised, and asked him, 'I wonder what takes her to South Africa?' He was soon to find out.

That night, as dinner was being served, Princess Radziwill arrived late and walked straight to Rhodes' table. She affected surprise that he should be sitting there and then asked, 'Is this chair engaged? May I have it?'

Rhodes was with Sir Charles Metcalfe, his company engineer, and Jourdan. They all rose and bowed, and she joined them. 'Of course,' noted Jourdan drily, 'she occupied the chair for the rest of the voyage.'

Sometimes, Jourdan also noted, the Princess expressed herself rather bluntly on delicate matters. 'Mr Rhodes could not suppress a blush.' She explained that her husband was 'a brute' and recounted examples of his cruelty in a way that impressed her listeners. Finally, she said she had decided to seek divorce, which in Russia would take a year. She wished to spend this year in South Africa. She had married when she was fifteen and a half. She had three children before she was nineteen and had lived in Berlin and Warsaw.

'She was not tall, inclined to be stout, had black hair and black shifting eyes. She could not be called handsome or pretty, and was about forty-seven years of age then,' wrote Jourdan.[19] She was actually forty-one. Contemporary photographs show her to have been slim, elegant, extremely well dressed and attractive.

The Princess always agreed with whatever opinion Rhodes expressed, but when Metcalfe or Jourdan differed from her own views, she would become excited and raise her voice 'to such an extent that everybody in the saloon could hear her.'

She complained that her heart gave her trouble, and then she would 'roll her eyes, sigh, and pant for breath in a most distressing way'. Once, sitting next to Rhodes on deck, she apparently fainted and collapsed against him.

Other passengers came to help her, but Jourdan recalled, 'I shall never forget the absolutely abject look of helplessness on his face. He was shy and at the same time very alarmed.' Thereafter Rhodes, never one to seek the company of women, kept mostly to his cabin.

When the ship docked he found that Cape Town had been decorated in honour of his return. Flags and bunting fluttered from tramway wires. Shops and offices were closed, and the dock was packed with people long before the *Scot* even came into sight. On the road to Groote Schuur Rhodes passed beneath banners lettered with 'Welcome Home' and 'CJR'. Later that day he received more than 100 loyal addresses in the Drill Hall, and the local band played 'See, the conquering hero comes' to an audience which rose to its feet in tribute to him.

Princess Radziwill stayed at Mount Nelson Hotel, the best in Cape Town, but fellow passengers on board ship who were friendly with Rhodes invited her to their houses and to various social functions. Her standing was greatly helped by a letter she had from Lord Salisbury, the Prime Minister, introducing her to Sir Alfred Milner, the new Governor of the Cape. Soon she was joining luncheon and dinner parties at Groote Schuur as the guest of Cecil Rhodes. To the wives of her new friends, the Princess described her unhappy marriage and gave the impression that she and Rhodes were about to marry. A second, and less favourable impression was that they were having an affair.

These rumours reached Rhodes, who was not best pleased. From being an apparently welcome guest, now, when the Princess sent a wire to say she would like to come to lunch or dinner, 'he showed signs of displeasure and tried to put her off'. He disliked being alone with her in the house and, to avoid meeting her, 'he would often bolt down his meal and drive off to some mythical appointment.'[20]

[19] *Cecil Rhodes his Private Life*, Philip Jourdan, John Lane, London, 1910.
[20] *Cecil Rhodes and the Princess*, Brian Roberts, Hamish Hamilton, London, 1969.

He became irritated with the Princess's political views and finally asked her not to discuss politics with him.

'One day he lost his temper, and told her point-blank that if she refused to comply with his wishes in this respect she had better not speak to him at all. Her visits after that became less frequent, but she still came. There was a strained feeling when she was in the house, and Mr Rhodes appeared uncomfortable.'[21]

Once, when Rhodes postponed meeting the Princess, Jourdan found her in his office, thumbing through private papers. Checking them when she left, Jourdan discovered that several were missing. He was reluctant to speak to Rhodes about this and, instead, mentioned the matter to Metcalfe, and asked his opinion as to what he should – or could – do. Metcalfe advised Jourdan to instruct a servant to wait by his desk whenever he was called away and his office was left unattended. This servant reported to Jourdan that in his absence the Princess had come into his office. Afterwards Jourdan found that the missing papers had been returned.

[21] Ibid.

CHAPTER 13

'REMEMBER THAT MR RHODES OWNS THIS PLACE.'

While the atmosphere in Groote Schuur between Rhodes and Princess Radziwill was growing strained, relations between Boers and British in South Africa had deteriorated into virtual collapse. The Anglo-Boer war was about to begin, basically for the same reasons that had encouraged Jameson to make his disastrous march to Johannesburg. It seemed that nothing had been forgotten by either side – or remembered.

British troop reinforcements about to land in South Africa, to augment regiments already there, had no idea whatever of the kind of war they might be required to fight. Their officers had not received training for any engagement that did not follow strictly orthodox military teaching. No one knew, or even imagined, that the ensuing conflict could change public perception of war for ever.

This would be the first in which British soldiers would wear khaki uniforms instead of their traditional red coats, so that the wearers would be made less conspicuous to the enemy. For the first time, too, automatic weapons would be employed on a huge scale; so would smokeless cartridges, shrapnel, camouflage, trenches and barbed wire. Units could be linked by field telegraph across miles of open country and film cameras would photograph action in a way never previously possible.

In the event, too, British Lee-Metford rifles were found to be less accurate than the Mauser rifles Kruger had bought from Germany, ironically with money paid in taxes by British Uitlanders. And, most important, the British army, lacking any knowledge of guerrilla tactics which the Boers would employ to such devastating effect, would face unnecessarily heavy casualties.

From the accuracy of Boer marksmen grew the British superstition that it was unlucky for a smoker to light three cigarettes from one match. When the first cigarette was lit, so it was said, the Boer sharpshooter would see the flame and pick up his rifle. At the second he would take aim. At the third he would fire.

In the beginning, however, most people in Britain thought, or were persuaded by political speeches and newspaper articles, that the conflict would be over very quickly. What could a crowd of Dutch farmers hope to achieve against the professional soldiers of the Queen?

Rhodes was in Cape Town when war finally seemed inevitable and Milner wanted him to stay there. He refused. 'My post is at Kimberley, yours at Cape Town,' Rhodes told him. As a boy, it is likely that Rhodes heard his father preach on the text, 'Where your treasure is, there will your heart be also' (Mat. 6.21). Kimberley was the primary source of his treasure. It required his immediate presence.

The people of Kimberley did not all agree. The Mayor, R.H. Henderson, cabled to Rhodes: 'Citizens generally feel that your presence here would serve to induce a rush with view to do the town, your company, and all our joint interests great damage. Under all circumstances would ask you kindly to postpone coming in order to avert any possible risks.'[1]

Kimberley at that time contained around 45,000 people, of whom 18,000 were Africans. De Beers employed a large proportion. The company was, in effect, Kimberley, just as Rhodes was synonymous with De Beers. Also, since some Kimberley diamond mines were only a few miles from the Orange Free State, and De Beers were producing more than 90 per cent of the world's diamonds it was, in Rhodes' view, clearly a prize the Boers could covet.

A British regular officer, 45-year-old Lt. Col. Robert George Kekewich, had been put in military charge of the town to make preparations for its defence and he did not subscribe to Rhodes' opinion. Kekewich was another bachelor and already going bald. 'His thin moustache overhung the corners of his mouth like two drooping feathers.' He was one year older than Rhodes, and, like him, running to fat.

Kekewich ordered earthworks to be built around the town and placed high look-out posts on the tops of heaps of waste from the mines. The land was so flat that a man with a telescope, standing on one of these look-out towers, could see any activity on the borders of the Orange Free State.

Kekewich had a conning tower on top of a mine headgear and also set up searchlights around the perimeter of the town, which extended to 13½ miles. These could sweep the area after dark. He was greatly helped by an ingenious American engineer, George Labram, who had built a crushing plant for De Beers, and was at that time the company's chief engineer and electrician.

On Saturday, 14 October, 1899, Kekewich was in the Kimberley telegraph office awaiting a cable from Cape Town when the line unexpectedly went dead. It had been cut. Kimberley was now on its own.

---

[1] *Kimberley, Turbulent City*, Brian Roberts, David Philip, Cape Town, 1976.

Thousands of men, women and children, black, white and coloured, now streamed into the town, which seemed safer than remaining in their outlying and isolated homes. Soon 400 were sleeping on the floor of the Town Hall. The Mayor, who had earlier urged Rhodes to stay away, now urgently sought his help.

Within half an hour Rhodes agreed to employ all men who were able to work, which would mean a wages bill of £8,000 a week. Their task was to repair roads, build new ones, dig trenches and replant parks.

Rhodes made his headquarters in the Sanatorium Hotel, which was originally intended to be a hotel for visitors as well as a hospital for patients. This project, like most in Kimberley, had been Rhodes' idea and was subsidized by De Beers. The verandah was now protected by sandbags and the whole building shored up with beams against possible artillery attack.

Throughout the siege, when Kimberley came under regular shellfire, Rhodes utilized the resources of De Beers to give every help possible to the townspeople. He raised a mounted corps, the Kimberley Light Horse, but he found it difficult t o hand over total defence of the town – his town – to Kekewich, with whom he had at the best little rapport, and for most of the time none at all.

To Rhodes, Kekewich represented all he disliked and despised in the rigid military mind and attitude. The two men were in fact totally incompatible. Kekewich was in charge of Kimberley's defences and his word and decisions on military matters should, therefore, be paramount. But Rhodes had been largely responsible for transforming Kimberley from a shambles of tin huts, tents, wooden shacks and wagons into a large and prosperous town with its own railway station and, most important, its huge diamond mines, the largest and most prosperous in the world. He was therefore not accustomed to bowing to other people's opinions if he did not respect either the speaker or what they had to say. In Kimberley, what Rhodes decided very few ever dared to contradict.

Kekewich was one of the few. Like some military men who in middle life have only achieved middle rank, he was of limited imagination. He did not consider Kimberley to be a prime target for Boer attack. He did not seem able to appreciate the fact that the town was a prize of incalculable value. In financial terms or in the wider terms of national prestige it was imperative that Kimberley should not fall. Rhodes realized how catastrophic it would be if the Boers captured – and then controlled – the mines. They had already announced that they would parade him through the streets of Pretoria in a cage, like a captured lion.

Kekewich imposed censorship on messages leaving the town. Rhodes did not see how this rule should, or even could, apply to him. He felt above such restrictions. He therefore employed his own messengers and through them kept in regular touch with the authorities at Cape Town and, by means of his Company offices there, with London. He wrote frequently to Sir Alfred Milner, urging 'immediate relief'.

'You ought to send relief here, and it is quite easy to get through from Orange River now with your present force, but commandos[2] round us are increasing daily and getting more impudent owing to our helpless position. I feel it is useless pressing this on Cape military authority, but wish to place fact on record.'[3]

A local physician, Dr Oliver Ashe, took a different view. 'The Boers openly gave out that they wanted to take Rhodes prisoner and to blow up his mines, and did not wish to injure anyone else.'[4]

Rhodes ordered that 3,000 African workers inside Kimberley should be allowed to return to their villages. This would reduce demands on Kimberley's food stocks, but the Boers on the veld refused to accept the Africans, who streamed back into Kimberley, arousing initial alarm that they might actually be the advance force of a Boer attack.

'Rhodes was now becoming more and more impatient at the delay which was taking place in the relief of Kimberley, and particularly so as Kekewich could give him no information as to what was being done in this matter by the Commander-in-Chief. The fact is that Kekewich was himself completely in the dark as to the intentions of his military superiors.'[5]

Rhodes could not allow this unsatisfactory situation to continue without attempting to change it. He had his own private code, which he used in his communications to Milner and to the Governor, but this could not cover every eventuality. Many of his messages were therefore virtually in clear, with odd words in code. For instance, on 2 November, 1899, he wrote to Milner:

'Boers around us oozing every side. . . . You myrtle (must) put heart into this philomena (place) which is practically defended by civilians. . . . Our spirit is excellent but calipash nicotian (cannot forever) stand prolonged strain.'[6]

And on the same day he sent a message to the Governor of the Cape stressing the urgency required to deal with the siege: 'We are absolutely invention (surrounded) by hordes enemy . . . Considering enormous nullify (numbers) women children in Kimberley . . . An immediate andante (answer).'[7]

[2] This word was first used in this war to describe a Boer army unit made up of the militia of an electoral district.
[3] *The Lion's Cage*, Brian Gardner, Arthur Barker, 1969.
[4] *Besieged by the Boers*, E.O. Ashe, Hutchinson, 1900.
[5] *Kekewich in Kimberley*, W.A. O'Meara, Medici Society, 1926.
[6] Rhodes Papers, 2 November, 1899. Quoted in *The Lion's Cage*.
[7] Rhodes Papers, 5 November, 1899. Quoted in *The Lion's Cage*

When the Commander-in-Chief of all the British forces in South Africa, General Sir Redvers Buller, learned of Rhodes' concern about the military situation in Kimberley he replied to Kekewich, 'Have heard nothing about this from you. Send appreciation of the situation immediately.'[8]

Kekewich was astonished at this request. He had not realized that, despite his orders regarding censorship, Rhodes was still in contact with such important people. Kekewich therefore sent a brief reply to the C-in-C: 'Situation in Kimberley not critical.'

On Saturday morning, 4 November, 1898, a detachment of Boers carrying a white flag approached Kimberley. They brought a message from the Boer Commandant, C.J. Wessels, to the effect that Kimberley must surrender unconditionally by six o'clock on the following Monday morning.

The Boer commander also said that he would receive 'all Afrikaner families who wish to leave Kimberley'. This notice would end at six o'clock on the morning of 6 November. The Boers would also offer 'liberty to depart' to all women and children of other nations who might wish to leave.

Kekewich drafted a reply which he sent to Rhodes at the Sanatorium Hotel for his approval. Rhodes said that the reply should only mention Afrikaner women and children, to show that the Boers had two classifications for white people – Afrikaners and British.

At six o'clock on the evening of 6 November, twelve hours after the ultimatum ended, the Boers fired two artillery shells into Kimberley. The mines used loud hooters to mark the start and end of shifts. Now they sounded warning of a possible attack. Boer artillery shelled the town regularly, but their explosives were of poor quality and most shells fell short.

The Boer big guns moved closer to the town and children found a new game. They scoured areas where shells had landed and picked up pieces of shrapnel to sell as souvenirs. Adults built dug-outs and made shelters with sandbags and sheets of corrugated iron.

General Buller thought that the war would be won or lost in Natal, and Kimberley, as a military target was, in his opinion, not of the first importance. Equally, he could not ignore personal messages from a Privy Councillor, the most famous man in South Africa, a man in direct contact with the High Commissioner in Cape Town and the Cabinet in London, where the Rothschilds were also stressing the importance of the diamond mines.

Redvers Buller therefore despatched a relief force of 8,000 men to Kimberley, under General Lord Methuen, who had recently arrived in South Africa. The Boers were believed to have rather less than this number under arms in the Kimberley area, but Methuen had very few maps and

[8] W.A. O'Meara, op. cit.

239

those he possessed proved of little tactical use; they simply showed farm boundaries rather than contours. Methuen therefore decided to advance along the railway line for what seemed to him to be a fairly simple action.

His force included the Guards Brigade, New South Wales Lancers and several hundred sailors with heavy guns, who made up the Naval Brigade. Methuen had sufficient men to ensure Kimberley's safety, but he lacked three vital necessities for the quick victory which he was confident he could achieve. He had no mounted troops to reconnoitre the situation, to ride at the head and on either side of his long marching column. He did not have any information about Boer tactics and, most important of all for any successful general, he lacked good luck.

His column, however, stretching for a mile, presented a formidable spectacle with sunlight glittering on polished brasswork and leather belts and, an unmissable target, marching beneath an enormous cloud of dust raised by their boots.

To prudent suggestions that he should bypass the main Boer position Methuen replied with the confident answer, 'I intend to put the fear of God into these people.'

In the early morning of 23 November, with this aim in mind, his troops attacked a rocky ridge where the Boers had dug themselves into trenches and behind boulders. Within twenty-five minutes seventy-one British soldiers lay dead and 220 were wounded. Then the Boers retreated, to regroup and fight again. First blood to them – and a shattering blow to British morale.

In Kimberley, meanwhile, Rhodes and Kekewich knew nothing of this setback, but relations between them were steadily deteriorating, most obviously at their regular meetings in the Sanatorium.

'You are afraid of a mere handful of farmers, armed with rifles,' Rhodes told Kekewich angrily. 'You call yourselves soldiers of an empire-making nation. I do believe you will next take fright at a pair of broomsticks dressed up in trousers. Give it up!'[9]

Boer shelling of Kimberley continued, except on Sundays, when it ceased because of their gunners' strict religious beliefs. Casualties were very slight, even after a barrage of 700 shells. One Boer woman in Kimberley was said to have died of fright; a cab driver broke his arm when his horse was shot and fell on him; two men received minor wounds.

The heaviest British artillery in Kimberley were seven-pounder guns, while the German-made Boer artillery fired shells of up to fifteen pounds. The Kimberley guns, which Rhodes contemptuously called 'pop-guns', did

9 Brian Gardner, op. cit.

succeed, however, in keeping the Boers at some distance, but this could not last for long because their ammunition was running low.

George Labram, with Rhodes' authority, now used the De Beers' foundry to build a huge gun. He had no previous experience of such a task or of the ammunition the gun might require, but he dissected unexploded Boer shells and then mixed dynamite and other explosives used in the mines to fill shell cases which his engineers could turn out very quickly and in large numbers.

This giant gun, with its huge wheels, took twenty-four days to construct and could fire a 28-pound shell through a 4.1-inch bore. Because of its long range, and in honour of Rhodes, it was called 'Long Cecil'.

Labram, as the builder, commanded it and each shell case was stamped in the foundry with 'CJR's comps'. When the gun fired, Kekewich reported that, through his telescope, he could see Boers fleeing 'in every direction in a frantic state'. It had a further advantage; its presence greatly raised the morale of everyone in Kimberley.

The troops in Lord Methuen's column, on the march again, sang 'Rule, Britannia', 'God Save the Queen' and 'Soldiers of the Queen'. Their cheerfulness was in sharp contrast to the inefficiency of their commanders. When they stopped for the night, for example, they found that the nearest pool of water was three-quarters of a mile away and extremely muddy. Food wagons arrived belatedly and only after dark; their drivers did not know where different units had bivouacked.

As a result, next morning the Naval Brigade had to set off without any breakfast and marched for three hours. They did not see any Boers, although scouts reported that as many as 500 Boers were on either side, but wisely keeping out of range.

The Brigade was out in open country when the Boers opened fire from behind the cover of rocks and trenches. Within an hour half the Naval Brigade had been killed or wounded. The survivors had been without food or water for eighteen hours in the heat of the day. Some crowded around locomotives on the railway line, desperate to sip steam or drips of water seeping from overflow pipes.

In Kimberley Rhodes was so concerned that the town might fall that he asked Kekewich to inform headquarters in Cape Town that he would personally raise, at his own expense, 2,000 horsemen to defend it. Kekewich claimed to be pleased at this proposal, but pointed out that they would take time to train and equip, and he would have to find suitable officers. Kekewich diplomatically suggested that Rhodes approach GHQ himself.

Kimberley had one searchlight, like so much else the property of De Beers, mounted on a wooden tower. With this watchers would rake the sky at night, peering into the darkness through telescopes, hoping they might see an answering searchlight from the relieving column. At last they saw a faint flickering with two letters in Morse code, 'M D'. This meant the Modder River. Kimberley answered with 'K B', to show the message was received.

Then came their first long message from the relieving force: 'Ascertain number on forefoot of mule omitted in Cape Town return.' That such a ludicrously trivial matter could occupy the minds of those who should be relieving Kimberley caused the standing of the British army in the town to fall sharply.

Then came a single word – 'Klokfontein'. This turned out to be a farm south of the Modder River. So the relief column were on their way at last. Because Methuen had no proper maps he had first kept to the line of the railway and then the river. Again his column marched steadily on into a complex ambush.

The Boers withdrew after this action, but the British lost seventy killed and 413 wounded, most in the first moments of the battle. They were still held up from approaching Kimberley, now only twenty miles away. Citizens, knowing that a relief force was so close, confidently expected its arrival at any hour. Then Kekewich received a message that the relief column could only pause in Kimberley when it did arrive and then go on. In the meantime, civilians could be evacuated.

Rhodes demanded to see this message. Kekewich informed him about it on the understanding that Rhodes would keep it to himself. Such an evacuation would involve at least 8,000 whites and 12,000 Africans, and so posed a very difficult problem of logistics as well as morale. Then Kekewich heard that the De Beers directors were discussing the matter.

He was further infuriated by the fact that Rhodes seemed able to send messages to Cape Town while he could hardly get a message to Lord Methuen twenty miles away. 'Kekewich was nearing a mental breakdown.'[10]

Kekewich now advised Methuen that he had information that the Boers were likely to try and halt the column at Magersfontein, a ridge of hills so long that it would be impossible to pass by a detour.

The Boers fully realized Magersfontein's significance. They dug a system of trenches nearly ten miles from end to end, concealed with grass, branches, and protected with a barbed wire fence on metal stakes. When Methuen sent out cavalry scouts to reconnoitre, they reported that they did not see any Boers. They also missed these hidden trenches.

Methuen ordered a heavy artillery barrage on the hills before he attacked, to try and neutralize any Boer defensive positions. What he did not know was that the shells simply passed harmlessly over the heads of the Boers in their trenches. When the British did attack they were caught on the wire and

---

[10] Gardner, op. cit.

massacred. The Guards Brigade and the Highland Brigade, two of the British army's crack units, had very high casualties.

In London this British defeat, with about 1,000 casualties inflicted within minutes, was greeted first with disbelief and then with horror. It seemed impossible that what many people in Britain still thought of as only a rabble of untrained Dutch farmers could inflict such a swift and savage defeat on the pride of the British army.

General Buller telegraphed to Methuen that he should retire to the Orange River, from where he had started weeks earlier. Methuen managed to delay this humiliating retirement; he believed he was facing a force of 16,000 Boers.

Later, when Rhodes heard this, he retorted contemptuously, 'Look over the census reports. Men cannot be made in a minute. It takes 20 years to make a man, and we know how many they had at the beginning of the war. The Transvaal only polled a little over 17,000 votes at the last election. No, we are exaggerating their numbers simply because, by doing so, we account for bad generalship without confessing it.'

The Empire – Australia, New Zealand and Canada – shared Britain's new determination that this humiliation must be speedily revenged. Lord Roberts, then nearly seventy, who had served for forty-one years in India, and the most famous Field Marshal in the British army, was put in charge – on the day he heard that his own son had been killed in South Africa. Major General Lord Kitchener of Khartoum, another charismatic figure, was his Chief of Staff and sailed with him for the Cape with strong reinforcements.

Methuen decided to wait until they arrived. He built a camp with railway sidings so that supplies coming from the Cape could be unloaded more easily. While his troops waited they had little to do. They organized games; Methuen presented a challenge cup for football matches between the different units.

Inside Kimberley Rhodes seemed totally unconcerned for his own safety. Some had criticized him previously for his preference, when sleeping in a tent in the veld, to sleep away from the door in case of being eaten by a lion. Now, as when he met the Matabele chiefs, he appeared indifferent to personal danger.

He would ride around the town in his white trousers, tweed jacket and soft felt hat, a target for any Boer sharpshooter. 'The very sight of him . . . was sufficient to inspire the fainthearted with confidence.'[11]

In addition to attempting to ensure that Kimberley would not fall, Rhodes never lost sight of his huge and continuing commercial obligations. One of his staff was marching with Methuen's column. Rhodes sent him a message

[11] *Kimberley: Turbulent City*, Brian Roberts, op. cit.

on Christmas Eve – to cable the Chartered company's office in Cape Town to wire London that they 'must pay De Beers' debentures by 1st January'.

The same day Rhodes sent another message about the telegraph line he planned as a link between South Africa and the North. This line would have to go across German territory, for which he had received permission from the Kaiser. He now cabled: 'German Emperor having signed agreement with me cable home they must proceed Tanganyika with all despatch. If not we shall be in our graves before telegraph reaches Egypt.'

On Christmas Day *The Diamond Fields Advertiser* printed a Christmas message from Queen Victoria which it had received by runner; and from De Beers' warehouses Rhodes produced plum puddings and toys for the children. Then, in the following week, food was rationed.

Rhodes organized a soup kitchen, run by the secretary of the Kimberley Club. Initially this provided 3,000 pints of soup a day; by the end of the siege it was producing 8,000 pints every day.

Bread was rationed at twelve ounces a day, meat at a third of this amount. Mules and old donkeys were killed for their meat, some of which went into the soup, which sometimes was so thick that people ate it with a knife and fork. Pet cats and dogs were disappearing, to be skinned and eaten. Morale steadily declined. Children, who lacked adequate amounts of milk or vegetables, were falling ill; many died.

The Boers brought up a 6-inch gun, 'Long Tom', to bear on the town. The Boers did not fire it themselves, but employed French mercenaries. Its huge shells now caused severe panic in Kimberley. Men strengthened the crude shelters with sheets of steel and railway sleepers – anything to give cover from Long Tom's shells and the scattering of shrapnel.

Kekewich heliographed to Methuen: 'Shelling has created consternation particularly among women. Endeavouring allay same by erecting bombproofs. Difficulty is providing secure cover for so large population. Position here becoming serious.'

Rhodes was furious that there still seemed no sign of a quick relief for the besieged town. He warned Kekewich that, unless he received within forty-eight hours exact details of what was being proposed in this connection, he would call a public meeting so that before Kimberley surrendered – as he claimed it might – the British people at home would know 'what I think of all this'.

The unpalatable truth was that Kekewich did not know when Kimberley would be relieved. Equally, he knew that a number of Boer supporters were in the town and they regularly smuggled out messages to the besiegers. News of a mass meeting, as Rhodes proposed, would be almost certain to reach the Boers outside Kimberley and would reveal the dangerously low morale of Kimberley's defenders.

One of the shells from Long Tom killed George Labram. He was in his bathroom in the Grand Hotel, washing before going to dinner, when the room suffered a direct hit. At first Rhodes hoped it would be possible to embalm his body and send it back to the United States in an airtight metal coffin. When this proved impractical, Labram was buried in Kimberley, but at night, in order not to attract a crowd of mourners, which might draw the attention of the French gun crew handling Long Tom.

After Labram's death Rhodes made arrangements for women and children to shelter in the mines. Latrines and adequate lighting and other facilities were organized and each evening guides marshalled queues who waited by the mine shafts. Every morning pails of hot milk were provided for the babies, and coffee, tea and bread for the mothers, with tubs of soup and sandwiches later in the day. Altogether 2500 people sheltered in these mines.

The Diamond Fields Advertiser printed an article[12] which somehow managed to avoid censorship. It was clearly based on Rhodes' own views.

'We have stood a siege which is rapidly approaching the duration of the siege of Paris. . . . Through the genius of Mr Labram we have been able not merely to supply ammunition for the pop-guns sent to Kimberley, but also to produce in our own workshops the only weapon capable of minimizing the terrible havoc and destruction caused by the enemy's six-inch gun. . . .

'We are fully aware that there are at the present moment 120,000 British troops in South Africa. . . . Arrayed against this vast army – the largest by far that England has ever got together since the Napoleonic Wars – are the burghers of two small republics . . . and why in the name of commonsense should Kimberley wait?

'We have now reached a situation when either a newspaper must speak out or it has no *raison d'être* and should cease to exist. . . .

'Is it unreasonable, when our women and children are being slaughtered, and our buildings fired, to expect something better than that a large British Army should remain inactive in the presence of eight or ten thousand peasant soldiers?'

Rhodes guessed that Kekewich might arrest the editor for publishing this without submitting it to the censor. To prevent this, he concealed the editor in one of the mine shafts.

Kekewich closed the newspaper. Rhodes then demanded that a statement which he had agreed with 'the twelve leading citizens in Kimberley' should be sent to Lord Roberts by heliograph. Kekewich told him that the message would be delayed because of the amount of messages the signallers were already handling.

[12] 10 February, 1900.

'You low damned mean cur!' shouted Rhodes, and would have hit him had not the Mayor of Kimberley pulled them apart.

Field Marshal Lord Roberts sent a message instructing Kekewich to urge on the Mayor and Rhodes 'as strongly as you possibly can disaster and humiliating effect of surrendering after so prolonged and glorious defence'.[13] Rhodes replied, explaining that they had 'never thought or spoken of surrendering'.

Now, at last, the watchers in their towers began to see a huge cloud of dust moving towards Kimberley like a living illustration of an Old Testament story. This was the relief column – at last; 25,000 infantry and cavalry, with 600 supply wagons and gun limbers. The Boers were astounded at the size of this huge force; they had never seen or even imagined such an army. To provide mounts for the cavalry in the numbers required, horses had been brought from as far away as Australia and the Argentine.

The Boers attempted to halt the column at Abon's Dam, to the north of the Modder River, but General John French, in charge of the column, did not falter or pause. Instead, he charged. Some Boers fled. Others died bravely where they stood, trampled by horses' hooves or lanced by their riders.

Rhodes knew what was happening here before Kekewich had any report of the engagement, because Rhodes had personal heliograph contact with a colleague riding with the column. Finally, on 15 February, 1900 – the 124th day of the siege – General French and his staff, with his force which had marched or ridden 120 miles in four days, were ready to enter Kimberley.

Kekewich, as the town's military commander, rode out to meet the General, but went in the wrong direction and so missed him. He returned to find General French and his staff drinking champagne as Rhodes' guests in the Sanatorium Hotel.

Kekewich felt too embarrassed to enter the building, but Rhodes saw him standing hesitantly in the doorway and told him sharply, 'This is my house. Get out of it!' However, one of French's staff officers had also seen Kekewich and took him in to meet the General in a side room.

French was not well disposed to Kekewich; Rhodes had already left him in no doubt as to his personal opinion of the commander. Afterwards a note of Kekewich's interview with General French came into Rhodes' possession.
Kekewich: I have borne with this man as long as I could.
French: Yes, but you should remember that Mr Rhodes, or 'this man' as you call him, owns the place, and that he is a power not only in the Empire but in Europe, and you should have tried to work with him.
Kekewich: I thought I was in supreme command.

[13] O'Meara, op. cit.

French: Command should always be exercised with discretion or it is apt to savour of tyranny.

Kekewich: Well, sir, I have done my best.

French: I don't doubt that, but you have done it in a way that has irritated.[14]

For most of that night Kimberley celebrated. De Beers promised £1,000 to any soldiers who could capture the Boer gun Long Tom, but the French crew successfully spirited it away.

Two days later the *Daily Mail* commented: 'Kimberley is won. Mr Cecil Rhodes is free. De Beers shareholders are all full of themselves and the beginning of the war is at an end. This is a great feat to have accomplished and the happiest omen for the future. There is no one like Bobs.' [Field Marshal Lord Roberts]

In an interview in the same newspaper Rhodes said: 'The marvellous thing about England is her luck. We have made the silliest mistakes, we have had some most incompetent generals, but we are coming out all right as we always do. Glad to have Kimberley relieved? Of course, we are all glad, but in heaven's name why was it not done sooner?'

Six days after the siege ended the Rev Arthur Gray Butler wrote to Rhodes from Oxford:

'We had a big supper at Oriel at the end of last term to celebrate our winning of the Association Football cup,' he explained. 'In proposing the health of the team, I alluded to the pleasure it would give Oriel men all over the world, *not forgetting one at Kimberley.* Then they stood up and cheered, and cheered, and cheered again.'

On the following day Rhodes told De Beers' shareholders, 'We have done our best to preserve that which is the best commercial asset in the world, the protection of Her Majesty's flag.'

Some time afterwards, when Rhodes was asked about Kekewich, he affected not to remember him.

'Kekewich? Who's he? You don't remember the man who cleans your boots.'

Possibly not, but Kimberley remembered Kekewich. Many citizens realized the difficulties under which he had attempted to carry out his orders. They invited him back in July, 1902, at the end of the Anglo-Boer War. This followed an earlier return visit by General French, who was given a sword in a golden scabbard to commemorate his relief of the town.

Kimberley men presented Kekewich with his own sword of honour; the women gave him a gold cigarette case. This must have been his only happy memory of his months in command, for twelve years later, in poor health

[14] Rhodes Papers, 2 March, 1900. Quoted in *The Lion's Cage.*

and a bitterly disappointed man, Robert George Kekewich committed suicide.

The siege had weakened Rhodes physically and emotionally. He had found it intolerable, as a multimillionaire and a Privy Councillor, accustomed to negotiating with heads of state, to be reduced to arguing and bickering with an obscure lieutenant colonel. Rhodes' breathing was now heavy, his face more blotched and blueish, his whole body thicker. He looked and walked like an old man.

When he returned to Cape Town he found that Princess Radziwill had been intriguing with the Bond, running up bills at her hotel, still hinting she was about to marry him.

Rhodes did not stay long – he had arranged to consult a specialist in London about his rapidly failing health – but before he sailed he paid all her bills, including her fare to England, and advised her most strongly to leave South Africa. This she did, following him to London.

Here she wrote various political articles and became involved in a curious incident in her London hotel. She was, as always, short of money to maintain her style of life and had pawned some jewels, said to be worth £25,000, for a fraction of this sum. She was now involved with pawnbrokers and money lenders who demanded huge rates of interest on any money they advanced.

One day, when she was lunching in her hotel with a friend, her maid rushed in to tell her that her suite had been burgled. The Princess immediately told the manager of the hotel that she had lost jewels worth £50,000. She repeated this story to a number of other people she knew in London – and to the newspapers. She visited Vine Street police station to report her loss officially and, under questioning, she made an extraordinary admission. The jewels she said she had lost were not worth £50,000. They were paste replicas, worth at the most £40. She explained that she had pretended they were real because she did not wish to admit to friends that they were false.

According to the police report, Princess Radziwill said 'she was engaged to Mr Rhodes who was assisting her to obtain her divorce, when he intended marrying her.'[15]

It was not difficult to persuade the police to do nothing further in this delicate matter, but the hotel manager put the Princess and her maid out of their suite. Rhodes had meanwhile returned to South Africa. She followed him, but by the time she arrived Rhodes had left Cape Town for Rhodesia. In the meantime, tradesmen in London sued her for unpaid bills and her remaining jewels were sold for £12,000.

[15] Quoted from a memorandum from the Metropolitan Police, 'C' Division, April 3, 1902, in *Cecil Rhodes*, John Flint, Hutchinson, 1976.

The Princess's troubles now began to multiply. A lawyer who had in the past worked for Rhodes issued a sum of £1,150 to the Princess on the basis of a promissory note forged with Rhodes' signature for £2,000. The money was not paid and the lawyer sued Rhodes and Princess Radziwill for this amount.

Rhodes returned in November, 1900. Oddly, despite his growing exasperation with Princess Radziwill, he gave her some money which she used to finance a newspaper, *Greater Britain*, which appeared from the following June to August. She advocated that Rhodes should concentrate on his associations with Jan Hofmeyr and the Bond and abandon Milner's policy of defeating the Boers.

The Princess proposed making peace between the Boers and the British, to allow Rhodes to return as Prime Minister, this time as premier of a federated South Africa.

Rhodes, however, was by now too ill to become involved in such matters. His eyes were on farther horizons than South African politics. He did not wish to spend time on them; he realized that at last his own time was all but over. His energies were largely concentrated on his plans for Scholarships; he also wished to buy an estate in Norfolk for his family, and to travel through Europe, ending his tour in Egypt.

The Princess sank steadily into deeper debt. She claimed to Milner that Rhodes was refusing to sign bills, as he had promised, because he did not agree with the policies she put forward in her paper. She also maintained that Rhodes had told her he would not prosecute her if she gave him letters that Milner had sent to her.

Milner's reaction was prompt and unequivocal; he ordered the Criminal Investigation Department to investigate. The head of the C.I.D. paid the Princess a visit and removed various letters involving Rhodes.

Desperate for money, the Princess forged Rhodes' signature on a bill for £4,500, then a promissory note endorsed with another forged signature for £6,300.

She was arrested and charged on altogether twenty-four counts of fraud and forgery. By means not revealed, funds fortuitously arrived from England and she was allowed out on bail.

Now she spread rumours that she possessed secret telegrams between Cape Town and London regarding the Jameson Raid. She threatened to make these public unless the prosecution was dropped. It was not dropped.

Rhodes returned from England in January, 1902, to give evidence against her. No one ever explained satisfactorily why he did so. There was no need for him to be present in person at her trial. He deliberately undertook the journey against the strong advice of his doctors, who feared that it would prove too much in his weak state of health. He could quite easily have given his evidence in London, but he was determined to face her accusations in person.

He had booked a passage late and the only cabins left were below the main deck and very airless and hot. When Rhodes was shown the cabin he had been allotted, he refused to occupy it. His secretary explained the situation to the ship's chief officer, who immediately offered Rhodes his own cabin on the boat deck, which had a porthole and an electric fan.

Rhodes was very grateful; his breathing was now extremely difficult. He caught a cold and tried to sleep on a writing table instead of in his berth, because he believed that he would be cooler there. The ship rolled unexpectedly, he fell off the table on to the floor and bruised himself severely. By the time he reached Cape Town he was in infinitely worse shape than when he set out.

To keep his arrival in South Africa as quiet as possible, because he now looked extremely old and ill, the ship anchored offshore and Rhodes, Metcalfe and Jameson transferred to a tug which took them in to the quay. A closed carriage then drove Rhodes to Groote Schuur.

The public had no idea of the severity of Rhodes' health and he did not wish to enlighten them. He always maintained he was in good health, because rumours that this was untrue could depress the stock market. For this same reason, because investors believed that whatever shares he advocated must appreciate, whenever Rhodes sold shares in a company he did so through nominees so that his action would not cause the shares to fall and other investors to lose money.

People in Cape Town awaited the court case involving the Princess with great interest. It was suggested that she could, and would if need be, produce documents which would have a devastating political effect.

Initially her counsel asked for an adjournment, but this was refused. When Rhodes appeared, his counsel showed him various notes bearing his signature; by now the sum of £23,000 was involved.

'They are all forgeries,' said Rhodes. 'I have signed no promissory notes . . . all absolute forgeries.'

The case was adjourned.

If the Princess did have copies of telegrams between Cape Town and London before the Jameson Raid, whatever she might claim about them would now be suspect. Since Rhodes had stated that his signatures on the promissory notes were forgeries, who was likely to believe her claims that any other documents she might produce were genuine?

If Rhodes had come to Cape Town to discredit Princess Radziwill in this way, he could have considered his journey worthwhile. But five or six years after the Jameson Raid any telegrams she might produce would have very little effect, politically or otherwise.

John Flint, in his biography of Rhodes, has a convincing explanation as to why he risked – and lost – his life by returning to South Africa in his terminal state of health. 'Rhodes had become heartily sick of the whole affair and wanted to make sure the Princess went behind bars.'[16]

Rhodes succeeded in this, if indeed it was his intention. When her case eventually came before the court at the end of April, she was found guilty and sentenced to two years' imprisonment in the House of Correction. By then, however, Rhodes, who she had tried so assiduously first to cultivate and then to implicate, was dead.

[16] John Flint, op. cit.

CHAPTER 14

'IF I'D HAD HIS EDUCATION THERE WOULD HAVE BEEN NO CECIL RHODES'

February and March that year had been unusually hot in Cape Town. Birds drooped. Animals in Rhodes' park around Groote Schuur stood listlessly under what shade they could find beneath the trees. The earth shimmered like a mirage during long dry afternoons; nights were very little cooler.

All the windows were open in Groote Schuur, but for Rhodes, with his laboured, painful breathing, the house still felt far too close and confined. He moved restlessly from room to room, trying to find some place where he could breathe more easily. His shirt was open to the waist and his hands stuck characteristically inside the belt of his trousers. His face shone with perspiration, simply from the effort of breathing.

In the large drawing room curtains had been drawn to keep out the heat of the sun, but even here the air felt stale and used up. Rhodes would lie down briefly on a couch, then move to an armchair, or go into the anteroom his secretaries used as an office. Then he would call for his new Wolseley car, of which he was both proud and possessive, to drive to Muizenberg and watch the great waves break across the wide arc of the beach. But even the stiffest and coolest breeze blowing in from the ocean could do little to help him.

Earlier, in happier times, he and Jameson, who was now with him constantly, had discussed death and especially the act of dying. Rhodes, aware of his heart condition, remarked that at least anyone dying from heart failure had a clean death. Jameson had not answered. Now the reason was becoming clear.

Some time before these final days Rhodes had been out riding with J.G. Macdonald, the manager of his estates in Rhodesia. Returning to Government House, he announced his intention to plant an avenue of trees and told Macdonald the story of the old admiral he had once met who was planting acorns.

'I'll plant an avenue here,' Rhodes announced. 'I see an avenue, with carriages going up the centre, and there will be ladies and gentlemen riding between the trees on one side, and there are nursemaids between the trees on the other side.'

Now, as Rhodes felt his strength steadily ebb away, he urged Macdonald to remember his instructions.

'Get that avenue going,' he told him. 'Make a success of it! We have got to fulfil our promise to give shade to the nursemaids in the afternoon.'

But for Rhodes, even in this little cottage so close to the sea, there was no shade. He could scarcely breathe if he lay down, and so for hours he would sit on the edge of his narrow bed, his hands flat under his thighs, leaning back against a broad canvas band stretched above the bed.

To try and improve the flow of air, an extra window had been knocked in one wall and holes cut above his head in the ceiling. An Indian-style punkah was fitted, with a servant to pull the rope day and night. Above this large tins were regularly replenished with ice cubes. But still he gasped and laboured for breath. Now and then he would doze and almost fall forward, and then wake up sharply.

Outside the cottage people would come and press their faces against the windows, hoping to catch a glimpse of 'the old man'. Lights burned in each room all through every night and, when Rhodes' breathing became too difficult and painful, Jameson and other doctors in attendance would give him oxygen from a cylinder by his bedside.

Important letters would be read to him. In the newspapers he would only read the regular and anodyne medical bulletins about his condition.

'There is something strange and pathetic at seeing a man of his wealth breathing away in a miserable, airless little cottage,' said a visitor, saddened by the sight. Rhodes was too ill now to move or be moved. Cables from Jameson to London all stressed how he was going 'steadily downhill'. His lungs were hardly acting at all. Heart failure was prevented only by the administration of oxygen.

Early one morning Jameson told Rhodes' secretary, Gordon Le Sueur, to fetch Sir Edmond Stevenson, a senior physician in Cape Town, because Rhodes' condition was worsening. At once Le Sueur set off in Rhodes' Wolseley.

Rhodes heard the engine start and asked Jameson who was using the car. Jameson explained that his secretary was taking it to Cape Town. Rhodes said angrily, 'Tell him not to use my car. It is *my* car, not his.'

In the evenings he would call out irritably to his companions keeping vigil in the next room, 'Why don't you play bridge, instead of sitting about doing nothing?'

Once, because one of his African servants from Groote Schuur had apparently annoyed him in some way, Rhodes made him sit upright, facing him, for several hours. When Rhodes dozed and the man tried to slip away, Rhodes would instantly start up, suddenly awake.

'Sit there!' he would command petulantly. 'Just sit there.'

Jameson slept in the room next to his bedroom and Rhodes' secretary would use a truckle bed across the open doorway. Once, when Jameson was briefly out of the room, Rhodes asked for his lawyer to be called; he wanted to provide for Jameson in his will. Jameson heard of this intention and would have none of it. When Rhodes attempted to write a codicil himself on a piece of paper, Jameson simply took the pen and the paper out of his hands. He did not want Rhodes' money; he simply wanted to be with him.

Rhodes announced one day that he was going to return to England. Passage was booked aboard the Royal Mail ship *Saxon*, sailing that Wednesday, and a cabin fitted with a special refrigerating plant, oxygen facilities and electric fans. But, as the date for departure approached, Jameson told Rhodes gently that the voyage was not feasible. Jameson knew that, in Rhodes' present condition, he would not survive long enough to reach the docks at Cape Town.

On 21 March Jameson sent a note to Lewis Michell warning him of the approaching end: 'Stevenson and I convinced case is hopeless. It has lasted longer than we expected, owing to extraordinary vitality, but the end is certain, though patient still anxious to sail on Wednesday.'

Jameson had regularly cabled other specialists in Cape Town and London about Rhodes' condition. He sent these cables in code, in case they should affect the Stock Market.

He was treating Rhodes with digitalis and strychnine to help his heart, and morphia for his pain. His legs swelled up with fluid, which had to be repeatedly drained through silver tubes. By Sunday, 23 March, he was being kept alive by oxygen and injections of ether.

Michell was sitting by Rhodes' bedside on Wednesday afternoon, while Jameson, who had been on duty for the previous day and night, was lying down in the room next door. Rhodes appeared more restless than usual. Once Michell heard him murmur, 'So little done, so much to do.'

'I heard him singing softly to himself, maybe a few bars of an air he had once sung at his mother's knee,' wrote Michell later. Then Rhodes called out for Jameson for the last time.

Cecil John Rhodes, one of the few men in history who gave his name to a country, and who achieved so much more besides, died at six o'clock that Wednesday evening, 26 March, 1902.

He had indeed sailed on Wednesday, as he planned, but on an infinitely longer voyage.

*　　*　　*

How did the years treat Rhodes' contemporaries after his death?

Fanny Barnato, Barney's widow, lived quietly in a London flat, with a house in Upper Colwyn Bay and another in Brighton. Oddly, she never appeared to have much money. When she died, aged 96, the jewellery that Barney had given her, and which had accentuated her good looks at the box he would take at the theatre, had long since disappeared.

The only items in her possession were a pearl necklace and a gold chain bracelet. On this hung a gold sovereign Barney had won at Kimberley in the boxing ring and a soft lead bullet, a memento of a shooting accident at a railway station on the Free State border. One day, waiting with Barney to change trains, a customs official accidentally fired his rifle and shot her in the leg. Barney retrieved the bullet and fixed it to his wife's bracelet as a lucky charm. She kept it all her life.

'In her later years,' wrote her grand-daughter, Diana Barnato Walker, 'Grandma Barnato was blackmailed. She couldn't have got through so much money otherwise. My father tried desperately to find out why or who, but to no avail. In the end he gave her a monthly then a vast weekly "allowance" but she still used it all up in spite of her simple living standard.'[1]

*　　*　　*

'Rhodes could never have achieved what he did at Kimberley nor in Rhodesia without Beit,'[2] wrote Lionel Phillips. Alfred Beit was a financial genius. He was not interested in politics; he left that to Rhodes. Beit was interested in making money. He did not make it for what it could buy – although latterly he owned a magnificent house in London and built a similar one for his mother in Hamburg – but for the good he could do with money, the help it would enable him to give to others less fortunate.

Beit had cultured tastes. He collected paintings and maintained a permanent box at Covent Garden, but he was a solitary man. Like Rhodes and Jameson, he was a bachelor. His most constant companions in England were a series of fox terriers, each one called Jackie.

Beit was genuinely concerned about the welfare of workers in the gold and diamond mines that had provided his prodigious fortune. He was also immensely shy – to such an extent that when he bought a country estate at Tewin Water in Hertfordshire, he specifically asked two friends, Earl Grey and Sir Lewis Michell, to come with him when he moved in for the first time.

Dr Sauer thought that Alfred Beit suffered a stroke when he visited a new diamond mine near Pretoria that was not under De Beers' control. The diamonds this mine was producing, in size and quality, he saw as a serious threat to De Beers' operations. This mine later produced the Cullinan diamond.

[1] Walker, op. cit.
[2] Phillips, op. cit.

Others thought that Beit's stroke was brought on when an imposter claimed that he could manufacture artificial diamonds far more cheaply than genuine stones could be dug out of the earth.

Alfred Beit died four years after Rhodes (and, at 53, four years older). He left millions to endow universities, medical and other charities, and the Beit Trust.

A bust in his memory stands in Kimberley. Its inscription encapsulates Alfred Beit's life and his simple endearing philosophy: 'Write me as one who loved his fellow men'.

★   ★   ★

Dr Jameson came back into South African politics and into power. He was appointed Prime Minister of the Cape, became president of the Chartered and was made a baronet. His poor health had meant he was released from jail early and for years he suffered severely from the effects of malaria and dysentery.

On Jameson's death on the afternoon of Monday, 26 November, 1917, his body was placed in a vault at Kensal Green cemetery until the end of the war. Later it was taken to Rhodesia to be buried in a grave cut in the granite at the top of the mountain Rhodes called 'The world's view'.

In life Jameson had always been loyally at Rhodes' right hand. In death they were not divided.

★   ★   ★

Paul Kruger, who had always declared he would not die under the British flag, lived up to his words.

'His army had been routed, his capital seized, he was forced to flee to Europe, yet he was hailed as a hero.'[3]

The Kaiser, although he had been willing to advance Kruger's chances when he believed that Kruger might be successful, did not allow him to settle in Germany.

Instead, France gave Kruger refuge – and acclamation. In Marseilles 400 people held a banquet in his honour. His speeches there, in Lyons and in Dijon, were all greeted with great applause.

Ironically, Kruger had lost everything on which throughout his life he had set his mind and heart. In their place he gained a fame long after it was of any practical use to him.

★   ★   ★

'Call no man happy until he dies,' wrote Herodotus. 'He is at best fortunate.'

Were Cecil Rhodes and Barney Barnato happy, or were they just fortunate? Both knew periods of happiness. Barney was probably happiest

[3] Apollon Davidson, op. cit.

facing an audience – in a theatre or addressing shareholders and bringing them round to his way of thought, or when visiting old friends in the East End.

Rhodes was possibly happiest when he was young and relatively fit, when he proved against all criticism that he could grow cotton; then that he could find diamonds, and so achieve his first ambition of becoming an Oxford undergraduate, at his own expense, on his own terms, indebted to no one.

In later life happiness certainly eluded him. On his last visit to Britain Rhodes rented a shooting lodge near Loch Rannoch in Perthshire and spent a holiday with old friends from early South African days.

He was by then too ill to join his own fishing or shooting parties, but one of his guests, the young Countess of Warwick, would join him for rides on hill ponies. On one of these outings she asked Rhodes whether he was happy. He agreed he had been happy when he was planning and dreaming of projects that would never be realized in his lifetime. But, she persisted, had he ever been happy with things as they were now?

'No,' Rhodes admitted. 'I was too busy when I was young. . . . I have had no time since.'

Barney had more reason to be the happier of the two. His health was always good and he did not suffer from premonitions of an early death. Had he lived, he would soon have won back the applause and approval of the public; honours would doubtless have been showered upon him. Most important, and unlike Rhodes, he had a wife and family of whom he was very fond and who loved him.

After his death, Fanny Barnato remarked to Tennyson Cole, the artist who had painted Barney's portrait, 'People thought my husband ugly, but to me he always seemed a very handsome man, with a smile that lit up the darkest room.'

Rhodes, who admitted that he could easily have become a Jesuit, followed the Jesuit belief that what is considered a worthwhile end justifies all means required to achieve it. His legacy is, surely, the thousands of young people who have benefited from his Scholarships. Had it not been for Rhodes, it is arguable that Bill Clinton, a Rhodes Scholar, might never have become President of the United States.

Rhodes' achievement, plus founding a country and driving railway and telegraph lines north against every kind of political and physical opposition, overshadowed Barney Barnato's financial genius. But, as Barney once remarked, 'If I'd had his education, there would have been no Cecil Rhodes.'

The two men's characters were complementary and both were creatures of their time. It is against that time that they should be judged, not by the softer standards of a later age.

Barney Barnato sought money as the only possible way of avoiding a future of poverty and despair. Cecil Rhodes sought money, not for what it would buy him, but for the power it represented. He needed Barney Barnato more than Barney needed him. Rhodes' ambitions were political and Barnato's financial, but, as Rhodes told General Gordon, 'It is no good having big ideas if you have not the cash to carry them out.' Barnato was able to provide much of that cash.

Had Barnato not bought as many mining claims as he could afford in Kimberley, the huge potential of that mine would probably have remained fragmented, with individual diggers owning small numbers of claims. Barney's decisive action, against much opposition, plus his genius in realizing that the biggest diamonds would lie in the blue ground that others considered worthless, made it possible for him to realize not only his dream, but Rhodes'.

Rhodes needed that mine to amalgamate with De Beers and so control the diamond industry. This might not have been possible if Barney had not been in full control and he had been forced to negotiate with a multitude of independent diggers.

While Rhodes is best remembered for his Scholarships, Barney Barnato is by no means forgotten. In Kimberley Barnato Street recalls the cheerful pioneer who Rhodes sometimes called – not condescendingly – 'The Little Prancer'.

The Big Hole, which gave them both wealth and power, is now a prime attraction for tourists. Digging in it stopped in 1909 after it had produced more than £50 million of diamonds.

Johannesburg, with more than 1,000 miles of streets, remembers Barney's name in the Barnato Park District of Berea, Barnato Place, Barnato View, Barnato Court.

The alchemists of old believed that the stars, planets and other earths were always in motion across the sky. They sought the inspiration of such perpetual movement, the prime mover, which, they reasoned, must be the source of all motion.

So far as the diamond industry was concerned, the original prime movers were Cecil Rhodes and Barney Barnato. They were the mainspring of De Beers. Their enterprise spread an initially small concern across the face of the earth with untold benefits to many nations.

Others were with them, of course; others of great and diverse talents and abilities joined them, but they were the first, and their success proved the catalyst for much of South Africa's subsequent economic growth.

The net asset value of what is now De Beers Consolidated and De Beers

Centenary stands at US$ 16.2 billion. De Beers employs 22,000 people around the world, and no less than 2,500,000 more are directly employed in the world diamond industry – mining diamonds and marketing, cutting, selling them.

Through its marketing arm, the Central Selling Organization, De Beers handle between 70 and 80% of the world's newly mined diamond production – and produce half of those diamonds in value terms. Diamonds are important to the economies of many countries – Australia, Angola, Namibia, Zaire, Tanzania, Botswana, Israel, India, Belgium, Russia, South Africa and the United Kingdom – through whose banking system flow the billions of dollars resulting from their sales – a record US $4.8 billion in 1996.

More than thirty years after the deaths of Barnato and Rhodes, the pioneer architects of this enormous undertaking, Dr Sauer, who had known them well, looked back on great events that had involved them, and which would eventually affect the world.

In so doing, he passed judgement with which few, even their harshest critics, could honestly disagree.

'Africa,' Sauer declared, 'will always have her surprises. . . . She will never lose her interest; but I may be pardoned for believing that never again will there be days quite like those early days, or men to equal those whom I knew and of whom I have tried to write.'[4]

BIBLIOGRAPHY

I would like to acknowledge my debt to the following sources:

E.O. Ashe, *Besieged by the Boers*, (Hutchinson, 1900).

Herbert Baker, *Cecil Rhodes by his architect*, (Oxford University Press, London, 1934).

Ian Balfour, *Famous Diamonds*, (Collins, London, 1987).

Alfred Beit and J.G. Lockhard, *The Will and the Way*, (Longmans, Green & Co., 1957).

George Beet, *Grand Old Days of the Diamond Fields*, (Maskew Miller, Cape Town, 1931).

Diana Barnato Walker MBE, *Spreading My Wings*, (Patrick Stephens, Yeovil, 1994).

Loius Cohen, *Reminiscences of Kimberley*, (Historical Society of Kimberley and the Northen Cape, 1990).

Ian Colvin, *The Life of Jameson*, (Edward Arnold & Co., London, 1922).

Lord Randolph S. Churchill, *Men, Mines and Animals in South Africa*, (Sampson Low, Marston & Co., London, 1922).

G.N. Clark, *Cecil Rhodes and his College*, (Oxford University Press, 1953).

P. Tennyson Cole, *Vanity Varnished*, (Hutchinson, London, 1931).

Conan Doyle, *The Great Boer War*, (Smith, Elder, 1901).

Oswald Doughty, *Early Diamond Days*, (Longmans, London, 1963).

Apollon Davidson, *Cecil Rhodes and his time* (translated from the Russian by Christopher English), (Progress Publishers, Moscow, 1988).

John Flint, *Cecil Rhodes*, (Hutchinson, London, 1976).

Sir Thomas E. Fuller, *The Right Honourable Cecil John Rhodes*, (Longmans, Green, London, 1910).

Brian Gardner, *The Lion's Cage*, (Arthur Barker, London, 1969).

Lawrence G. Green, *Like Diamond Blazing*, (Robert Hale, London, 1967).

John Hayes Hammond, *Autobiography*, (Farrar & Rineheart Inc., New York, 1935).

Sir David Harris, *Pioneer, Soldier and Politician*, (Sampson Low, London, 1931).

George Honour, *What Cecil Rhodes thought about 'the native question'*, (The New Rhodesia, Vol. 8, 1951).

Stanley Jackson, *The Great Barnato*, (Heinemann, London, 1970).

Edward Jessup, *Ernest Oppenheimer – A Study in Power*, (Rex Collings, London, 1979).

Stanhope Joel, *Ace of Diamonds*, (Frederick Muller, London, 1959).

Frank Johnson, *Great Days*, (Bell, London, 1940).

Philip Jourdan, *Cecil Rhodes, his private life*, (John Lane, London, 1910).

Sam Kemp, *Black Frontiers, Pioneer Adventures with Cecil Rhodes*, (Harrap, London).

W.M. Kerr, *The Far Interior*, (Sampson Low, London).

John Lang, *Bullion Johannesburg*, (Jonathan Ball, Johannesburg, 1985).

Olga Levinson, *Diamonds in the Desert*, (Tafelbert Publishers, Cape Town, 1993).

Richard Lewinsohn, *Barney Barnato* (translated from the French by Geoffrey Sainsbury), (Routledge, London, 1931).

Gordon Le Sueur, *Cecil Rhodes – the Man and his Work*, (John Murray, London, 1913).

Sir F. Maurice, *Official History of the War in South Africa*, Vol. I, Vol. II, (Hurst & Blackett, 1906, 1907).

André Maurois, *Cecil Rhodes*, (Collins, London, 1953).

J.G. McDonald, *Rhodes: A Life*, (Chatto & Windus, London, 1941).

Sir Lewis Michell, *The Life of the Rt. Hon. Cecil John Rhodes 1853–1902* (in two volumes), (Edward Arnold, London, 1910).

A. Monnickendam, *Secrets of the Diamond*, (Frederick Muller, London, 1941).

W.A. O'Meara, *Kekewich in Kimberley*, (Medici Society, vol. 8, 1951).

Lionel Philips, *Some Remininscences*, (Hutchinson, London, 1924).

William Plomer, *Cecil Rhodes*, (Nelson, London, 1933).

C. Radziwill, *Cecil Rhodes: Man and Empire Maker*, (Cassell, London, 1918).

Terence O. Ranger, *Revolt in Southern Rhodesia, 1896–7*, (Heinemann, London, 1967).

Harry Raymond, *B. I. Barnato*, (Isbister & Co., London, 1897).

Brian Roberts, *Kimberley, Turbulent City*, (David Philip, Cape Town, 1976).

Brian Roberts, *Cecil Rhodes and the Princess*, (Hamish Hamilton, London, 1972).

Brian Roberts, *The Diamond Magnates*, (Hamish Hamilton, London, 1972).

Roberts I. Rotberg, with Miles F. Shore, *The Founder: Cecil Rhodes and the Pursuit of Power*, (Oxford University Press, New York, 1988).

Dr Hans Sauer, *Ex Africa*, Geoffrey Bles, London, 1937).

W.T. Stead, *The Last Will and Testament of Cecil John Rhodes*, (London, 1902).

Anthony Trollope, *South Africa*, (Chapman & Hall, London, 1878).

'Vindex', *Cecil Rhodes, his politcal life and speeches*, (Bell, London, 1900).

Leo Weinthal, *Memories, Mines and Millions*, (Simpkin Marshall, London, 1929).

Basil Williams, *Cecil Rhodes*, (Constable, London, 1921).

Derek Wilson, *Rothschild*, (Andre Deutsch), London, 1988).

Also to the following newspapers:

Diamond News, Kimberley; *Diamond Fields Advertiser*; *Cape Argus* (South Africa).

The Times, London; *Daily Telegraph*, London; *Willesden Chronicle*, London, and to reports of various Parliamentary Debates.

INDEX

Barnato, Jack, 21
Barnato, Leah, 225
Barthelemy, Father, 205–6
Bastards: *see* Griquas
Basutoland, 116
Basutos: *see* Bantus
Bechuanaland, 49, 113–16 *passim*;
    149, 158, 162, 163, 170, 188,
    190
Bechuanaland Exploration
    Company, 151, 155
Bechuanas: *see* Bantus
Bees, Fanny: *see* Barnato, Fanny
Beit, Alfred, 116, 118–21 *passim*;
    127, 132, 135, 142, 144, 158,
    191; pays fines, 201; cable
    from Rhodes, 215; his help to
    Rhodes, 255; stroke and
    death, 255–6
Beit, Siegfried, 118–19
Beresford, Lord Marcus, 4
Bismarck, Otto von, 115, 157
Bloemfontein, 215
Bodley, J.B., 44
Boers, 7, 8, 16, 33, 35, 44, 65, 71,
    87, 89, 105–6, 133, 149, 189,
    202; lifestyle, 12–14; victory at
    Majuba Hill (1881), 113;
    excellent marksmen, 113, 187,
    235; cultivated by Germany,
    114, 187, 195; Rhodes' co-
    operation with, 122, 183;
    government in Pretoria, 133;
    Churchill's description of,
    178; maligned community,
    180; resistant to change, 181;
    no vote in Transvaal, 184;
    treble charges for rail
    transport, 185; 'irritating',
    186; follow Jameson and trap
    his column, 190–3; fear
    uprising, 199; religious beliefs,

211; anti-British campaign in
    Transvaal, 214–15; alleged
    plot against, 222; collapse of
    relations with Britain, 235;
    wish to capture Rhodes and
    blow up mines, 238; demand
    surrender of Kimberley, 239;
    shelling of Kimberley, 240;
    attack Naval Brigade, 241; at
    Magersfontein, 242–3;
    defeated, 246
Bower, Graham, 214
Boyes, Lorenzo, 17, 18, 35–6
Brand, President, 159
British North Borneo Company,
    155
British South Africa Company,
    158, 166, 169, 173, 175, 188,
    189, 192, 201, 202, 208, 213,
    244; cost of Matabele
    rebellion to, 203; telegrams
    about Jameson's raid, 213
Buffalo River, 20
Bulawayo, 149, 153–5 *passim*; 160,
    164, 167, 170, 172, 202
Buller, Sir Redvers, 239, 243
Bultfontein, 36, 43
Bushmen, 11
Butler, Rev. Arthur Gray, 84, 229,
    230, 247

Caldecott, Harry Stratford, 130,
    132
Campbell, Rev. John, 15
Cape Argus, 61, 109
Cape Colony, 14, 19–21 *passim*,
    36, 60, 82, 83, 113, 130, 160,
    183, 185; vote in, 181; discord
    with Transvaal, 184
Cape of Good Hope, 11, 13, 30
Cape of Good Hope Bank, 122,
    132

negotiations over French Company, 124; teams up with uncle Barney over investment in gold mines, 144–5; engages architects for Barnato Buildings, 146; arrested, 196; visited by wife, 198; sentenced and fined, 199; chairman of Johannesburg Stock Exchange, 216; persuades Barney to return to South Africa, 218, 219; fails to save Barney, 220; takes control of Barnato operations in South Africa, 221; receives threatening letter from 'Kismet', 221–2; possibly Barney's murderer, 224; his ambition, 225; swindled Barney, 226; paradoxical character, 226–7; makes Woolf (son) bankrupt, 227; successful racehorse owner, 227

Joel, Stanhope, 223, 224

Joel, Woolf, 4, 98, 125, 127, 143, 148, 221, 224, 225; goes to Kimberley, 98; pays bail for brother, 107, 108; wrongly identified as Isaac Joel, 110; sues, 110; in favour of negotiations over French Company, 124; meets 'Kismet', 222; murdered, 223

Joel, Woolf (son of Solly), 226–7

Johannesburg, prospects of, 175; description of, 184; railway to Vaal river, 185; rights of Uitlanders in, 186; Rhodes prepares raid on, 187–8; conditions there after Jameson's raid, 196

Johannesburg Chamber of Mines, 180

Johannesburg Consolidated Investments, 216, 222

Johannesburg Stock Exchange, 216, 221

John II, King or Portugal, 11

Johnson, Frank, 162, 163

Jourdan, Philip, 203, 231; learns shorthand, 137–8; chief clerk to Rhodes, 138; attack of malaria, 140; negotiations with Matabele, 204, 206; legacy from Rhodes, 232; description of Princess Radziwill's appearance and behaviour, 232–3, 234

Kaffirs: see Bantus

Kalahari Desert, 11, 113, 153

Kann, Rodolphe, 123

Kekewich, Colonel Robert George, 236–7, 238, 239, 241; nearing breakdown, 242; serious position in Kimberley, 244; closes Diamond Fields Advertiser, 245; interview with General French after relief of Kimberley, 246–7; invited back to Kimberley, 247; commits suicide, 248

Kemp, Sam, 27–28, 166

Kerr Brothers, 95–6

Khartoum, 117

Kimberley, mine foundry in, 8; named after Lord Kimberley, 38; £50,000-worth of diamonds taken from, 52; Barney sees Kimberley for first time, 65; Barney meets Cohen in Kimberley, 67; working conditions in, 94, 181;

his death, 135, 136; unease with women, 136, 233; employs Philip Jourdan as secretary, 137–8; resentment over Harry Palk, 138–9; Jack Grimmer only person he fears, 139; habitually gives away clothes, 140; lives by proxy through secretaries, 141; knew nothing of gold mining, 142; believes Lobengula obstacle to central Africa, 150; allows Lobengula's indunas to go to London, 155; petitions Crown for Royal Charter, 156; gives evidence for Dr Prince, 159; proposes to kidnap Lobengula, 162; funds expedition to north, 163; promises claims to Pioneers, 166; sells shares to finance Matabele War, 169; arrives in Salisbury, 171; calls new country Zambesia and changes name to Rhodesia, 173; appointed Privy Councillor, 173, 213; concentrates on politics, 181; creates fruit industry, 181; calls election, 182; relationship with Kruger, 183, 184; relies on Hammond's advice, 186; reaction to Sauer's accurate shooting, 187; preparations for raid on Johannesburg, 188–91; objects to Jameson's activities, 190; urged to stop Jameson, 192; despair after Jameson's raid, 193–4, 199; pays fine, 201; raid costs him £800,000 and premiership, 201; dismissed as director of Chartered Co, 203; negotiates with Matabeles, 204–7; eating habits, 205; interest in religion, 205–6, 257; ends Matabele uprising, 207; admired by Africans, 207; high reputation, 208; buys Groote Schuur, 208; erotic nature of library, 209; prefers company of men, 209–10; generosity, 211, 231; visits England for enquiry into raid, 213; meets Kaiser, 214, 228; disbelief in war between Boers and British, 215; receives honorary degree at Oxford, 228–31; writes final will, 231; leaves Groote Schuur as residence for Prime Ministers, 231; buys stallions, 231; meets Princess Radziwill, 232; irritation with her, 233–5; dislike of Kekewich, 237, 240, 244; urges relief of Kimberley, 238; commercial obligations, 243–4; telegraph line, 244; allows women and children to shelter in mines, 245; relief of Kimberley by General French, 246; advises Princess Radziwill to leave Africa, 248; gives evidence against her, 249–51; final illness, 252–4; 'happy or fortunate?', 256–7; his achievements, 257; need of Barnato for his ambition, 257–8; best remembered for Scholarships, 258; prime mover of diamond industry, 258–9

Rhodes, Elmhirst, 23
Rhodes, Francis William, 22–3, 76; character, 24

Sylvester, Rev, 168

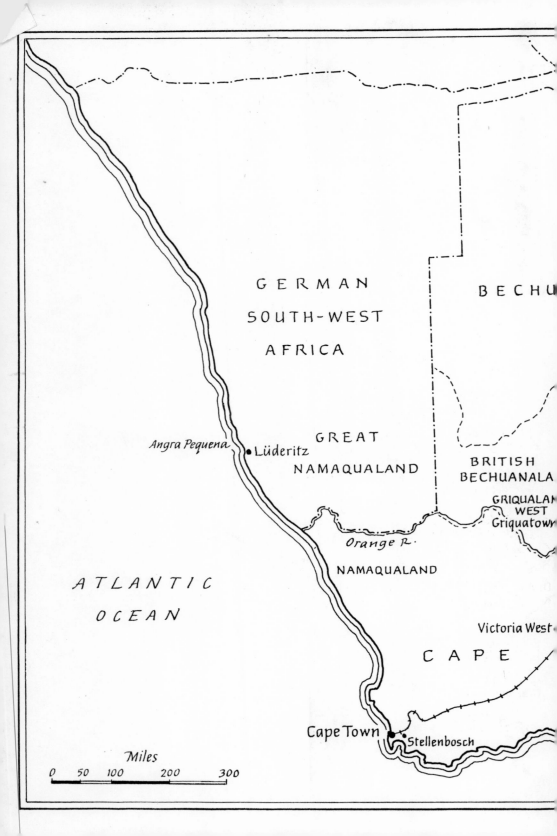